Parenting
Beyond
Belief

| SECOND EDITION |

Parenting Beyond Belief

On Raising Ethical, Caring Kids Without Religion

| SECOND EDITION |

DALE McGOWAN

With contributions by

Richard Dawkins, Julia Sweeney, Dr. Phil Zuckerman,
and more

AMACOM

AMERICAN MANAGEMENT ASSOCIATION

New York • Atlanta • Brussels • Chicago • Mexico City • San Francisco •
Shanghai • Tokyo • Toronto • Washington, D.C.

Bulk discounts available. For details visit:
www.amacombooks.org/go/specialsales
Or contact special sales:
Phone: 800-250-5308
Email: specialsls@amanet.org
View all the AMACOM titles at: www.amacombooks.org
American Management Association: www.amanet.org

Library of Congress Cataloging-in-Publication Data

Names: McGowan, Dale, editor.
Title: Parenting beyond belief : on raising ethical, caring kids without
  religion / [edited by] Dale McGowan ; with contributions by Richard
  Dawkins, Julia Sweeney, Dr. Phil Zuckerman, and more.
Description: 2nd Edition. | New York : Amacom, 2016.
Identifiers: LCCN 2016031076| ISBN 9780814437414 (pbk.) | ISBN 9780814474266
  (previous edition) | ISBN 9780814437421 (ebook)
Subjects: LCSH: Parenting--Religious aspects. | Religious education of
  children. | Free thought.
Classification: LCC BL2777.R4 P37 2016 | DDC 649/.7--dc23 LC record available at
https://lccn.loc.gov/2016031076

About AMA
American Management Association (www.amanet.org) is a world leader in talent development, advancing the skills of individuals to drive business success. Our mission is to support the goals of individuals and organizations through a complete range of products and services, including classroom and virtual seminars, webcasts, webinars, podcasts, conferences, corporate and government solutions, business books, and research. AMA's approach to improving performance combines experiential learning—learning through doing—with opportunities for ongoing professional growth at every step of one's career journey.

10 9 8 7 6 5 4 3 2 1

To Becca, Connor, Erin, and Delaney.

All the best things I know about parenting, I learned from them.

ACKNOWLEDGMENTS

Thank you to all of the phenomenal contributors to both editions for pouring your hearts and minds into this project.

Thanks to the thousands of nonreligious parents who attended my workshops and talks in cities from San Francisco to Miami and Ottawa to Mexico City in the decade since the first edition was published, as well as countless virtual correspondents and blog readers. You've shaped and refined my understanding of nonreligious parenting better than anything else could have done. Except for the actual parenting, I suppose.

Thanks to my agent, Uwe Stender, of TriadaUS Literary Agency and the remarkable crew at AMACOM, including my patient editors: Christina Parisi for the first edition, and Ellen Kadin for the second. Thanks as well to Barry Richardson, Miranda Pennington, Beth Metrick, and Kaitlyn Sparta for improving the manuscript at various stages and in various ways.

Deepest thanks to Becca, my brilliant wife of 25 years, and Connor, Erin, and Delaney, our cool and amazing kids. They have endured with good humor something that must be galling to any kid: a parent who writes parenting books.

CONTENTS

Preface to the Second Edition   xi

CHAPTER 1 ▪ PERSONAL REFLECTIONS

Introduction   1

Navigating Around the Dinner Table   3
     Julia Sweeney

Good and Bad Reasons for Believing   8
     Richard Dawkins

Growing Up Godless: How I Survived Amateur Secular Parenting   16
     Emily Rosa

Excerpt from *Autobiography*   20
     Bertrand Russell

Raised Without Religion   21
     Other voices of kids and adults raised in nonreligious families

Authentic Secular Parenting: Letting Children Choose   25
     Be-Asia McKerracher

My Father's House   31
     Dan Barker

Passing Down the Joy of Not Collecting Stamps   37
     Penn Jillette

Additional Resources   40

CHAPTER 2 ◼ LIVING WITH RELIGION

Introduction   41

Introducing Kids to Things We Don't Believe   45
Wendy Thomas Russell

10 Commandments for Talking to Kids About Religion
    When You're Not Religious   51
Wendy Thomas Russell

When Your Child Is Terrified You're Going to Hell   55
Neil Carter

Managing Dissonance with Religious Relatives   62
Libby Anne

Parenting Across the Belief Gap   68
Dale McGowan

Choosing Your Battles   90
Stu Tanquist

Secular Schooling   99
Ed Buckner, Ph.D.

Additional Resources   107

CHAPTER 3 ◼ HOLIDAYS AND CELEBRATIONS

Introduction   109

Humanist Ceremonies   111
Jane Wynne Willson

Losing the "Holy," Keeping the "Day"   117
Dale McGowan

POINT/COUNTERPOINT: The Question of the Claus: Should the
    Santa Story Stay or Go in Secular Families?

    Point: Put the Claus Away   126
    Tom Flynn

    Counterpoint: Santa Claus: The Ultimate Dry Run   129
    Dale McGowan

Additional Resources   132

CHAPTER 4 ■ ON BEING AND DOING GOOD

Introduction   135

Raising Ethical Children   139
  Marvin W. Berkowitz, Ph.D.

Spare the Rod—and Spare Me the Rest   146
  Dale McGowan

Morality and Evil   150
  Gareth B. Matthews, Ph.D.

Behaving Yourself: Moral Development in the Secular Family   155
  Jean Mercer, Ph.D.

Take Two Tablets and Call Me in the Morning   165
  Yip Harburg

Double Vision: Teaching Our Twins Pride and Respect   166
  Shannon and Matthew Cherry

Seven Secular Virtues: Humility, Empathy, Courage, Honesty,
  Openness, Generosity, and Gratitude   171
  Dale McGowan

Excerpt from "Morals Without Religion"   180
  Margaret Knight

Additional Resources   181

CHAPTER 5 ■ DEATH AND CONSOLATION

Introduction   185

Before and After   189
  Yip Harburg

Helping Your Child Live with Grief without Religion   190
  Rebecca Hensler

Where All Roads Lead   199
  Dale McGowan

The First Really, Really Hard Good-Bye   204
  Dale McGowan

Small Comforts   207
  Yip Harburg

Dealing with Death in the Secular Family   208
  Rev. Dr. Kendyl Gibbons

Additional Resources   220

CHAPTER 6 ■ WONDERING AND QUESTIONING

Introduction 223

Little Bessie Would Assist Providence 227
    Mark Twain

A Nose Is a Nose Is a Nose 229
    Yip Harburg

Of Curious Women and Dead Cats 230
    Dale McGowan

Repurposing Noah's Ark: How to Inspire Your Kids with
    the Science of Evolution 233
    Katherine Miller, Ph.D.

We've Come a Long Way, Buddy 244
    Yip Harburg

Teaching Kids to Yawn at Counterfeit Wonder 245
    Dale McGowan

Parenting and the Arts 251
    James Herrick

Additional Resources 257

CHAPTER 7 ■ COMMUNITY AND IDENTITY

Introduction 259

"What Are We?" 265
    Katherine Ozment

Being Secular, Finding Community 270
    Phil Zuckerman, Ph.D.

Summer Camp Beyond Belief 275
    Amanda K. Metskas and August E. Brunsman IV

Live Better, Help Often, and Wonder More 279
    Sanderson Jones

Additional Resources 282

Glossary 285
Notes 289
Index 295

PREFACE TO THE SECOND EDITION

DALE McGOWAN, Ph.D.

The good life is one inspired by love and guided by knowledge.

—Bertrand Russell

When the first edition of this book was written in 2006, my children were 10, 8, and 5. Writing a parenting book by myself with kids that young would have been pretty nervy. So in addition to my own thoughts, I pulled together 27 other writers with a wide range of experience and expertise.

There was no question about the need for the book. Although millions were already raising their children without religion, there had to that point been virtually no resources to help them navigate the specific issues that arise from that decision. There were almost no nonreligious parent groups, online forums, or books for nonreligious parents in 2006.

It didn't help that even the larger community of nonbelief was still finding its feet. Richard Dawkins's *The God Delusion,* which helped bring the existence of the nonreligious into cultural awareness, was not yet released when *Parenting Beyond Belief* went to the publisher, and few specific nonreligious resources existed for many of the human needs religion has fulfilled for its own adherents, from processing grief and loss to organized volunteering and charitable giving to the creation of mutually supportive communities.

What a difference a decade has made. The religiously unaffiliated have grown from 15 percent of the U.S. population to 23 percent, and a full third of millennials (born 1981–96) now identify as nonreligious.[1] Books, online resources, and organizations have risen up to meet the needs of this growing population. More public figures have identified as nonreligious than ever before. And many political analysts credited the religiously unaffiliated as a deciding factor in the reelection of President Barack Obama in 2012—something unimaginable 10 years ago.

The world of secular parenting has grown and matured as well. After *Parenting Beyond Belief* came the practical follow-up *Raising Freethinkers* (2009) and a number of other books by and for secular parents, including Wendy Thomas Russell's *Relax, It's Just God* (2015) and Katherine Ozment's *Grace Without God* (2016). In 2006, I could find only one small secular parent support group in the United States; now there are hundreds. A tiny handful of secular parenting blogs and forums has given rise to entire networks and scores of articulate, insightful blogs by experienced secular parents. A group called Grief Beyond Belief addresses grief, loss, and talking to children about death, all in a nonreligious context. Foundation Beyond Belief gives secular families and individuals a nonreligious option for regular volunteering and giving, and Sunday Assembly has done the same for nonreligious gathering. In ten years, Camp Quest, the secular summer camp that had grown from one location to six in the decade before the first edition, has grown from six to sixteen in the decade since, including locations in the United Kingdom, Norway, and Switzerland. And the global Sunday Assembly movement, a brilliant and inspiring secular alternative to religious congregations, wasn't even a glimmer in its founders' eyes in 2006. Born with Sunday Assembly London in 2013, it has grown to seventy Assemblies in eight countries.

The most common reader response to the first edition was, "I thought I was the only one raising my kids without religion." Though many parents remain isolated on the local level, the last ten years have made it likely that they at least know they are far from alone.

Even though the community has grown, the issue remains the same: How can nonreligious parents find all of the undeniable benefits religious parents enjoy without the equally undeniable detriments of religion?

Approach and Focus

This is not a comprehensive parenting book. It will be of little help for dealing with diaper rash, aggression, or tattling. It is intended as a resource of opinions, insights, and experiences related to a single issue: raising children without religion.

Although our contributors include experts in child development and education, there's little attempt to dictate authoritative answers. Our writers suggest, inform, challenge, and encourage without claiming there's only one right way.* This is also not a book of arguments against religious belief, nor one intended to persuade readers to raise their children without religion. It is meant to support and encourage those who have already decided to do so and to help them do it well.

Parenting is already among the toughest of jobs. Living secularly in a mostly religious world is among the most difficult social choices. Combining them can be daunting to consider. But it helps to realize that no matter where you live, even in an outwardly religious area, there are people around you doing the same thing. You might assume that every parent on your block, everyone cheering in the stands at the soccer game or walking the aisles of the supermarket, is a churchgoing believer. It's the assumed default in our culture. But it isn't true. Just realize that they are making the same assumption about you. You are not remotely alone—and given the recent explosion in nonreligious identity, you are even less alone than ever before.

Nearly half the content is new to this edition, including 17 new essays and dozens of new resource reviews. In addition to encores from Julia Sweeney, Richard Dawkins, Dr. Jean Mercer, and more, you'll meet such rising stars in secular parenting as Wendy Thomas Russell, Katherine Ozment, Neil Carter, Be-Asia McKerracher, and Libby Anne. We also have several new experts on board, including Dr. Marvin Berkowitz, on secular moral development; Dr. Katherine Miller, on evolution education; Dr. Phil Zuckerman, on community without religion; Rebecca Hensler, on secular grieving; and Sanderson Jones, on the exciting global phenomenon of Sunday Assembly.

As before, one thread runs throughout: Encourage a child to think well; then trust her to do so. Removing religion doesn't guarantee kids will think independently. In order to really think for themselves about religion, kids must learn as much as possible about religion as a human cultural expression while being kept free of the disturbing idea that they will be rewarded in heaven or punished in hell based on what they decide—a bit of intellectual terrorism we should never inflict on our kids, nor on each other. They must also learn what has been said and thought in opposition to religious ideas. If my kids think

---

* Unlike a child-care guide I can see on my shelf right now with the subtitle "The Complete and Authoritative Guide." Holy Moses!

independently and well, then end up coming to conclusions different from my own—well, I'd have to consider the possibility that I've gotten it all wrong. Either way, in order to own and be nourished by their convictions, kids must ultimately come to them independently. Part of our wonderfully complex job as parents is to facilitate that process without controlling it.

As the editor of this collection, I've encouraged the authors to retain their individual styles and approaches, even to articulate contrasting opinions on a given question, confident that you as a secular parent can handle the variety and would want nothing less. This is big-tent secularism, offering many different perspectives on living without religion. The authors' approaches are at turns soberly academic, off the cuff, inspiring, irreverent, angry, joyful, confident, confused, revealing, and empowering. Skip around, dip, and dive, and be sure to challenge your natural inclinations.

I hope you find this a worthwhile contribution to the bookshelf for those of us taking on the wonderful and humbling task of raising the next generation of people inspired by love and guided by knowledge.

Parenting
Beyond
Belief

| SECOND EDITION |

1

Personal Reflections

INTRODUCTION

The first and most important task of *Parenting Beyond Belief* is to let secular families know they are not alone—that millions of other families are wrestling with the same challenges and asking the same questions. This chapter includes personal reflections by freethinking parents and children, as well as adults recalling when they were children, all grappling with familiar issues and offering hard-won advice.

This chapter is framed by a perfect pair of bookends to illustrate the range of approaches to secular parenting. We start with Julia Sweeney, who describes raising her daughter, Mulan, to make her own choices while making peace with her Catholic background and devout parents. At the end is Penn Jillette, who applies his famously uncompromising life philosophy to secular parenting.

Because Richard Dawkins thinks religion greatly and negatively impacts the world, his disrespect for many religious claims leads him to passionate and strident denunciation of what he sees as a real and present danger. After the attacks of September 11, Dawkins wrote, "My last vestige of 'hands off religion' respect disappeared in the smoke and choking dust of September 11th 2001, followed by the 'National Day of Prayer.'"[1] He believes that religion is dangerous and must be actively opposed. While it is perfectly acceptable for readers to disagree with such an opinion or with the way in which it is expressed, this impassioned and well-informed voice should no more be excluded from the conversation than thoughtful religious nontheists at the other end of our big tent.

Secular kids themselves are well represented by Emily Rosa, who describes an upbringing that kept her "itching for the truth" and a fourth-grade science experiment that briefly catapulted her into the national spotlight. She also offers some serious advice to secular parents to relax, play, laugh, lighten up—so as not to raise a grim generation of obsessive debunkers. And this edition adds the thoughts of several other kids and adults who were raised, or are being raised, without religion.

Also new to the second edition is Be-Asia McKerracher, a talented author, podcaster, and rising voice in secular parenting and the black atheist movement.

Dan Barker rounds out the chapter with a fascinating dual perspective: First, as an evangelical minister, Dan raised four children in a Christian home; then he lost his faith, divorced, remarried, and is now raising a daughter in a home actively devoted to freethought.

Though each of these stories is unique, common threads run throughout these essays, including courage, honesty, and optimism. There are many good ways to raise children, with or without religion. These examples are not models to follow but invitations to find your own way—and assurances that you will.

■ ■ ■ ■ ■ ■ ■ ■ ■ ■ ■ ■ ■

NAVIGATING AROUND
THE DINNER TABLE

JULIA SWEENEY

I loved being Catholic. Well, most of the time. I mean, I didn't like it when people didn't answer my questions or take my sporadic natural skepticism seriously. But other than that, I felt lucky. I mean, being Catholic was cool to me. I felt sorry for the people I met who weren't. Which were hardly any people. Because everyone I knew was Catholic. And they belonged. Not just to parishes and schools, but to this great big club called Catholic. And there were rituals we all knew and outfits we wore—school uniforms. And the priests wore all black except when they were saying a Mass, when they wore a cape! I mean, come on, it rocked. Plus there were all the other medieval-like things associated with being Catholic. You knelt in obedience and submission, but to me this was not humiliating—it was like you lived in a castle! And incense was strewn through the church on occasion, and that, too, seemed mystical and otherworldly. And then there was the fact that everybody I knew, knew everybody else and where they went to school and where their parents went to school. It was a close-knit, safe feeling.

But then I grew up, opened my eyes, and realized I didn't think there was any supernatural reason for doing all these things. I didn't think there was any good evidence for a God at all, let alone one who cared who showed up at church. And I moved away from Spokane to Los Angeles, a place where Catholicism didn't knit the community in the way that I had experienced. Even when I did go to a Catholic church in L.A., my mind had this pesky habit of actually listening to the words being said at Mass. I would inevitably leave angry, or bemused and distant like an anthropologist, but certainly not connected. Eventually I stopped going and just got used to describing myself as an atheist. Then I got proud of saying I was an atheist. And during this time, I adopted a little girl from China.

It didn't dawn on me right away that I wasn't raising her with any religion. I mean, religion to me meant those old ritualistic ceremonies that we went to when we visited my hometown. And it was still a little fun to go—I mean, my dad or my brother would hold my daughter, and she wriggled like the other two- and three-year-olds. But then a couple of things happened that changed everything.

The first thing was that my dad died.

Wow. Just saying that shows you I had changed. I didn't say he "passed away," because he didn't pass away. He died. My daughter was four and a half at the time and very close to my father. He was the guy she made Father's Day cards for on Father's Day, the man whom she liked to have hold her. My dad used to take naps next to my daughter on the bed, and I remember seeing them in there—my father with his oxygen machine and my daughter curled up next to him— and it was all so dreamy and loving and cute. And so, it was a big deal when he died. And my daughter had questions.

When she asked, "What happens after we die?" I said, "To be honest, darling—we decompose." And she wanted to know what that meant. A bird had died in our backyard and so we watched how it disappeared a little bit every day. When I tell this story to people, they look at me horrified. Like I was forcing some horrifying truth onto a little kid too small to understand it. But actually, she got it just fine, possibly because I didn't *only* say that. I said two more things. "When you die, your body decomposes," I said. "It breaks down into all these teeny parts you can't even see—like dirt or air even. And then those particles become part of something else." And my daughter said, "Like what?" And I said, "Well, like a flower or air or grass or dirt or even another person." And she said, "Well I want to be another person!" And I said, "Yes, I understand. But even if some of your molecules became part of another person, it wouldn't be you. Because You are You, and when You are gone, there will never ever be another You in this world. You are so special and unique that this world will only ever make one of You. With You they broke the mold, so that's it! Only You. Right here, right now."

And she seemed to kind of get that. In fact, it made her feel special.

And then I told her a second thing: that her grandfather did live on after he died, inside of the people who were remembering him. And in the ways he influenced those people, even when they weren't thinking of him. Like how Grandpa just loved orange sherbet. Now, because of that, we eat orange sherbet too, and we remember him when we do it. Or even things that we might not think about him while we do them, like when we watch some basketball on TV. We might do that because of Grandpa, who loved to watch basketball on TV. Because of him, we are different. In probably thousands or even millions of ways. And that difference is what makes him live after he dies.

And she really got that.

Only one problem: Her friends at school were asking her if her grandfather was up in heaven. And she was thrown, because to say no sounded bad and to say yes wasn't what I had told her. One day we were walking home from the park with one of her friends, and the friend said, "Did you see your grandfather's spirit fly up to heaven when he died?" And my daughter looked at me and said, "Did it?" And I said, "No, we don't believe in things like that." And my daughter parroted me, "Yeah, we don't believe in that." And for a second she looked confident repeating me, and then her face crinkled up and she frowned and directed her eyes downward.

> 66 I was seized with compassion for my little girl and how she will be navigating herself in a world where she will be a little bit different. I didn't have this burden. I was told what everyone else was told. 99

Suddenly I was seized with compassion for my little girl and how she will be navigating herself in a world where she will be a little bit different. I didn't have this burden. I was told what everyone else was told. Grandpas died and went to heaven. You would see them later when you died. Vague memories arose of my own childhood images of heaven, of a long dining table with a gold tablecloth and a feast. It was easier for me, in that way, than it will be for her.

But while I was having all these thoughts, my daughter and her friend had nonchalantly moved on to talking about their American Girl dolls. No biggy. But that moment, I think, is when all of the "what we believe" discussions began. And it made me uncomfortable. My daughter would often start conversations with me by saying, "So, we believe that . . ." And frankly I hated the whole word "believe," and I also hated that she was just taking what I said as absolute truth, because in the perfect world of my head, she wouldn't be indoctrinated with anything. She would come up with her own answers, and she would never say things like, "We believe" or "We don't believe." But then I got more seasoned as a mother and realized that basically that's what we do all the time as parents, no matter what we "believe." Our job is to socialize our kids, and they have evolved to look to us for answers. Not providing those answers is wrong.

I got a little more comfortable saying things about what we "believe." Like, we believe it is good to take the garbage out. Honestly, it seems silly now that I write it. But that's how I got comfortable with that word. We believe in treating people nicely. We believe you shouldn't tell people lies. We believe that you should do your homework. That kind of believe.

Finally, I would say things like, "Lots of people believe that after someone dies, they live on. But I think that is just their way of not feeling as sad as they might about whoever they loved who died. I think that when people die, they die. And we should feel really sad and also feel happy that the flower of that person ever got to live at all." And even though many of my friends thought this was too big of a concept for a four- or five-year-old, after explaining it several times, I do think she got it.

That didn't mean, of course, that other people, like my mother, weren't also telling her what they believed about my dad's death. When we visited my mother, she and my daughter would make cookies, and I would hear my mother going on and on about how Grandpa was in heaven and we were going to see him again and he was there with Mike, my brother who passed away. And later, when my daughter asked about this discrepancy, I just said, "We believe different things." And amazingly, Mulan got that just fine—even though it sort of made me mad. Because what story is going to seem better? The one where someone decomposes or the one where he's at a big dinner table in the sky with other people who died? Decomposition does not stand a chance against the dinner table. But for me and Mulan, those discrepancies or different stories didn't become as traumatic as I thought they would.

A few months after this, Mulan started kindergarten at our local public school. And as part of her day at school, she said the Pledge of Allegiance. She proudly repeated it to me, and the "under God" part made me flinch. "You don't have to say 'under God,' you know," I said—and her eyes widened with fear. "What do you mean?" I said, "You can just keep your mouth closed during that part. I don't believe in God. These people in the government allowed that to get stuck in there much later. I wouldn't say it if I were you."

A few days later she came home and said, "I have to say it. Because it's nice, it's being nice to say it. You have to be nice and so you say it." I don't think I have ever heard a more heartbreaking sentence from my child. I am probably more sensitive to this, for many more reasons than religion. I have tried for years and years to stop doing things automatically because they are "nice," because I find myself drowning in doing a million things for people because it's "nice." On the other hand, it's expedient to pressure children to conform. It makes sense. It encourages community and all the behaviors that we are trying to instill in them. I understood her dilemma.

Fortunately, a friend of mine suggested a solution. "How about telling her to say, 'under laws' instead of 'under God?'" Brilliant! I told my daughter the idea. She looked at me like I was from Mars. It was her first truly I've-got-an-insane-mother look. But now when she comes home from school, as the year has worn on, she'll tell me, "Today I said, 'under God.'" Another day she will report that she said "under laws." And I figure she will find her own rhythm.

Recently I was in Spokane with Mulan on Memorial Day. The whole family was making their way up to Holy Cross Cemetery, where many members of our family are buried. Even though this is a Catholic cemetery, and icons litter the lawns, I love it there. I am all for burial in a plot with your family. I find it extremely comforting. I have picnicked there on days when it wasn't Memorial Day. In fact, everyone in our family does this. It's a destination for us. And I love it.

Well, we were heading toward the cemetery, and my daughter was in an ornery, crappy, poopy mood. She didn't want to go. My mother, who was driving, made the mistake of saying, "God wants us to go." She was mostly trying to be funny. But my daughter yelled out, "I don't believe in God! I only believe in things that you have evidence for and there is NO EVIDENCE FOR GOD!" The way she said it was petulant and snotty. I was so angry with her. But in that instant, even though I had to reprimand her for her "tone" and demeanor, and even though she started a tantrumy cry and begged for a cheese stick and began kicking her legs and I wanted to throttle her for it—in spite of all of this, I knew instantly that ultimately she would be okay. She had spirit and gumption, and she could say something that was unpopular (at least in that car at that moment). And more than not believing in God, that seemed like the best influence I could ever have on her.

Grammy Award–winning comedian JULIA SWEENEY is also an actor, playwright, and monologist. Since her years on Saturday Night Live, *Sweeney has been featured in films, including* Pulp Fiction, Stuart Little, *and* Monsters University. *Her monologue* Letting Go of God, *which chronicles her journey from faith to philosophical naturalism, was Critics' Choice for the* Los Angeles Times. *She received the 2006 Richard Dawkins Award for raising public awareness of the nontheistic life stance and serves on the advisory board of the Secular Coalition for America. Her adoptive daughter, Mulan, 16 at this writing, was not named for the Disney character.*

■ ■

GOOD AND BAD REASONS FOR BELIEVING*

from *A Devil's Chaplain*

RICHARD DAWKINS

Dear Juliet,

Now that you are ten, I want to write to you about something that is important to me. Have you ever wondered how we know the things that we know? How do we know, for instance, that the stars, which look like tiny pinpricks in the sky, are really huge balls of fire like the sun and are very far away? And how do we know that Earth is a smaller ball whirling round one of those stars, the sun?

The answer to these questions is "evidence." Sometimes evidence means actually seeing (or hearing, feeling, smelling . . .) that something is true. Astronauts have traveled far enough from Earth to see with their own eyes that it is round. Sometimes our eyes need help. The "evening star" looks like a bright twinkle in the sky, but with a telescope, you can see that it is a beautiful ball—the planet we call Venus. Something that you learn by direct seeing (or hearing or feeling . . .) is called an observation.

Often, evidence isn't just an observation on its own, but observation always lies at the back of it. If there's been a murder, often nobody (except the murderer and the victim!) actually observed it. But

---

* © 2003 used with permission from the Orion Publishing Group (London) and Houghton Mifflin Harcourt.

detectives can gather together lots of other observations which may all point toward a particular suspect. If a person's fingerprints match those found on a dagger, this is evidence that he touched it. It doesn't prove that he did the murder, but it can help when it's joined up with lots of other evidence. Sometimes a detective can think about a whole lot of observations and suddenly realize that they fall into place and make sense if so-and-so did the murder.

Scientists—the specialists in discovering what is true about the world and the universe—often work like detectives. They make a guess (called a hypothesis) about what might be true. They then say to themselves: If that were really true, we ought to see so-and-so. This is called a prediction. For example, if the world is really round, we can predict that a traveler, going on and on in the same direction, should eventually find himself back where he started. When a doctor says that you have the measles, he doesn't take one look at you and see measles. His first look gives him a hypothesis that you may have measles. Then he says to himself: If she has measles, I ought to see . . . Then he runs through the list of predictions and tests them with his eyes (have you got spots?); hands (is your forehead hot?); and ears (does your chest wheeze in a measly way?). Only then does he make his decision and say, "I diagnose that the child has measles." Sometimes doctors need to do other tests like blood tests or X-rays, which help their eyes, hands, and ears to make observations.

The way scientists use evidence to learn about the world is much cleverer and more complicated than I can say in a short letter. But now I want to move on from evidence, which is a good reason for believing something, and warn you against three bad reasons for believing anything. They are called "tradition," "authority," and "revelation."

First, tradition. A few months ago, I went on television to have a discussion with about fifty children. These children were invited because they had been brought up in lots of different religions. Some had been brought up as Christians, others as Jews, Muslims, Hindus, or Sikhs. The man with the microphone went from child to child, asking them what they believed. What they said shows up exactly what I mean by "tradition." Their beliefs turned out to have no connection with evidence. They just trotted out the beliefs of their parents and grandparents, which, in turn, were not based upon evidence either. They said things like: "We Hindus believe so and so"; "We Muslims believe such and such"; "We Christians believe something else."

Of course, since they all believed different things, they couldn't all be right. The man with the microphone seemed to think this quite right and proper, and he didn't even try to get them to argue out their differences with each other. But that isn't the point I want to make for the moment. I simply want to ask where their beliefs came from. They came from tradition.

Tradition means beliefs handed down from grandparent to parent to child, and so on. Or from books handed down through the centuries. Traditional beliefs often start from almost nothing; perhaps somebody just makes them up originally, like the stories about Thor and Zeus. But after they've been handed down over some centuries, the mere fact that they are so old makes them seem special. People believe things simply because people have believed the same thing over the centuries. That's tradition.

> **Traditional beliefs often start from almost noth- ing. . . . But after they've been handed down over some centuries, the mere fact that they are so old makes them seem special. People believe things simply because people have believed the same thing over the centuries.**

The trouble with tradition is that, no matter how long ago a story was made up, it is still exactly as true or untrue as the original story was. If you make up a story that isn't true, handing it down over a number of centuries doesn't make it any truer!

Most people in England have been baptized into the Church of England, but this is only one of the branches of the Christian religion. There are other branches such as Russian Orthodox, the Roman Catholic, and the Methodist churches. They all believe different things. The Jewish religion and the Muslim religion are a bit more different still; and there are different kinds of Jews and of Muslims. People who believe even slightly different things from each other go to war over their disagreements. So you might think that they must have some pretty good reasons—evidence—for believing what they believe. But actually, their different beliefs are entirely due to different traditions.

Let's talk about one particular tradition. Roman Catholics believe that Mary, the mother of Jesus, was so special that she didn't die but was lifted bodily into Heaven. Other Christian traditions disagree, saying that Mary did die like anybody else. These other religions don't talk about her much, and, unlike Roman Catholics, they don't call her the "Queen of Heaven." The tradition that Mary's body was lifted into Heaven is not an old one. The bible says nothing on how she died; in fact, the poor woman is scarcely mentioned in the Bible at all. The belief that her body was lifted into Heaven wasn't invented until about six centuries after Jesus' time. At first, it was just made up, in the same way as any story like "Snow White" was made up. But, over the centuries, it grew into a tradition, and people started to take it seriously simply because the story had been handed down over so many generations. The older the tradition became, the more people took it seriously. It finally was written down as an official Roman Catholic belief only very recently, in 1950, when I was the age you are now. But the story was no more true in 1950 than it was when it was first invented 600 years after Mary's death.

I'll come back to tradition at the end of my letter, and look at it in another way. But first, I must deal with the two other bad reasons for believing in anything: authority and revelation.

Authority, as a reason for believing something, means believing in it because you are told to believe it by somebody important. In the Roman Catholic Church, the pope is the most important person, and people believe he must be right just because he is the pope. In one branch of the Muslim religion, the important people are the old men with beards called ayatollahs. Lots of Muslims in this country [the United Kingdom] are prepared to commit murder, purely because the ayatollahs in a faraway country tell them to.

When I say that it was only in 1950 that Roman Catholics were finally told that they had to believe that Mary's body shot off to Heaven, what I mean is that in 1950, the pope told people that they had to believe it. That was it. The pope said it was true, so it had to be true! Now, probably some of the things that that pope said in his life were true and some were not true. There is no good reason why, just because he was the pope, you should believe everything he said any more than you believe everything that other people say. The present pope* has ordered his followers not to limit the number of babies they have. If people follow this authority as slavishly as he would wish, the results could be terrible famines, diseases, and wars, caused by overcrowding.

Of course, even in science, sometimes we haven't seen the evidence ourselves, and we have to take somebody else's word for it. I haven't, with my own eyes, seen the evidence that light travels at a speed of

---

* John Paul II when this letter was written.

186,000 miles per second. Instead, I believe books that tell me the speed of light. This looks like "authority." But actually, it is much better than authority, because the people who wrote the books have seen the evidence and anyone is free to look carefully at the evidence whenever they want. That is very comforting. But not even the priests claim that there is any evidence for their story about Mary's body zooming off to Heaven.

The third kind of bad reason for believing anything is called "revelation." If you had asked the pope in 1950 how he knew that Mary's body disappeared into Heaven, he would probably have said that it had been "revealed" to him. He shut himself in his room and prayed for guidance. He thought and thought, all by himself, and he became more and more sure inside himself. When religious people just have a feeling inside themselves that something must be true, even though there is no evidence that it is true, they call their feeling "revelation." It isn't only popes who claim to have revelations. Lots of religious people do. It is one of their main reasons for believing the things that they do believe. But is it a good reason?

Suppose I told you that your dog was dead. You'd be very upset, and you'd probably say, "Are you sure? How do you know? How did it happen?" Now suppose I answered: "I don't actually know that Pepe is dead. I have no evidence. I just have a funny feeling deep inside me that he is dead." You'd be pretty cross with me for scaring you, because you'd know that an inside "feeling" on its own is not a good reason for believing that a whippet is dead. You need evidence. We all have inside feelings from time to time, sometimes they turn out to be right and sometimes they don't. Anyway, different people have opposite feelings, so how are we to decide whose feeling is right?

> People sometimes say that you must believe in feelings deep inside, otherwise, you'd never be confident of things like 'My wife loves me.' But this is a bad argument. There can be plenty of evidence that somebody loves you . . . outside things to back up the inside feeling.

The only way to be sure that a dog is dead is to see him dead, or hear that his heart has stopped, or be told by somebody who has seen or heard some real evidence that he is dead.

People sometimes say that you must believe in feelings deep inside, otherwise, you'd never be confident of things like "My wife loves me."

But this is a bad argument. There can be plenty of evidence that somebody loves you. All through the day when you are with somebody who loves you, you see and hear lots of little tidbits of evidence, and they all add up. It isn't a purely inside feeling, like the feeling that priests call revelation. There are outside things to back up the inside feeling: looks in the eye, tender notes in the voice, little favors and kindnesses; this is all real evidence.

Sometimes people have a strong inside feeling that somebody loves them when it is not based upon any evidence, and then they are likely to be completely wrong. There are people with a strong inside feeling that a famous film star loves them, when really the film star hasn't even met them. People like that are ill in their minds. Inside feelings must be backed up by evidence, otherwise you just can't trust them.

Inside feelings are valuable in science, too, but only for giving you ideas that you later test by looking for evidence. A scientist can have a "hunch" about an idea that just "feels" right. In itself, this is not a good reason for believing something. But it can be a good reason for spending some time doing a particular experiment, or looking in a particular way for evidence. Scientists use inside feelings all the time to get ideas. But they are not worth anything until they are supported by evidence.

I promised that I'd come back to tradition and look at it in another way. I want to try to explain why tradition is so important to us. All animals are built (by the process called evolution) to survive in the normal place in which their kind live. Lions are built to be good at surviving on the plains of Africa. Crayfish are built to be good at surviving in fresh water, while lobsters are built to be good at surviving in the salt sea. People are animals, too, and we are built to be good at surviving in a world full of—other people. Most of us don't hunt for our own food like lions or lobsters; we buy it from other people who have bought it from yet other people. We "swim" through a "sea of people." Just as a fish needs gills to survive in water, people need brains that make them able to deal with other people. Just as the sea is full of saltwater, the sea of people is full of difficult things to learn. Like language.

You speak English, but your friend Ann-Kathrin speaks German. You each speak the language that fits you to "swim about" in your own separate "people sea." Language is passed down by tradition. There is no other way. In England, Pepe is a dog. In Germany he is *ein Hund*. Neither of these words is more correct or more true than the other. Both are simply handed down. In order to be good at "swimming about in their people sea," children have to learn the language of their own country and lots of other things about their own people; and this means that they have to absorb, like blotting paper, an enormous amount of traditional information. (Remember that traditional information just means things that are handed down from grandparents to parents to children.) The child's brain has to be a sucker for traditional information. And the child can't be expected to sort out good and useful traditional information, like the words of a language, from bad or silly traditional information, like believing in witches and devils and ever-living virgins.

> 66 Once something gets itself strongly believed— even if it is completely untrue and there never was any reason to believe it in the first place—it can go on forever. 99

It's a pity, but it can't help being the case, that because children have to be suckers for traditional information, they are likely to believe anything the grown-ups tell them, whether true or false, right or wrong. Lots of what the grown-ups tell them is true and based on evidence, or at least sensible. But if some of it is false, silly, or even wicked, there is nothing to stop the children believing that, too. Now, when the children grow up, what do they do? Well, of course, they tell it to the next generation of children. So, once something gets itself strongly believed—even if it is completely untrue and there never was any reason to believe it in the first place—it can go on forever.

Could this be what has happened with religions? Belief that there is a god or gods, belief in Heaven, belief that Mary never died, belief that Jesus never had a human father, belief that prayers are answered, belief that wine turns into blood—not one of these beliefs is backed up by any good evidence. Yet millions of people believe them. Perhaps this is because they were told to believe them when they were young enough to believe anything.

Millions of other people believe quite different things, because they were told different things when they were children. Muslim children are told different things from Christian children, and both grow up utterly convinced that they are right and the others are wrong. Even within Christians, Roman Catholics believe different things from Church of England people or Episcopalians, Shakers or Quakers, Mormons or Holy Rollers, and are all utterly convinced that they are right and the others are wrong. They believe different things for exactly the same kind of reason as you speak English and Ann-Kathrin speaks German. Both languages are, in their own country, the right language to speak. But it can't be true that different religions are right in their own countries, because different religions claim that opposite things are true. Mary can't be alive in Catholic Southern Ireland but dead in Protestant Northern Ireland.

What can we do about all this? It is not easy for you to do anything, because you are only ten. But you could try this. Next time somebody tells you something that sounds important, think to yourself: "Is this the kind of thing that people probably know because of evidence? Or is it the kind of thing that people only believe because of tradition, authority, or revelation?" And, next time somebody tells you that something is true, why not say to them, "What kind of evidence is there for that?" And if they can't give you a good answer, I hope you'll think very carefully before you believe a word they say.

Your loving Daddy

Oxford ethologist RICHARD DAWKINS *is among the most celebrated living contributors to the popular understanding of science. His first book,* The Selfish Gene *(1976), was an international bestseller, and was followed by the seminal classic* The Blind Watchmaker *(1986). With the publication of* The God Delusion *in 2006 and his subsequent formation of the Richard Dawkins Foundation for Reason and Science, he became one of the most prominent advocates of atheism and naturalism. Dawkins is a Fellow of both the Royal Society and the Royal Society of Literature. He is vice president of the British Humanist Association. He has one daughter, Juliet.*

■ ■

GROWING UP GODLESS: HOW I SURVIVED AMATEUR SECULAR PARENTING

EMILY ROSA

In 1987, I was born a seven-pound godless heathen, content with enjoying and exploring the world around me. My mother was delighted with my natural state.

Mom determined that, as much as possible, I would grow up without the intrusion of religion—or atheism. She, and later my stepfather, believed that when I reached a certain level of maturity and experience, I could decide such matters for myself.

Mom set out early to teach me the things she values: honesty, fairness, freedom, the fun of exploration and looking for evidence, and the notion that hard work pays off.

Things progressed well through my wee toddler years when Mom had control over things. She allowed me the time and the opportunity for exhaustive study of my environment. So when I became determined to break into neighbors' cars with an old key, she followed after me down the street as I tried the locks to my heart's content. Once she stood by as I asked every shopper in the grocery store whether they had a penis or vagina.

The first intrusions of religion came in preschool. My mother won't lie, so when the Santa Claus myth came up, she told me right off that he was make-believe, and that she could be his helper (wink, wink) if I wanted. One year I really wanted to enjoy the fantasy, so I ordered my mom, "Don't tell me about Santa being make-believe." I still knew the score and didn't have the letdown that my friends did later.

The truly hardest time was learning about death. I had seen the animated movie *Land Before Time,* in which the beloved mother dinosaur dies, though her spirit occasionally appears to give advice to her son. The thought of losing my own mom was devastating, and I even started to contemplate my own death. Teachers at preschool noticed my depression. They kindly advised my mom to comfort me with hope of an afterlife. She couldn't honestly do that, yet felt at a loss for how to comfort me except to be with me as much as possible during that difficult time. Since then, death has probably been more on my mind than it has with most kids, and it may account for my abiding interest in forensic sciences and my appreciation for how precious life is.

When my first science fair loomed in the fourth grade, I chose to do a boring color separation experiment with M&M's but lost interest when I realized I couldn't eat the candy. My attention wandered to a videotape showing nurses claiming to heal people by waving their hands over them. These nurses were practicing "Therapeutic Touch" (TT), which they explained was an ancient religious practice called "laying on of hands," but with a lot of extra Eastern mystical ideas. Among these was the idea that a "human energy field," or HEF, exists around every person, and that TT practitioners touch and manipulate it with their hands. The HEF felt spongy, they said, like warm Jell-O, and even "tactile as taffy."

Given these religious aspects, some adults might not have questioned TT any further. But with my upbringing, I was itching for the truth. Could those nurses really feel something invisible with their hands?

I asked Mom if I could test TT for the science fair, and she replied, "Sure, if you can figure out a way to test it." With a little thought, I had my testable hypothesis: If these nurses can feel a real HEF, then they should be able to feel it when they aren't looking.

The cardboard display boards used at the fair gave me the idea of how I could shield the nurses' vision. The nurses would put their hands through holes in the cardboard; I randomly put my hand near one of theirs and asked them which of their hands felt my HEF.

I tested some very nice TT practitioners who couldn't detect the presence of an HEF any better than guessing (with 48 percent correct answers). Everyone who entered the science fair got a blue ribbon, but I also got my answer.

My experiment was repeated for the TV program *Scientific American Frontiers*, and the combined results (only 44 percent right) were statistically significant and published in *JAMA* (*Journal of the American Medical Association*). It became a sort of Emperor's-New-Clothes event that the media jumped on. James Randi gave me his Skeptic of the Year Award, and *Skeptic* magazine, recognizing the potential of kid experimenters, launched *Jr. Skeptic*. I also had a great time at the Ig Nobel Awards* as a presenter that year.

---

*The Ig Nobel Awards are a parody of the Nobel Prize. Sponsored by the Annals of Improbable Research, a humorous parody of a scientific journal, the Ig Nobels recognize weird, funny, or otherwise odd scientific (or pseudoscientific) "achievements."

TT practitioners came up with silly explanations for why they didn't pass my test—the air-conditioning blew away my HEF, for example—and continue the practice religiously. But to date, none has ever refuted my experiment with another one.

My hometown didn't take much note of my experiment, so I could go back to being a regular kid. Kids mostly just want to play with their friends, and religion isn't that big a deal—though it is, unfortunately, to parents. I could ask a friend, "Do you think God really exists?" and only get a shrug in return. But I soon learned that if I asked that within a parent's earshot, I could be banished from their home, and even be labeled a weirdo. I can remember some neighborhood boys throwing rocks at me and calling me "satanic." (I asked Mom why they called me "Titanic.")

Circumstances made me learn ways to appear an acceptable playmate. If asked what church I attended, I would answer truthfully, "Well, my mom and stepdad don't go to church, and my dad and stepmom are Catholic. I haven't decided yet." This put me in the damned-yet-savable category. While that made me a target for conversion, I thought it an acceptable trade-off for having someone to play with.

Having parents who take on creationism or the Pledge of Allegiance also put a strain on my social life. Though my folks would ask my approval before intervening, I couldn't always predict what I was in for. Some kids reflected their parents' attitudes and shunned me. Fortunately for me, I had a few really good friends who would still sit with me at lunchtime.

> 66 Kids mostly just want to play with their friends, and religion isn't that big a deal—though it is, unfortunately, to parents. I could ask a friend, 'Do you think God really exists?' and only get a shrug in return. But I soon learned that if I asked that within a parent's earshot, I could be banished from their home, and even be labeled a weirdo. 99

My parents put their foot down when it came to "youth group." I'd been invited by friends to attend this gathering of teens for Christian rock, food, and Bible lessons. My parents relented when they learned it was also a place for me to meet atheist teenagers who had been sent there by their parents to be brought back into the fold.

Atheist philosophy was easier to sort out than the value of being an atheist. I found many atheists, well, unpleasant. While I have met some remarkable atheists who are actively involved in making the world more civilized, I am frequently disappointed by atheists who gather only to indulge in rude jokes and angry religion bashing. Give me the company of happy-go-lucky religionists any day.

My best advice to secular parents is to try not to raise grim, cynical, god-obsessed atheist children. Along with the usual secular values (such as appropriate tolerance/intolerance, morality, critical thinking, appreciation for reason and science), don't forget to impart social graces, playfulness, and humor. Those go far in our short existences.

> 66 Along with the usual secular values (such as appropriate tolerance/intolerance, morality, critical thinking, appreciation for reason and science), don't forget to impart social graces, playfulness, and humor. Those go far in our short existences. 99

And as for my parents' naïve plan to keep me from religion until I became an adult—frankly, it didn't work. I suggest instead that children be given lots of information about all sorts of religious concepts. Satisfy their natural curiosity. Trust them to sort out the real from the unreal.

EMILY ROSA grew up in Colorado. In 1998, the appearance of her study on Therapeutic Touch in the Journal of the American Medical Association *created a media sensation and put her in the* Guinness Book of World Records *as the youngest person to publish serious medical research, conducted two years earlier at age nine. She later experimented with "healing magnets" and in eighth grade won first place in her division at the Colorado State Science Fair for measuring the circumference of the world with homemade instruments and unique units of measurement. She studied forensic psychology at the University of Colorado Boulder.*

■ ■

EXCERPT FROM *AUTOBIOGRAPHY*

BERTRAND RUSSELL

My father was a Freethinker, but died when I was only three years old. Wishing me to be brought up without superstition, he appointed two Freethinkers as my guardians. The Courts, however, set aside his will, and had me educated in the Christian faith. . . . If he had directed that I should be educated as a Christadelphian or a Muggletonian, or a Seventh Day Adventist, the Courts would not have dreamed of objecting. A parent has a right to ordain that any imaginable superstition shall be instilled into his children after his death, but has not the right to say that they shall be kept free from superstition if possible. . . .

I was taken on alternate Sundays to the (Episcopalian) Parish Church at Petersham and to the Presbyterian Church at Richmond, while at home I was taught the doctrines of Unitarianism. . . . At [age 15] I began a systematic investigation of the supposed rational arguments in favor of fundamental Christian beliefs. I spent endless hours in meditation upon this subject. I thought that if I ceased to believe in God, freedom and immortality, I should be very unhappy. I found, however, that the reasons given in favor of these dogmas were very unconvincing. . . .

Throughout the long period of religious doubt I had been rendered very unhappy by the gradual loss of belief, but when the process was completed I found to my surprise that I was quite glad to be done with the whole subject.[1]

RAISED WITHOUT RELIGION

OTHER VOICES OF KIDS AND ADULTS RAISED IN NONRELIGIOUS FAMILIES[1]

I don't know what growing up in a religious home is like, so it's hard to describe growing up in a nonreligious home. I am happy not being religious. I think I get to learn more accurate science and history. If you grow up with just one belief, you don't really get to understand all the other beliefs. My parents make sure I know about lots of different belief systems, and they say I can choose one if I like. This makes me happy, because they are letting me make my own decisions and I know they will love me and support me, no matter what.

WILLA (11)

My parents were nominally Christian—presently, my father is a Freemason and my mother appears to have no faith—but this nominal belief was a label I later ascribed. Back then, religion just didn't feature. This was the key. I had no religion pressed upon me; I was not forced to go to church and follow rituals. I went to Sunday school and left stomping one day. It wasn't for me.

Going to boarding school from age seven also had an effect, allowing me to distance myself from my parents to become who I wanted to be. The result of this freedom was that religion wasn't hard-coded. I adopted the Christianity of my school, which I later worked out was theologically utterly inaccurate—I just didn't understand it.

Traveling and the Problem of Evil put paid to this belief early on. This freedom allowed me to grow and flourish and follow evidence to a much greater degree. I didn't have to overcome a psychologically embedded worldview in order to work out the "truth" of the world, as it were. I was born neutral, I was brought up neutral, and I forged my own path with an intellectual freedom that was itself embedded. I was given the tools, not the conclusion.

**JONATHAN PEARCE (39), philosopher and author,
Fareham, Hampshire, United Kingdom**

Being raised without religion is cool. After school my friends all have to go to CCD [Catholic religious education classes] or communion classes and I don't, so I can just do my homework and then have fun and do other things. Also, I don't have to worry about some guy up in the sky watching me all the time, which I kind of think is really creepy. It makes me feel nervous. Is he dead? Why is he watching me? It makes no sense that he's just up there staring at us. I think there's just sky, sky, and more sky up there.

I get a little nervous when I think about dying and not being together with my family anymore. I wish that we could always be together, and it scares me that we might not be since nobody knows what happens. But I'm glad we don't believe in god because that part just doesn't make sense. Plus my friends all say church is boring and on Sundays we always do family stuff, which is definitely not boring.

REESE (8), New Jersey

I was born in the late '70s in Green Bay, Wisconsin, so when I was growing up it seemed like everyone else went to church on Sundays. I was told that I was going to hell a few times, but my family always made being secular seem so normal. My two sisters and I grew up to be very ethical adults without any sort of formal religious upbringing. One of my sisters is an atheist, but my other sister and I are more agnostic. My parents always encouraged a lot of reading, and I feel that a good background in mythology, Shakespeare, and classics teaches just as much about morality as going to church. I actually ended up going to a Jesuit university and found the religion courses to be very interesting since it wasn't something that I was forced to learn as a child.

Being raised secularly was wonderful because I wasn't taught that I was better than others because of some belief. We are all the same and we respect others' beliefs. My husband was also raised secularly and our marriage has benefited. We just don't have the same hang-ups that we might have had otherwise. There's no fear of God. We just want to be good people, and that's exactly how we are raising our children.

CARRIE (36), Milwaukee, Wisconsin

I think one of the benefits is being more open to possibilities. Let your children choose which religion they want because if you don't, the child might rebel more.

TARYN (10), North Carolina

At 66 years old, raised in the Philadelphia Ethical Society since age 14, my fondest memory is the whole family, Mom, Dad, and my six siblings riding the bus to Rittenhouse Square every Sunday morning or piling into the family car (didn't acquire that until I was 16) and driving down. There was a vibrant congregation and Sunday school with a different level for each of us from me on down. As far as Ethical education, I learned so much about other religious traditions because each of us in my grade level had assignments to research and present about Eastern and Western belief systems.

Now I am a member of the Washington Ethical Society. Developing my spiritual fitness at WES is a great way for me to start the week. It is a congregation that adheres very well to the Ethical Movement tradition of service to humanity and the environment.

SHEILA WALTERS (66), Washington, DC

I was brought up nonreligious in northern Virginia. My parents had spent their lives abandoning culture: when they'd moved north to leave the race issues and politics of the South, they had also left their Christianity behind. Their parental tactic for addressing all of these things was largely not to talk about them.

This was fine until I was 11 and a friend tried to convert me. She was genuinely worried about my lack of religion. All of the science and critical thinking I had been brought up with did nothing to protect or inform me in that situation. Her concern made me feel as if there was something wrong with me. It was an awful year. I quietly considered myself a Christian for a short while, then finally found a word to describe myself that made me feel proud of my nonreligious state: I was an atheist. When I told my parents, they were disgusted at the word, even though they were nonbelievers themselves.

MICHELLE CLAY (37)

I loved attending Sunday school at the Brooklyn Society for Ethical Culture. We had discussions, played cooperative games, learned about different traditions, created things, explored ethics, and were encouraged to share what was important to us (be it an item, a joke, or an idea). It was never a chore, although waking up early was often challenging. My favorite part of Ethical Culture is our seasonal festivals because they are unique multigenerational celebrations full of music, stories, and laughter.

My parents chose Ethical Culture because they came from different religions (one was Catholic and one was Jewish) and did not want to be solely responsible for their children's moral upbringing. It was important to them that my brother and I had a religious community of caring people who would nurture our ideas and inspire us to look at life from different views. As a family, we still have difficult discussions on our beliefs, but always find common ground on our values. I greatly appreciate that my parents taught us to share both with them and others.

EMILY NEWMAN (30), communications director,
American Ethical Union, Brooklyn, New York

My mom always encouraged me to challenge arbitrary authority and explore, even when it came to religion. For the latter, I went to different churches, watched different denominations worship (without participating myself), and even tried temple with my Jewish friends. These religions claimed to know ultimate truths about the universe—claims based on faith, not evidence. I could find no reason to elevate one religion's claims over the others as more likely to be true. When I later read Edward Gibbon's piece about philosophers regarding all religions as equally false, it was less a revelation than a confirmation of something I'd realized in my early spiritual wanderings. Thanks Mom!

An early exposure to laughing at the sacrosanct or mocking sacred cows might be critical to raising freethinkers. My family had two Easter traditions: egg hunt with the kids and watching Monty Python's *Life of Brian* together. That early experience of laughing at the ridiculous, even if some people find it sacred, was instrumental in being able to challenge other religious ideas. If we treat an institution as sacred or infallible, its ideas become unassailable—no matter how absurd. Learning early on that ideas should stand or fall on their merits, and not on how deeply or faithfully someone believes in those ideas, contributed significantly to my atheism.

ANDREW SEIDEL, constitutional attorney,
Freedom From Religion Foundation, Madison, Wisconsin

AUTHENTIC SECULAR PARENTING: LETTING CHILDREN CHOOSE

BE-ASIA McKERRACHER

It was when my oldest daughter turned five that I saw her for the person she'd always been. Essence is resilient, fiercely independent, and unabashedly logical in her approach to the world. Even at five, these qualities shone strong. It was the Picture Day fiasco, the day kids learn to dread but parents love—at first.

Essence chose her outfit: a long dress, with layers of pink lace nearly to the ground. It's an elegant garb for a dainty little girl. Instead of soft white or petal pink shoes to match her over-the-top ensemble, my daughter wore her Velcro, strap-across sandals. I despised these sandals. They were hideous: The pink had faded, an inch of brown covered the bottom half, all of the fake bling had fallen off, the Velcro strips were almost two inches longer than the shoes' width—and they smelled. Bad.

My hatred of her shoes didn't really matter to Essence; she had this outfit chosen the day she came home with the picture packet. There would be no changing her mind. And while she floated safe in the security of her coming day, I spent a full week fixated on that pair of shoes. If she took pictures in those sandals, it would ruin everything—for me.

(Hold that thought.)

When she rounded the corner into the living room on picture day, she was so proud of herself—from top to bottom—shoes included. She had listened to me say (in so many words) that I didn't want her to take a picture in those shoes, but Essence turned down every offer for something different. She didn't want new ones, she refused to let me clean those, and she saw nothing whatsoever wrong with them. She left the house ready for picture day and all I could do was shake my head.

I'd wanted to raise a freethinking child—and I had!

Parenting affords us the luxury of children who want to be themselves in all areas of their lives and as secular parents, we are more than happy to oblige them. But I didn't learn this powerful parenting skill on my own, and I now know individuality in children is not limited to what they wear. Beyond clothing or vegetable choices, children have a sense of individuality that must be nurtured on every level as they grow and mature.

While there may be a plethora of parenting books designed to offer advice and guidance, few offer a method. But I stumbled across an author video that moved me from "parenting" children to teaching them. The author's name was Barbara Coloroso. She was utterly captivating, but initially, her respect for children left me swirling in confusion. Many of us first-generation secular parents came from a world of obedience and respect—for adults, that is. Children were seen and not heard. The notion of giving children the authority—the power— over their wants and desires simply didn't happen.

But Coloroso's methods come from a child-centered perspective, one that most secular parents have absorbed. The plain truth is that you cannot force children to do anything without breaking who they are inside. Children, like adults, are people who yearn to understand and have ownership in their lives.

Superficial power is a start, but if we are to raise independent critical thinkers, we must go further. Coloroso's method for helping parents raise self-controlling and positive children centers on what she calls the six critical life messages parents must convey to their children through our actions, our words, and our deeds. Those messages are simple, focused, and worth adopting as secular parents. They say:

- ◆ I believe in you.
- ◆ I trust in you.
- ◆ I know you can handle this.
- ◆ You are listened to.
- ◆ You are cared for.
- ◆ You are important to me.

As I fumbled through my parenting, I used Coloroso's critical messages as my light in the darkness. I devoured her book *Kids Are Worth It!: Giving Your Child the Gift of Inner Discipline*. Those messages are the foundation to raising children who are just as empathetic to the plight of the dying bumblebee population as they are to children in war-torn areas. If we want children to have the self-confidence to stand up to bullies (in child or adult form), then they need to know that behind their words are parents who say, "I know that you can do this."

And while Barbara Coloroso was not herself a secular parent, taking those six critical life messages that she developed and moving them into the realm of nonreligious parenting affords us an opportunity for a new kind of conversation.

One subject that tests this commitment to raising independent, self-determining kids is the right of a freethinking child to adopt a religious identity if he or she so chooses.

Such a conversation may sound absurd, but the reality is that we are raising freethinkers—young people who are afforded a life that revolves around critical thinking, choice, and using reason and logic to view the world. These are the basic principles of secular parenting. But what if a secular child uses that freedom to choose faith? Is such a thing possible? Can faith be a choice?

Instead of keeping this conversation in the shadows, I propose that we begin as a secular community to sound the alarm of rationality. Of course a secular child can become a believer in adulthood. According to the Pew Research Center's 2014 Religious Landscape Survey, of the 9.2 percent of American adults who say they were raised in religiously unaffiliated homes, nearly half came to identify with a religion at some later point. The reasons these young adults decided against a secular life vary, though many experts suspect the main culprit is marriage or relationship conformity.[1]

Sadly, the secular community has taken the bait of those who abhor rational discussion on the topic of faith, scrambling to come up with reasons for the data. We have succumbed to the fear of becoming invisible once again. Instead of embracing religious literacy for our children, secular parents often shelter their kids from religious texts and religious spaces. For some reason, we have shrunk against the pressure of reality. This is not the way to raise a genuine freethinker. Instead of shielding our babes in hopes of keeping them secular, we must allow them to breathe.

> 66 Instead of embracing religious literacy for our children, secular parents often shelter their kids from religious texts and religious spaces. . . . This is not the way to raise a genuine freethinker. Instead of shielding our babes in hopes of keeping them secular, we must allow them to breathe. 99

So how do we encourage free choice of worldview for our children while upholding the principles of secular parenting? On the surface, the answer is straightforward: Free choice *is* one of the principles of secular parenting. But putting that principle into practice takes some doing.

The first step revolves around those same principles that Coloroso beautifully gifted the parenting community with not so long ago. When we say, "You are listened to," to our freethinking children, secular parents commit ourselves to an open and honest dialogue about faith and the choices they have. We are committing ourselves to something that our parents couldn't or wouldn't do for us. To do that in reality, we need to add to Coloroso's list. Here are a few important truisms secular parents need in order to really listen to our kiddos as they work to create their own worldview. We need to be willing to say:

- My reality is not your reality.
- Faith cannot divide us.
- We can love each other and disagree at the same time.

This really hit home for our family when we took our then thirteen- and fourteen-year-old daughters to Europe. As much as I hated going to church as a kid—and I really did hate going—my reality isn't their reality. They were mesmerized by the churches and cathedrals in London. Before we even entered, their eyes were drawn to the sheer size and craftsmanship of these great artifacts of history. They took dozens of pictures, lit prayer candles, and had quiet moments in the churches that they visited. As a family, we descended the stairs of Saint Martin's Church in London and created intricate brass rubbings, all while in the company of the religiously devout.

The beauty of these experiences was that we as a family were safe in our secularity; that is, we had no fear of conversion or coercion. That's because as parents, we embraced the mantra that says, "Our reality is not your reality."

Yes, most secular parents were forced, bullied, or guilt-tripped into faith as children. But for secular children being raised by first-generation secular parents, things are different. They can be exposed to concepts like prayer, ritual, and orthodox tradition with an open, skeptical mind. In this way, faith as an exploration becomes a family goal—something for everyone to get excited about. Our girls went to those churches not because they were forced to go, or to save their souls, but because of their natural curiosity. They found them charming, and because at the end of the day they knew that the second truism, "Faith cannot divide us," reigns supreme in our home, they spent that time making connections instead of worrying about ill intentions. The drive to know and learn, present in all children, is particularly cultivated in those raised by secular parents.

This is the legacy that we want to leave our children. We must combat the apprehension and anxiety religious spaces cause us by knowing that our children's choices are not ours to make. You cannot choose your child's faith any more than your parents were able to ultimately choose your faith. Our responsibility as secular parents is to remind our kids of this one real fact: No matter their choice of faith, our love for them will stay forever true. It is when parents reactively do the opposite—shelter their children to keep them uninformed—that we encourage them to "leave the fold." How else can secular kids get the knowledge their minds crave if parents are not creating opportunities for understanding? This strains family relationships and creates tension—and the cycle of faith-based trauma continues.

It all boils down to this: What is our intention as secular parents? Is it to make an army of little atheists and agnostics in the war against faith? Or do we want to raise educated citizens, capable of making their own decisions about everything, including faith? Secular parenting is about offering more than a shelter from the damaging effects of faith. We cannot parade our young ones into the chapel or the mosque and simply walk back out the door. Considerations of age, maturation, and actual desire all come into play. We also cannot fear the reality of choice: that our children may not grow up to be secular adults. Fearing this reality will not keep it from happening.

Our chief goal as secular parents is to instill a real passion for critical thinking and evaluation. The world our children will inherit is masked in a shroud of sexual innuendo, deceptive advertising, and the cruel manipulation of those not clever enough to understand the game. If we fail to allow our little freethinkers a chance to flex their critical thinking muscles often, and about issues that affect their worldview, then we have failed to prepare them for the most important struggles that lie ahead: those that are fought inside their own minds.

When we as secular parents focus on instilling critical thinking and positive self-awareness, we are helping them free themselves from the undue influence of media and culture that threatens to make their decisions for them. The idea of a child choosing faith over a secular life then becomes something that is not to be feared; child choice becomes a celebration.

When my daughter spent two months researching Buddhism—and seriously considering conversion—I didn't harass her. I chose not to bully her into my choice of secularism. I took her to the library, we watched videos, and I tried to find a Buddhist temple for her to investigate. Had she moved to convert, I can't say how I would have handled it. As children, many of us had our paths chosen for us—forced by tradition and mental manipulation. Our children, however, do have a choice, and we are the ones as secular parents responsible for enabling such options.

This is the crucial difference—not between secularism and religion, but between choice and choicelessness.

If secular parenting is to survive and thrive in the current millennium, it will need to adjust. Part of that is knowing that not all children born and raised secular will choose that path in their adult lives. As long as communication is open and love is apparent, we will have left a lasting legacy of freethought, and we, as secular parents, will have thoroughly done our job.

BE-ASIA McKERRACHER is the author of Secular Parenting in a Religious World *(2014). She holds a master's degree in English from Truman State University and teaches English at the high school and college levels. Her website, The Secular Parent (thesecularparent.com), focuses on a wide range of issues affecting secular parents and their children. Be-Asia lives in Kansas City, Missouri, with her husband and two children.*

■ ■

MY FATHER'S HOUSE

DAN BARKER

When I was a child I thought of childish things:
Eternal life in paradise with angel wings,
A father up in heaven who would hover over me,
And tell me what to think, tell me what to be;
But now that I have grown,
It's time to use my own good mind.

I'm outa here! Let me outa here!
I found my own place—
I've left my father's house behind.

A normal Dad is really glad to realize
His little child has now become, before his eyes,
An independent person who can stand on steady feet,
An equal human being with character complete.
But God is not that way—
He orders me to stay his child.

For God so loved the world he gave his only son—
A sacrifice to pay the price for everyone—
And if you believe that this deserves a Fatherhood Award,
You can move in with the guy, and he will be your Lord.
But listen to this song:
Forever is a long, long time!

—Lyrics from "My Father's House" © 2004 by Dan Barker

My mother-in-law, Anne Gaylor (founder of the Freedom From Religion Foundation), claimed that you can't raise children. Children raise themselves. We parents are simply facilitators. If we are the birth parents, we bequeath some of our genetics, for better or worse. We give them a home, an environment in which to feel safe and grow, access to education, resources, health care, love, and friendship. Then we let nature take its course. It's not as though if we failed to do some critical task the kids would never grow up, never find a way through life. Anne's four children grew up just fine; I married one of them.

I'm not an expert on child raising. I don't think anyone really is. My only claim to credibility is that I do have five children. Having children of your own does make you a kind of expert, though that is probably because much of our learning comes through our mistakes.

Kids should not be forced into a straitjacket of parental expectations. I think parents who obsess about how to raise their children may actually do more harm than good. This is the children's world too, and they are finding their way just like we did. Thinking back on how I was raised, I am surprised to remember that I never once thought of myself as "the son of my parents." Yes, of course, I had a mom and a dad, and they were great parents, good examples, and I was proud of them and love them dearly, but I never considered it was my purpose in life to be an extension of their lives. I never saw myself as little Norman Barker, put on this earth to make him look good. What child has ever thought that way? (The dedication to my book *Losing Faith in Faith: From Preacher to Atheist* is, "To Norman Barker, my only father." If we do need a father figure, it may as well be a real person. My dad is someone who has truly earned my respect.)

I think most freethinking parents have similar feelings. We don't want to force our kids into any mold, unless reason and kindness are molds—well, no, reason and kindness are open ended, not constricting. What we truly want is the satisfaction of seeing our children become mature, self-reliant human beings, at any age, thinking for themselves, free and happy. Parents who want anything else are obsessed with control and not free and happy themselves.

My first four children were the product of a Christian marriage, from the time when I was a minister. They are all great human beings: generous, thoughtful, caring. The three girls are now raising children of their own and doing a wonderful job. My son is still single, a chef and a guitar player. Even though we took them to church as children and tried to instill "Christian" values, they ended up thinking for themselves. In this case, the religion didn't seem to do too much damage. My Christian wife and I divorced, mainly for religious reasons,* and this clearly had an impact on the four kids, as all divorces do. However, I think we were lucky. My former wife and I decided that we would never place the children in a position where they were forced to choose between parents. My love and support for the kids

---

* Editor's note: To learn more about Dan's deconversion, see *Godless: How an Evangelical Preacher Became One of America's Leading Atheists* (2008).

has always been unconditional, and they know it. I repeatedly told them that they are free to think their own thoughts. They don't have to agree with me. They don't have to be atheists or agnostics in order to earn my respect. Consequently, at least two of them now have views that I would call freethinking, and the other two, although perhaps nominally religious, are quite liberal and open in their beliefs, which also counts as freethinking where the rubber meets the road in their daily lives. I don't think any of them go to church, not regularly, although one was attending a Unitarian fellowship for a while. To my former wife's credit—she later remarried a Baptist minister and remains a conservative believer—her love for the kids has not been tempered by the fact that we all don't agree.

I married Annie Laurie Gaylor in 1987. She is a third-generation freethinker and editor of *Freethought Today*. She and I are now co-presidents of the Freedom From Religion Foundation. Our daughter, Sabrina, a fourth-generation freethinker, is currently in high school. She has been raised with a complete lack of religion. She went to a friend's bat mitzvah some years ago, but beyond that has never been to a church or worship service other than the occasional Unitarian fellowship where Annie Laurie or I have spoken or performed. Most Unitarians are freethinkers, and our "service" was nonreligious.

When Sabrina was little, she had a vivid imagination, like most children. (She still does.) We all had a lot of fun pretending, playing games with imaginary creatures and friends. That is a healthy part of learning and growing. Rather than tell Sabrina that the Tooth Fairy and Santa Claus were lies, we told her that we were pretending they were real, just like characters in a book or cartoon. She never had to go through the process of unlearning Santa or the Easter Bunny. We figured that this would allow her to have the fun of childhood imagination, not deprived of anything that her friends might have, yet not having to deal with the thought that her parents had deceived her. She "got it" from the very beginning.

When Sabrina was about three or four, I reminded her that we were just pretending and wanted to confirm that she truly grasped the concept of imagination. I guess I was a little worried that she might think we were expecting her to actually believe the stories, but she didn't. She was quite clear and sensible. "I know it's just pretend, Dad. But it's fun."

So I asked her, "How do you know the difference between what is pretend and what is real?"

"It's easy," she said immediately. "Things that are pretend can do things that you can't do."

Wow. She pretty much summed up naturalistic philosophy in those few words. "Things that you can't do" was her way of saying "things that can't be done." We never explicitly taught her this worldview. We had not been taking her to "atheist Sunday school" in order to indoctrinate her as a materialist. We were not making her memorize "agnostic scriptures" or sing "naturalistic hymns." She was simply a normal child in an environment that allows for individual thinking, and left on her own was quite capable of making natural distinctions.

> Imagination is an amazing thing. It can be a fount of creativity, or, if taken seriously, a source of immense confusion. Just think what the world would be like if the Apostle Paul or Muhammad or Joseph Smith had been cautioned not to take their imaginations literally.

Of course, over the years, Sabrina has heard Annie Laurie and me talking about freethought and state/church separation. She has come to some of the meetings of the Freedom From Religion Foundation and listened to many of the speeches. So perhaps this amounts to a kind of "freethought education," though it is all voluntary.

I should be careful when I say that Sabrina is being raised as a fourth-generation freethinker. That is technically not correct. She is a freethinker, and we are a freethinking family, but a person's identity is not tied to their family. Sabrina knows that she is free to choose otherwise. She knows that she has the liberty to become a Buddhist, Catholic, Mormon, or Pentecostal. She also knows that if she made such a decision, we would be disappointed, and that we would be equally free to argue with her about it. However, we all agree that her choices are not mandated by her parents' disappointment. In any event, there seems to be little danger that someone like Sabrina, having grown up in a freethinking environment, would be attracted to dogmatism.

In his book *The God Delusion*, Richard Dawkins denounces those who identify children by the religion of their parents. There is no such thing as a Christian child or a Muslim child or an atheist child, he insists. We should call them children from a Christian or Muslim or atheist family. To call someone a Catholic child is to claim that the views of parents can be forced into the minds of children. Children might indeed grow up to adopt the views of their parents, as so often happens with religious indoctrination—and we have to wonder how truly "free" such a choice is—but the children, as children, are not free to responsibly choose their own lifetime religious identity.

Steven Pinker's great book *The Blank Slate* shows that we come prepackaged with a basic human nature that is not as malleable as many religious, political, and philosophical systems imagine. We are who we are, biological organisms in a natural environment, and we get into deep trouble if we try to deny it.

I think the greatest problem with religious systems such as Christianity is their pessimistic view of human nature. If you teach a generation of children that they are sinful creatures by nature, that left on their own they are morally corrupt, deserving of eternal torment in hell, that they are not to be trusted to think their own (selfish, evil) thoughts, all of this can become—has become—a self-fulfilling prophecy. Whole segments of the population grow up with a negative self-image, thinking they really are rotten, in need of a savior or father figure. They are told they are bad, so they act like it. Their religion exaggerates and demonizes normal human feelings, turning them into cosmic struggles with evil, creating devils to be fought instead of problems to be solved.

At the 2005 World Religions Conference, I was asked to represent atheism, sitting on the stage with a Buddhist, Muslim, Christian, Jew, Sikh, Hindu, and Native American spiritualist. (I accepted the invitation only after making it clear that atheism is not a religion, and they agreed to include it as a "world philosophy.") The theme of the conference was salvation, and each of us was asked to summarize our respective positions on that topic. After pointing out that sin is a religious concept, hence salvation is merely a religious solution to a religious problem—would we respect a doctor who ran around cutting people with a knife in order to sell them a bandage?—I ended with these words: "If salvation is the cure, then atheism is the prevention."

> 66 If you teach a generation of children that they are sinful creatures by nature, that left on their own they are morally corrupt, deserving of eternal torment in hell, that they are not to be trusted to think their own (selfish, evil) thoughts, all of this can become—has become—a self-fulfilling prophecy. 99

Many in the audience laughed at that comment, some who should not have been laughing. They got the point: Much of religious education is an endeavor to solve a nonproblem. It is a confusing waste of time.

It is better to tell children that they are okay the way they are. Most secular parents are optimistic about human nature. We do not make our children feel bad for being—well, children. We do our best to affirm the positive potential of our children, and of ourselves. That is the major difference between religious and secular parenting.

DAN BARKER is the author of Godless: How an Evangelical Preacher Became One of America's Leading Atheists *(2008) and* God: The Most Unpleasant Character in All Fiction *(2016). With his wife, Annie Laurie Gaylor, he is copresident of the Freedom From Religion Foundation, an organization working to keep state and church separate and to promote freethought. Dan has five children and has written three books for children:* Just Pretend: A Freethought Book for Children *(2002),* Maybe Yes, Maybe No: A Guide for Young Freethinkers *(1990), and* Maybe Right, Maybe Wrong: A Guide for Young Skeptics *(1992).*

■ ■

PASSING DOWN THE JOY OF NOT COLLECTING STAMPS

PENN JILLETTE

St. Ignatius Loyola, the founder of the Jesuit Order, once said, "Give me the child until he is seven and I will show you the man." Some web pages say that might really be a Francis Xavier quotation, others say it was "some Jesuit" who said it, and all the careful web pages credit it to "some guy."

Little kids have to trust adults or they die. Trust has to be built in. So while you're teaching them to eat, stay out of traffic, and not drink too much of what's underneath the sink, you can abuse that trust and burn in the evil idea that faith is good. It'll often stick with them longer than not drinking bleach. It seems if someone snuck the idea of faith into you at an early age, you're more likely to do it to your own kids.

If your childhood trust was not abused with faith, or if somehow you kicked it in your travels down the road, your work is done. You don't have to worry too much about your kids. You don't ever have to teach Atheism. You don't have to teach an absence of guilt for things they didn't do. As Atheist parents, you just have one more reason to keep your kids away from priests. Tell your kids the truth as you see it, and let the marketplace of ideas work as they grow up. I don't know who said, "Atheism is a religion like not collecting stamps is a hobby," maybe it was Francis Xavier, or more likely The Amazing James Randi, but, some guy or gal said it, and it's a more important idea than any Jesuit ever came up with. You have to work hard to get kids to believe nonsense. If you're not desperately selling lies, the work is a lot easier.

> 66 Tell your kids the truth as you see it, and let the marketplace of ideas work as they grow up. I don't know who said, 'Atheism is a religion like not collecting stamps is a hobby,' . . . but . . . it's a more important idea than any Jesuit ever came up with. 99

My kids are really young, they're still babies, they can't even talk yet, but what the hell, we're still a little bit careful what we say. When someone sneezes we say, "That's funny," because it is. We don't have any friends who are into any kind of faith-based hooey, so our kids will just think that "damn it" follows "god" like "Hubbard" (or something) follows "mother." That's cool. That's easy.

I know this is unfashionable in the Atheist community, but truth just needs to be stated; it doesn't have to be hyped. (This is the point where you check again who wrote this. Remember what Bob Dobbs said: "I don't practice what I preach because I'm not the kind of person I'm preaching to.")

There is no god, and that's the simple truth. If every trace of any single religion were wiped out and nothing was passed on, it would never be created exactly that way again. There might be some other nonsense in its place, but not that exact nonsense. If all of science were wiped out, it would still be true and someone would find a way to figure it out again. Without hype, Lot's salt-heap ho would never be thought of again. Without science, the Earth still goes around the sun and someday someone will find a way to prove that again. Science is so important because it's a way to truth, but the truth doesn't depend on it. Reality exists outside of humans; religion does not. The bad guys have to try to get the kids early to keep their jive alive. We good guys should try to get the truth out there, but the stakes just aren't as high for us. Most anyone who is serious about science will lose some faith. Maybe not all their faith, but they'll lose a hunk of it before getting that Nobel Prize. No matter how bad the polls on Americans look, the people who do science for a living aren't being fooled. The polls on belief in evolution make the USA look bad, but maybe Turkey is the only Western country with worse pollsters than the USA—ever think of that?

Evolution is the truth. And with truth comes a lack of panic. I don't lose sleep over creation myths being taught in public schools. Who trusts anything from government schools? "Better to be uneducated than educated by your government" (that quotation is mine). The bad guys always have to fight for their ideas to be taught. They must cheat. Government force, propaganda, and hype are the tools you desperately need when you're wrong. Truth abides.

Dr. Richard Dawkins had a christian education, but he kicked that away before taking his seat in the Darwin BarcaLounger at Oxford. The bad guys got the Dawk until he was 7. So what? That race has been run; they fought the truth and the truth won. I went to Sunday school and the reality of the creationist myth stayed as true for me as the certainty that the Greenfield High School football team was going to win the Turkey Day game because we had P . . . E . . . P . . . PEP! PEP! PEP! Jesus christ, doesn't anyone but Paul Simon and me remember it was all crap we learned in high school anyway and all the kids always knew it?

Evolution was true before Darwin. Evolution was true in the 16th century when Loyola did or didn't start that quotation. Evolution has been true as long as there has been life on Earth, and it always will be true. If you pick your side carefully, you don't have to fight as hard.

All this assumes you're an out-of-the-closet Atheist parent. Truth doesn't live in the closet. You have to make it clear to everyone including your kids that there is no god. If you're not doing that every chance you get, then the other side will win. They'll win only in the short term; we only get to live in the short term. You don't have to fight, but you have to do your part—you have to tell the truth. You have to be honest. You don't have to force schools to say there's no god, but you have to say it. You have to say it all the time. No one can relax in a closet.

Those of us who are out-of-the-closet Atheist parents have all that extra time on Sunday mornings to love our kids. We can use that time to hold them, laugh, and dance around together. Tell your kids there's no god and be done with it. Jesus christ, your kids aren't stupid.

PENN JILLETTE is the Emmy Award–winning illusionist/entertainer/ debunker of the duo Penn & Teller; author of several books, including God, No!: Signs You May Already Be an Atheist and Other Magical Tales *(2011); and star and producer of such films as* The Aristocrats *and* An Honest Liar *and the Showtime series* Bullshit! *(which debunks such frauds as alien abduction, magnetic cures, and talking to the dead). Penn is married to producer Emily Zolten Jillette, with whom he has two children, Moxie CrimeFighter (born 2005) and Zolten (born 2006).*

■ ■

ADDITIONAL RESOURCES FOR "PERSONAL REFLECTIONS"

Many books have included heartfelt personal reflections by those who have found their way out of religious faith and into naturalism. Many of these include stories of childhood and parenthood; all are fascinating reading. Most are intended for adult readers, but you know your kids best.

Barker, Dan. *Godless: How an Evangelical Preacher Became One of America's Leading Atheists.* Ulysses, 2008. The personal journey of a searching mind from the pulpit to atheism, a journey made painful not by his conscience but by those around him. Teens and adults.

Sweeney, Julia. *Letting Go of God.* DVD. Julia Sweeney Blum, 2006. In this hilarious, honest, insightful monologue, comedian Julia Sweeney describes her journey from a Catholic upbringing to religious doubt and finally to atheism. This is the one to hand to a friend who is questioning his or her religious convictions or just wants to know more about atheists and atheism.

The God Who Wasn't There. DVD. Beyond Belief Media, 2005. Former fundamentalist Brian Flemming takes viewers through his years in a strict Christian school where hell was promised to those who doubted. But he doubted anyway, first terrified and then intrigued by his growing realization that though the wheel of religion keeps spinning, there's no hamster.

Willson, Jane Wynne. *Parenting Without God: Experiences of a Humanist Mother.* Educational Heretics Press, 1999. Don't judge this book by its rather basic cover, or by the years that have passed since it was written. This slim volume of reflections by one of the leading lights in British humanism is a gem, one of the finest contributions to the literature on nonreligious parenting. Buy it used for a song on Amazon or Amazon.co.uk.

2

Living with Religion

INTRODUCTION

Religion is an understandable response to being human. It's not always a good response—sometimes it's counterproductive, and often downright dangerous—but it is an understandable impulse. Our brains have evolved to seek patterns and find causes. This pattern- and cause-finding is a good thing, something that has served us well for millions of years. And when we don't know the answer, we guess—also a good thing, as long as you stay open to whatever new and better answers might float by.

I loved "religion" growing up and spent countless hours reading about it—though it wasn't the religion of my neighbors and relatives I was soaking up, but the religion of ancient Greece and Rome, better known now as myths. I found the stories fascinating and recognized them as creative attempts to understand the world. They revealed something not just about being Greek or Roman or ancient, but about being human. The ancients marveled at the stars, just as I did, and feared death, and wondered why spring came so reliably, year after year, why Africans and Europeans look different, how the world began, how spiders got so good at weaving, why we go to war and fall in love. They didn't reveal much about the world, these myths, but they spoke volumes about humanity.

The similarities between cultural myths can be striking. A deity miraculously impregnates a mortal woman, who then gives birth to a great leader and deliverer of men. A father, on divine instructions, prepares to sacrifice his only son, only to be stopped at the last moment by the arrival of a ram. A little guy defeats a giant with one blow. A divine one miraculously turns a paltry plate of food into a banquet to feed the many. If you were born into Western civilization after the fourth century, you'll clearly recognize these as stories from the Jewish and Christian scriptures. If you were born before then, however, you'd have recognized them as Greek and Roman myths. They are both.

Cultural legends and myths are among our greatest inheritances from the past. They are real treasures, insights into the human condition, diminished not one whit by the fact that most were once thought true by the great majority of those who heard them. Persian, Greek, Roman, Sumerian, Norse, Celtic, and Egyptian mythologies passed into the category of recognized fiction, while the Abrahamic mythologies are still considered religions by many. They too will most likely pass into recognized fiction, whether 10 or 10,000 years from now, almost certainly to be replaced by new religions, most of which will borrow mythic archetypes from their predecessors—and on turns the great karmic wheel.

I sometimes claim that I have "set religion aside." Actually, that's a bit like saying someone who rides a bike to work has set traffic aside. I'm still in it, still surrounded by it, and I always will be. For better and worse, religion is likely to be a permanent part of the human world. Our job as secular parents is not to work toward some fantasy of a world free of religion, but to help our kids learn to coexist with religion.

Coexistence does not mean silent acceptance of all consequences of religious belief. On the contrary, silence and inaction in the face of dangerous immorality is itself immoral. We have to engage religious people and institutions in just the way we wish to be engaged ourselves, as co-participants in the world. We should reasonably but loudly protest the intolerance, ignorance, and fear that are born of religion while at the same time reasonably and loudly applauding religious people and institutions whenever charity, tolerance, empathy, honesty, and any of our other shared values are in evidence. An important part of this is recognizing that not all expressions of religion and not all religious people are alike. Be sure to help kids recognize that the loudest, most ignorant and most intolerant religious adherents—whether raving radical Muslim clerics or raving radical Christian televangelists—do not represent all believers, nor even the majority. Though institutional religion itself is an unfortunate thing, the majority of individual believers are decent and thoughtful people with whom we have more in common than not. Saying that to yourself once in a while, and to your kids, can move the dialogue further forward than just about anything else.

The vision we should encourage in our children is not a world free of religion but one in which no idea or action is granted immunity from discussion and critique—including, of course, our own. That is the vision of living with religion to which this chapter is devoted.

Some of the authors in this chapter warn against the ill effects of religious evangelism, including the demonization of honest disbelief and the erosion of our religiously nonpartisan public schools. Others are optimistic about the prospects of cooperation, right down to the sharing of a home and marriage between a believer and a nonbeliever.

New to this edition is Wendy Thomas Russell, author of *Relax, It's Just God*, who addresses both the how and why of teaching children about things in which we ourselves do not believe. Neil Carter, creator of the popular Godless in Dixie blog, describes the heartrending experience of becoming an atheist while the children he had taught to believe continue to do so—and now with the added worry that Dad is destined for hell.

Libby Anne of the blog Love, Joy, Feminism writes about a situation that most nonreligious parents know all too well: the challenge of raising freethinkers in the shadow of grandparents who are fervently religious.

Living with religion is a literal reality for a nonreligious parent with a religious partner. I have some experience with this myself, having married a Southern Baptist who remained a Baptist for the first 13 years of our marriage. It's more common than most people think: 59 percent of the religiously unaffiliated who are married have a religious partner. In this chapter, I offer an essay about the specific parenting challenges that arise from the religious/nonreligious mixed marriage and some strategies that have worked well for many such couples.

The chapter finishes with two returning favorites from the first edition, Stu Tanquist and Ed Buckner, on what church-state separation does and doesn't means for kids in public schools.

The "Additional Resources" section includes several resources for religious literacy. One of the most enlightening and gentle ways to help children accept myth for its insights into humanity while keeping it distinct from fact is to steadily trace the patterns of the complete human mythic tapestry. Buy a good volume of classical myths for kids, and buy Chrystine Trooien's *Christian Mythology for Kids*. To whet kids' appetites and introduce the pantheon of gods, read a few of the basic myths: Cronos swallowing his children, Zeus defeating the Titans and dividing the tripartite world, Icarus, Phaeton, and so on. Then begin interweaving Christian and Jewish mythologies, matched if you can with their classical parallels. Read the story of Danae and Perseus, in which a god impregnates a woman, who gives birth to a great hero; then read the divine insemination of Mary and birth of Christ story. Read the story of the infant boy who is abandoned in the wilderness to spare him from death, only to be found by a servant of the king who brings him to the palace to be raised as the king's child. It's the story of Moses—and the story of Oedipus. No denigration of the Judeo-Christian stories is necessary; kids simply see that myth is myth.

Ideally, kids can come to a view of our mythic inheritance, including Judeo-Christian myth, as a creative attempt to understand an incomprehensible world when there were few other means to do so. With the rise of science, our real understanding has dwarfed even our richest mythic creations for pure wonder and awe inspiration, but the myths remain dazzling, mesmerizing tributes to our collective imagination, to be admired and enjoyed. A child whose exposure to the explosive wonder of science grows in parallel to his or her engagement with myth is unlikely to allow them to mix. Our creative fictions and our marvelous facts are each too precious in their own domains for us to do without either. The more we bring children to a real understanding of religious belief, the greater chance they will have of coming to terms with it, of living with it—and of having believers learn at last to live with and understand them in return.

■ ■ ■ ■ ■ ■ ■ ■ ■ ■ ■ ■ ■

INTRODUCING KIDS TO THINGS WE DON'T BELIEVE

WENDY THOMAS RUSSELL

When I first set out to write a book about how secular parents could and should address religion with their kids, I emailed the communications director of an atheist group in New York. I was in search, I explained, of secular parents who might talk about how they had introduced their own kids to religion.

"As an atheist," she wrote back, "I did not introduce my children to religion. And nobody I know [in this group] would introduce their kids to religion."

Too often, it seems, parents (both religious and non) equate religious literacy with religious indoctrination and simply dismiss or ignore concepts they don't personally believe to be true or valuable. It's a shame.

Not only is religious literacy a necessary part of being an educated citizen in today's world, but it's also an important part of instilling in our kids empathy and genuine tolerance for people who hold different worldviews.

Perhaps no one knows this better than E. D. Hirsch, the renowned author of the *Dictionary of Cultural Literacy*. "A religiously diverse society like ours should encourage students to range outside of their religious comfort zone in order to encourage respect for other faiths," Hirsch wrote. "Religious literacy is, in part, crucial so we have the necessary knowledge and motivation to actively welcome those of other faiths and particularly religious minorities.[1]"

Some years ago, a consortium of 17 major religious and educational organizations released the handbook *Religion in the Public School Curriculum: Questions and Answers*, which made a strong case for the importance of religious studies. "Omission of facts about religion," it says, "can give students the false impression that the religious life of humankind is insignificant or unimportant. Failure to understand even the basic symbols, practices, and concepts of the various religions makes much of history, literature, art, and contemporary life unintelligible.[2]"

Religious literacy has other advantages as well. Several nonreligious parents I interviewed have made clear, for example, that religious knowledge can serve a more practical purpose: It can prevent embarrassment and even bullying. One woman raised within the pantheistic Eckankar religion told me her ignorance of mainstream religion made her feel isolated as a child.

"Having grown up with a parent in a religion far from the norm," she said, "I have an idea about the feelings of 'otherness' my kids could experience. At the age of 12, I had no idea what the word 'priest' meant. . . . I hope to do things a bit different than my parents, and give my kids lessons in religious literacy so they don't feel so foreign at times."

A mom told me her family was "accused of being devil worshipers" because her daughter didn't know who Jesus was when asked about him on the playground. Had the little girl simply been familiar with the concept of the Christian messiah, the entire episode might have been avoided.

This is not to suggest that children should feel compelled to lie or cover up their families' belief systems just to avoid conflict—not at all! But knowledge is powerful, particularly for kids growing up among very religious peers. When kids have shared knowledge of holidays, stories, characters, or beliefs, they often are better equipped to focus their attention on what they have in common with religious kids rather than what they don't. That can go a long way toward cooling tensions.

"So far my son's religious literacy is hiding the fact that we don't believe," said one mother, who was making it a priority to teach her son about Christianity. "Plus, he may very well end up believing—so if and when any negative impacts occur [among peers], it will be as a result of his actions and decisions."

What We Mean When We Say "Religious Literacy"

When people hear the words *religious literacy*, their eyes tend to glaze over. It sounds like work—work for the kid, work for the adult. So let's start with a little demystification.

First, you do not need to be a religious scholar to give your kids a foundation for the vast network of beliefs and customs that we call religion. In fact, you don't need a formalized plan at all. Religious literacy requires only that you look for opportunities in your everyday life to point out religious symbols, explain religious concepts, or ask religious questions. In this way, you relate religion to the here and now, and you set yourself up as your child's go-to person for religious and spiritual inquiries. You are the person your child approaches when he confronts religion in the world around him; you are the guide who sets things straight, talks through confusion, and supports him as he reaches his own conclusions about supernatural beliefs.

Second, the importance of religious literacy lies not in what you say but in how you say it. When you speak about religion factually—that is, you try your best to keep your personal biases and judgments out of your talks—and when you make your conversations fun and engaging, you show your child that you see value in discussing religion openly and in the spirit of kindness. You encourage children to treat people on the content of their characters, not the fundamentals of their faith. And you show your little ones that you don't view religion as something threatening or boring or beneath you, all of which can sabotage religious literacy, not to mention religious tolerance.

Consider the words of Esther Boyd, a humanist working at Johns Hopkins University as an interfaith chaplain:

> Religious literacy requires that we are not afraid to discuss religion in public, whether it is in the classroom or a cocktail party. It removes the taboo from discussing what we believe and why and how we live it out and how others respond to us and how we respond to the lived practices of others. Religious literacy is learning how to navigate the exploration of other faiths and traditions, of learning to be respectful and sensitive, and of learning to shed our preconceived ideas.[3]

I really love how she words that—"not afraid to discuss religion." It makes for an excellent goal: to give kids enough understanding that they aren't afraid to explore religion on their own.

Five Tips for Engaging Your Kids in Religious Discussions

Religious literacy, like religion, is no science. How you address the topic will depend largely on your child's (and your own) personality and interests. So will the "when" and "where" of your talks. Personally, I've found car rides to be a great setting for conversations with my daughter—not just because we pass by so many things that prompt dialogue, but because we both tend to be more thoughtful in the car. The monotony lends itself to more existential questions and deeper conversations about a wide variety of beliefs. Bedtime also seems to be a natural fit for us, perhaps because I sometimes bring home library books relating to one particular religious belief or custom or legend or holiday.

Here are some more tips:

Start early. Sometimes parents underestimate their kids' intelligence as a subconscious excuse to get out of uncomfortable situations; please don't be one of them. If you open up discussions when kids are young—around, say, age four or five—they are likely to be quite interested in what you have to say and to ask great questions that will undoubtedly deepen their knowledge. No, they may not understand or remember everything, but the greater good is that you get the ball rolling. The longer you wait, the more likely discussions will become awkward, unnerving, contrived, or difficult. Waiting until kids are teenagers to talk about religion can backfire. By then, kids may already have formed some pretty strong opinions—opinions that may be unfair, inaccurate, or unkind. What's more, you may miss your window. Most teens are far more interested in what their friends have to say than in what you have to say.

Get "faith literacy" out of the way first. Before there can be literacy in religion, there must be literacy in faith. *Religion* is a big word, entailing everything from dogma and life-cycle traditions to history and world politics. But the word *faith* entails only one thing: belief in things that cannot be proven. So start there. Tell your child the difference between fact, fiction, and belief. Explain why faith is personal and varies from person to person. Tell them that people often change their beliefs over time, and point out the many different reasons people have faith: because they were brought up that way, because faith gives them comfort, because they feel deep down that God is real and can't imagine not believing, and so on. And remember to pepper these conversations with, "That's what others think, but what do you think?" If we parents truly want our children to make up their own minds, we need to talk less and listen more.

Don't overthink it. Being religiously literate doesn't require a Ph.D. in religious studies. Much of what you want to pass on to your kids you know already; the rest you can look up as needed. (Wikipedia is your friend.) The very act of defining a religious word for your child—*baptism*, for instance—is literacy. Buying your kid a dreidel around Hanukkah is literacy. Pointing out Moses in a painting is literacy. Watching a YouTube video of whirling dervishes is literacy. Oh, and don't beat yourself up if you don't know or can't remember an answer, or don't know *how* to answer. Just say, "Great question, I'll get back to you on that."

Celebrate religious holidays. In my mind at least, the minimum religious literacy required of American parents involves giving kids some basic information about all major world religions: Hinduism, Buddhism, Judaism, Christianity, and Islam. The easiest way to do this? Mark your calendar. When Rosh Hashanah and Ramadan and Buddha's birthday come around, don't ignore them. Instead, find out a bit about them and then share the interesting stuff with your kids. You might eat apples and honey with your dinner on Rosh Hashanah (explaining that that's how Jewish people bring in a "sweet" new year); go out and ponder the phases of the moon on Ramadan (explaining that Muslims do not eat or drink anything from sunup to sundown for an entire month); show your child a picture of the Buddha on his birthday (explaining that Buddha is always pictured in a meditation posture because meditation is how he devised the all-important Four Noble Truths). And don't forget to make Fox News proud and put the Christ back in Christmas! This impossible-to-ignore and massively commercialized holiday is a perfect opportunity to share one of the world's most famous stories, the Nativity, with our curious children.

Humanize religion. Make connections between your children and the people in their lives who believe differently than they do. Instead of telling kids not to talk about religion in mixed company, encourage them to show interest in other people's customs and traditions. As long as you stay abreast of what your children are learning elsewhere, and remind them that it's not okay for people to foist their beliefs onto them (or vice versa), you have very little to worry about. You can sit back and relax and know that you're doing a great job as a parent. (And you really are. You know that, right?)

Building understanding and compassion between groups of people who oppose each other's ideology isn't just some wishy-washy, feel-good idea. It's essential to creating a better, more peaceful, less divisive future. We wouldn't ignore the fact that people are different races or ethnicities, or that people come from different socioeconomic backgrounds or political perspectives. So why ignore religion? Kind people deserve to be treated with kindness. No matter what people look like, where they come from, how much money they have, who they vote for, or what god they worship, they are individual people—as we are—and will benefit from our open minds and willingness to see them that way. The earlier we share that message with our children, the longer they'll have to live it.

> " Building understanding and compassion between groups of people who oppose each other's ideology isn't just some wishy-washy, feel-good idea. It's essential to creating a better, more peaceful, less divisive future. "

WENDY THOMAS RUSSELL *is the author of* Relax, It's Just God: How and Why to Talk to Your Kids About Religion When You're Not Religious *(2015). A former newspaper reporter, Wendy hosts the blog* Natural Wonderers *for the Patheos network, writes an online parenting column for PBS NewsHour, and is cofounder of the independent publishing company Brown Paper Press.*

■ ■

10 COMMANDMENTS FOR TALKING TO KIDS ABOUT RELIGION WHEN YOU'RE NOT RELIGIOUS

WENDY THOMAS RUSSELL

Secular parents are by no means a cohesive unit; our struggles are hardly singular. But most of us—whether we consider ourselves atheist, agnostic, humanist, deist, or nothing at all—do share a common goal: to raise kind, happy, tolerant kids capable of making up their own minds about what to believe.

What many of us lack, however, is a clear path for how to get there. We can't always rely on what we were told as children. We can't always trust ourselves to handle things gracefully. Where our parents or grandparents were guided by the well-defined teachings of their faith, we are left to chart a new course for our families.

Here are 10 commandments to help clear the path.

1. **Expose your kids to many religions.**

    Have you ever noticed how religion can get in the way of a religious education? Either children are schooled in one particular belief system, or they're not being taught a damn thing. But a good religious education is one that covers the basics of many religions from a cultural and historical perspective, without a whole lot of emotional investment. What is religion? Why did it come about? And why is it so important to people? Pick up some books and educate yourself about various religions; tell your kids what you're learning. Put major religious holidays (such as Diwali, Vesak, Rosh Hashanah, Easter, and Eid al-Adha) on your calendar, and use them as opportunities to talk about history and tradition. Point out signs and symbols, religious clothing. Seize opportunities to visit places of worship. Religious literacy is a gift; give it.

2. **Embrace the "idol" of science.**

    Idolatry is described as valuing anything in place of God—whether it be other gods or demons, power, pleasure, or money. Because science is something that can be valued in place of God, it's possible to consider science an idol. So be it. For every religious idea they hear, tell your kids one cool thing about the real world. Evolution, the stars and planets, you name it. But remember, you need not set up religion and science as opposing forces, the way religious people often do. Present the facts. Your kids likely will figure the rest out on their own, and it will mean more when they do.

3. Don't saddle your kids with your anxiety over the word *God*.

The Pledge of Allegiance. The Girl Scout Promise. The motto written on American money. There is religion all around us, even in school. But it need not be a crisis. Let your kid know that God is a part of our culture's language, its songs, its poetry, its monuments, and its works of art. God is a part of human history, and there's nothing wrong with that. Not everything needs to be loaded with meaning. Kids might pledge their allegiance to "one nation under God" not because of religion but because of tradition, the same way they might sing Christmas songs or say "Bless you" when someone sneezes. If your kids prefer to draw battle lines for themselves on these matters, great! Just be sure you're not nudging them toward the battle.

4. Keep in mind: there's nothing wrong with faith.

Faith in the supernatural is only as good or bad as the people who possess it. Most of the people your kids will meet during their lifetimes will have something wonderful to offer the world; that something may be accomplished despite belief in a higher power, or it may be accomplished because of it. *Religion* has become a loaded word, referring more to dogma than the simple underlying belief in God, and that's unfortunate in a way. Because religion is like a fingerprint; everyone's is slightly different. Consider the chances, for instance, that any two people envision heaven in exactly the same way. Or interpret all the major biblical passages in the same way. Or inject religion into their politics and social mores in the same way. Not bloody likely. In the end, then, to say someone is Christian or Jewish or Muslim means very little. Knowing someone's religion is a far cry from knowing her beliefs; knowing her label is a far cry from knowing her heart. So when you speak of religion around children, try to be as neutral as possible. And if you do choose to speak of religion in negative terms, be sure to explain exactly what you oppose and why. Rarely do people oppose faith itself, but rather the actions that can arise out of faith. It's important that kids understand the difference.

5. Honor your mother's faith.

Just because you're a nonreligious parent doesn't mean you have to shield your child from religious family members. If you give your child a context in which to hear about Grandma's religion—or Cousin Suzie's or neighbor Bob's—you won't mind so much when those conversations arise. It may benefit Grandma to be able to talk with your child about her faith, and it may benefit your child to hear about faith from someone he knows and loves. And as long as you've set the scene up front in a gentle, nonjudgmental way, there should be very little worry. For example, you might say: "Some people believe that a magic power, often called God, created the universe and is watching over us. And many people say that if you believe in God, you will go to live with God in a place called heaven after you die. That's why it's so important to Grandma that you believe what she does." One caveat: If there's a risk a family member will say something harmful or hateful to your child, the faith-sharing privilege is off the table. Luckily, I think most religious folks are capable of having conversations with children without invoking images of hell or condemning anal sex.

6. Don't kill your kid's good time.

One of the many problems with ardently opposing religion is that it's so damn boring. If you're preoccupied, for example, with explaining to your kids that Adam and Eve weren't the first humans and that those who believe such things are irrational, you're probably not telling the Adam-and-Eve story very well. And that's a shame. Because it's a really great story! A child's age, certainly, will dictate the tenor of your conversations about God and which stories are appropriate to share. But don't forget to have some fun. Go to the library and dig up as many interesting-looking books as you can. The more pictures the better. And don't just offer flat readings of the stories; inject the stories about Jesus with all the drama and excitement with which they were probably intended. The same goes for tales of Abraham and Shiva and Muhammad and Zeus and all the other religious figures, both past and present. The more fun the stories are, the more your kids will want to hear them, and the more likely they'll be to remember them. And that's good. What kids don't know can hurt them, and that's especially true when it comes to religion.

7. Don't be a jerkwad.

Here's the thing: When it comes to religion, most humans believe their way is the best way, the right way. But conviction need not translate into being snarky, arrogant, or mean. There is nothing at all wrong with criticizing people for saying hateful things or doing harmful things. But let's cut the vitriol. You may discuss, oppose, even argue. But try to do it without name-calling, generalizing, or degradation—even when you see theists name-calling, generalizing, and degrading nonbelievers. Yes, it's possible to fight fire with fire. But, in the end, it's all just fire.

8. Don't steal your child's ability to choose.

If you're going to teach children that it's okay for people to hold religious beliefs, you must be willing to let your children hold religious beliefs as well. Otherwise the words sound hollow—and they are. There's no shame in wanting your kids to believe the way you do. So guide them. Teach them the value of science. Explain the difference between fact and faith, between dogma and freethinking. Teach them morals and ethics. Tell them about religion from a dispassionate viewpoint. And then let them take it from there. Let them know they are free to choose what they want to believe, and encourage them to change their minds as often as they like. If they want to experiment with religion, support them. They'll probably come around to your way of thinking eventually anyway. And if they don't, it doesn't matter. What does matter to you is that they grow up to be kind and happy. Right?

9. Don't lie about your own beliefs.

Everyone has the right to his or her own thoughts and beliefs, and that includes you. Don't hide them! Not only would you be sending a message that religion is an uncomfortable/scary/ intimidating subject, but you'd be making it clear that it's okay to be ashamed of your beliefs. You can put off the conversation for a while, but eventually your kids will ask. Admit when you are confused or don't have all the answers. Tell them that the existence of God, in any shape or form, is something no one can prove or disprove, which is what makes it so easy to debate. Let kids know that yours is a household that talks openly and respectfully about tough subjects—including religion.

10. **Respect the religious without tolerating intolerance.**

Teaching your kids to respect religious people is important. But that doesn't mean they must respect religious intolerance. It doesn't mean they must respect immoral, unethical, or hateful words and actions simply because they come under the heading of religious righteousness. Will kids say mean things on the playground? Yes. Do all those mean things need to be treated seriously? No. Fights will break out; feelings will be hurt. It's a part of growing up. But hurting or terrorizing another child—or anyone—in the name of religion is no different than terrorizing a child for any other reason. Bullying is bullying and should be treated as such. The bottom line: Don't hold religious beliefs against people who are being nice. And don't hold them in favor of people who are being mean.

WHEN YOUR CHILD IS TERRIFIED YOU'RE GOING TO HELL

NEIL CARTER

Most fathers enjoy the luxury of sharing their beliefs with their children unguarded, without fear of reprisal. It's the kind of entitlement you hardly even notice until it is taken away. Back in the charmed early days of parenting each of my four beautiful daughters, I enjoyed that luxury myself. But our family dynamic eventually changed, and now I find myself separated from them by a deep ideological chasm. I myself am no longer a Christian, while virtually everyone else whom I love still is, including my children.

Over the years, I've tested the waters to see if there is room in my girls' mental worlds for the kind of skepticism that now characterizes my own, but I have found that even the tiniest movement in that direction meets with visceral opposition. See, the brand of Christianity into which their mother and I introduced them doesn't countenance competing moral or philosophical viewpoints. Their world is not the wide, tolerant ocean of liberal religion; it is the landlocked lake of evangelical Christianity.

In my precarious situation, I find myself torn between two opposing instincts: On the one hand, as their father I want to expose them to an exciting, adventure-filled world much larger than the cultural enclave they currently inhabit. But on the other hand, I am painfully aware that their programming predisposes them to recoil from anything resembling one of many forbidden fruits. With each attempt to introduce another verboten idea, I run the risk of teaching them to be afraid of their own father. The Good Book warns them that the Devil himself masquerades as an angel of light. Why couldn't he just as easily come to them disguised as their own poor, misguided father?

> 66 With each attempt to introduce another verboten idea, I run the risk of teaching them to be afraid of their own father. 99

Given the complexity of my current situation, I am forced to walk a fine line. As the only atheist in their limited social world, I cannot come right out with my views without damaging our relationships. I've seen that happen again and again with every other relationship I once had, and I have lost them all, one way or another. I can't bear to see that happen with them as well. But my girls remain immersed in a reality alternative to my own, enclosed within an epistemic bubble that I am cursed to both fully understand and yet despise for all its antihumanistic distortions. I want to connect with them inside that bubble, showing them another way to view themselves and the world, but I must do it in such a way that I do not alarm them for all of our differences. I cannot be both "the other" and one of them at the same time.

Through trial and error, I've discovered for myself what I think is the way forward to get me through this challenge. To explain what I feel I have learned, I will share the story of a conversation I had with one of my girls because it illustrates the intricate dance I must do. In the end I'll summarize what moments like this have taught me about how to be a father to a family who believes I am destined for destruction.

"Why Are You Crying?"

My youngest daughter "got saved" during the past year, making her profession of faith and then getting baptized the way our tradition prescribes. I baptized two of the other three myself years ago, so I knew all too well the series of events that would soon follow. I knew that her grandparents, aunts, uncles, and Sunday school teachers would all congratulate her for her "new birth," reinforcing for her that her own eternal destiny was now secure. Because she had put her trust in Jesus, when her life is finally through, she can look forward to being reunited again with all her deceased loved ones in the life hereafter.

Except for her father. Because he's not a Christian anymore, the poor sap.

Of course, I present a confounding problem for Baptist theology because anyone who knows me can attest to the authenticity of my Christian zeal throughout the 20 years I was a committed believer. I was as sincere as any other person I knew, so my departure upset a great many people. Baptists believe that once you're saved, you stay that way. So when someone truly devout leaves, you're not left with much choice but to conclude that the one who left must not have ever been a true believer. The cognitive dissonance has to be rough.

Because I know what children are told about people who don't trust in Jesus, I didn't have to guess why, one night as I sat on the edge of her bed, just a few short days after her baptism, my seven-year-old was weeping. It did take me a while to get the reason for her tears out of her, but a few pointed questions revealed that the eleven-year-old had encouraged her to start praying for the restoration of my condemned soul.

"It's just that . . . I want you to be . . . to be with me in . . . in heaven!" she cried, sobbing uncontrollably. It took me nearly 10 minutes to calm her down. I picked her up and held her for a while. When she regained her composure enough to speak intelligible sentences, she lay back on her pillow and recounted for me how she had learned that everyone who believes in Jesus will go to heaven when they die, but the people who don't will not be allowed in.

She never mentioned hell, interestingly enough. I think some things are too horrific for first graders to wrap their little heads around, or at least it was for her. Instead her anguish stemmed from the idea that we would be separated from one another for all eternity. The thought of it terrified her and broke her heart.

What would you say to your child in this situation? How would you react? Would you sit her down and tell her the whole thing is made up? Do you confront the foundation of her entire belief system and tell her that there's nothing after you die, so all of this is simply a fairy tale? Would there be any use in doing that if you are the only person in her life who believes that, knowing that you are going up against an enveloping community that univocally tells her the opposite of what you are saying? Remember, I live in the Deep South, in JesusLand.

What would you do?

Walking a Fine Line

I'll tell you what I did. I talked to her as calmly and as gently as I could, and I began to ask her some questions, encouraging her to think about things from a slightly different perspective.

I told her, "Listen, honey. You know that adults can be wrong, right? I mean, clearly we disagree on belief in God, and we can't all be right about that, right?" She nodded, still frowning and one breath away from crying again.

I continued, "Well, another thing even Christians disagree with each other about is what gets people into heaven. Not everybody thinks that people will be kept out just because they don't believe the right things. So isn't it possible that people can be wrong about that?" She shrugged, and then nodded. "I guess," she said, still clearly unconvinced.

I nudged a little further. "Now let me ask you another question. As your father, don't you think I would do whatever it took to keep you safe? Even if it meant keeping you from doing things to hurt yourself?" She nodded again, still listening.

"Well, God is supposed to be a father, right? And he's supposed to be a good one, right?" Again she nodded. "And do you suppose I am a better father than God is?" For the first time she cracked a half smile and said, "No," with just a touch of nervous laughter.

"And do you think that God loves *you* and the rest of the family more than he loves *me*?" She rejected that thought right away. It didn't sit well with her at all.

"Well, then, don't you suppose that if God is a father, and a good one, and that I'm not any better at it than he is, then he will not let anything as bad as that happen to me? Because that's what good fathers do?" Her nods were getting bigger, and now I could even see her little body relaxing before my eyes, her breaths growing a little deeper.

I reassured her in the end that I know how scary all of this is, and that I understand why she was upset. But I also reiterated once more for her that adults don't always agree with each other, even about really important things like this. She will have to decide for herself what she thinks about all of it and what makes the most sense to her.

I scooped her up from her bed again and held her for a long time, letting her relax even more into my arms until she was comfortable enough to fall asleep. I got her a Kleenex and made sure she was past this scary conversation, then got her ready for bed. In a matter of minutes, she was fast asleep.

Next I had a conversation with the eleven-year-old. That was a fun one as well. I'll spare you the details of that one, but I ran her through the same logical breakdown that I presented for the seven-year-old, asking her to please stop scaring her younger sister because it wasn't really helping anything. She apologized for freaking her out and agreed to think harder about which religious conversations were constructive to have with someone that young. I also encouraged her to bring her issues to me in the future so we could talk about them face-to-face, and thankfully she has.

"You're Doing It Wrong"

One of the fun things about being a writer is how putting my personal life on display entitles complete strangers to tell me how to talk to my children. Upon publishing stories like the one I just recounted, I become inundated with self-appointed child-development experts who insist that I'm going about this all wrong. They reprimand me for accommodating my children's theism, telling me instead that I should sweep the legs of their faith, exposing the whole system for the fairy tale that it is.

These people have no idea what they are talking about.

First of all, they don't know my children in particular. They don't know my life situation as well as I do, and I guarantee the people who offer this slash-and-burn approach don't understand how utterly entrenched these beliefs are in the social world in which my children live. People who tell me to "cut the crap" with my girls have no idea what it takes to maintain a good relationship with them amid a culture that speaks with one voice about Jesus and sin and salvation.

But more than that, as an educator I can assure you that this is no way to teach children something new. Experienced teachers understand that when introducing novel ideas, especially those with far-reaching consequences, you must start by engaging the prior understandings of the young minds you want to influence. You cannot invalidate everything they believe they know about the world and expect them to just absorb that. You have to find a point of contact with what they already

❝ You cannot invalidate everything they believe they know about the world and expect them to just absorb that. You have to find a point of contact with what they already believe and build on that, offering them an alternative way of looking at what they see. ❞

believe and build on that, offering them an alternative way of looking at what they see.

That is what I did for my youngest daughter that emotional night, and in a way it is what everyone has to do who wants to influence others into a more skeptical direction. Our goal as freethinkers should not be telling others what they should believe. We should be helping people come to appreciate the value of thinking for themselves. We are teaching people critical thinking skills, not merely alternate beliefs, and our conversations with them should reflect that difference.

This requires that you first labor to understand other people's way of thinking. You cannot engage what they believe if you do not accurately understand it in the first place. If you don't understand their mental world, you will misrepresent what they believe, and they will turn you off. Nothing is learned.

This is why I love Daniel Dennett's advice about conversing with people who believe differently from you. He charged that you should first learn to state the other person's beliefs so clearly and accurately that even she will have to admit she couldn't have said it better herself. Now her defenses will be lowered, and she will be ready to listen to what you have to say. You've just eliminated 90 percent of what consumes conversations like this, namely that each person has to feel that his own view isn't being misrepresented. Once you've gotten past that moment, real conversation can begin.

Making It Up As I Go

Finding my voice in my own religious family is not an easy task. Before I left my faith (or rather it left me), I could speak my mind without encountering much opposition. Things are different now, and I have to pick my battles. Not every matter is a cause for a fight, and people in my situation have to walk circumspectly, choosing carefully which matters are important enough to disturb the peace. Personally, I remain as supportive as I can be toward my children's participation in religious activities, not because I am happy about what they are being told but because I don't really have many options. Other people may find themselves in a different situation, but mine is precarious, so I have to be careful.

When I hear my girls regurgitating self-talk that is negative, I counter that by telling them I don't think that is healthy. When I hear them rehearsing condemnation toward the choices and lifestyles of other people, I try to speak up when I feel they aren't treating others with the same compassion they would want others to show toward them. My next great challenge as my girls enter the throes of their teenage years is to counter the body shame their religion subtly instills in them through the pernicious and pervasive purity obsession that's become an institution in evangelical youth culture.

I've really got my work cut out for me, and I will be the first to tell you that I don't have this all figured out. But I trust that if I continue to love my children to the best of my ability, never holding back from them anything that they need, in time they will come to see that their infidel father loves them just as passionately as does anyone else in their lives. They will see that good people come in all kinds, and that their religious sect doesn't have the corner on the market of ideas or values in the world. In the end, a life well lived is the best argument I have.

NEIL CARTER is a high school teacher, a writer, a father of four, and a former evangelical living in the heart of the Bible Belt. Finally putting his master's in biblical studies from Reformed Theological Seminary to good use, Neil spends the bulk of his writing energy unpacking his own religious deconversion under the name Godless in Dixie, a blog hosted on Patheos. He truly does not care what you believe as long as you treat others with respect and compassion.

■ ■

MANAGING DISSONANCE
WITH RELIGIOUS RELATIVES

LIBBY ANNE

I grew up in a religious household. I was homeschooled, and my family attended an evangelical megachurch. We were members of a weekly evening Bible club, and my mother read the Bible aloud to us each morning after breakfast as part of our curriculum. We were also required to read the Bible on our own before breakfast, and in the evening my father prayed with us before bed. As I grew older I took apologetics classes with a family friend who was also a professor at a local theological seminary. Religion was integrated into every part of our lives.

Today, I am raising my own kids in a nonreligious household.

As I parent my two young children, I face several challenges. How do I raise my children with the freedom to form their own beliefs that I never had, while at the same time having strong convictions of my own? How do I balance both my own desire for peace with my parents and my children's deep love for their grandparents with the freedom with which I am raising my children? How do I parent differently from my parents without splash damage hitting my children? None of these questions has an easy answer. In many ways, I've spent my children's lives flying by the seat of my pants. Still, I've learned some things.

I've learned that raising children with freedom means letting go. I've learned that raising open-minded children in an often narrow world means showing respect for a variety of different beliefs and ideas while also providing them with specific values and skills. I've learned that negotiating between the freedom I am giving my children and my relatives' religious certainty requires setting boundaries and expecting them to be respected.

Let's go back to where this story starts. I grew up in a very happy home. There were problems, yes, but there was so much good. I loved church, and Bible club, and apologetics class. I spent time in the church library after services searching for new Bible commentaries or books on creationism to read in my spare time. I was passionate, and earnest, and content. I no longer hold the beliefs I did then, but my biggest objection to my upbringing is not the specific beliefs I was taught but rather the expectation that I must conform.

I didn't realize how heavy this expectation was, or what it really meant, until I was in college. It was there that I was exposed to mainstream science, and after thorough study I became a theistic evolutionist. I still believed God created the world; I simply believed he'd done it through evolution. I didn't realize that that seemingly small change in belief would entirely transform the way my parents viewed and treated me. I cried so many times as I watched my parents' rigid expectations destroy our relationship. It felt like my entire world was shattering. I don't want my children to ever have to face that.

How do I, as a parent, ensure that my children have the ability to meaningfully make their own choices free from the constraints of parental expectation? Much of that hinges on how I, as a parent, respond to the choices they make as they grow, and on how I treat others. It does mean balance, though. I want my children to grow up to be kind, caring, honest adults who have the ability to recognize and navigate through and around abusive structures, ideas, and relationships. Simply put, I want them to have tools.

Over time I've come to realize that I care more about teaching values and skills than about teaching specific beliefs. I want my children to have the freedom to explore various religions and beliefs, to make their own life journeys. I don't want them to feel obligated to believe something just because I do, or to feel judged because they believe something different. As they prepare for their life journeys, I can give them overarching values—kindness, empathy, honesty—to guide them, and specific skills—critical thinking, awareness of abusive structures, the ability to stand up to unjust power—to protect them.

But even when I give my children values and skills, I still can't determine whether they will adopt those values or use those skills. As a parent, all I can do is equip them and then let them fly. And sometimes flying means falling.

I had a landlady once whose daughter had been in an abusive relationship as a young adult. My landlady told me that she had voiced her concerns but then had

> As a parent, all I can do is equip them and then let them fly. And sometimes flying means falling.

focused on just being there for her daughter and loving her. She realized that her daughter had to see the problems for herself, and that if she continued bringing them up she would only drive a wedge between them. After several years, her daughter recognized the warning signs herself and left her abusive partner. The first person she went to was her mother, who had been there for her and who hadn't judged or pushed the issue.

I am sure there will be times, once my children are grown, when they will end up in situations that I find genuinely concerning. I can't change that. All I can do is provide my children with tools and set them free to make their own decisions.

While I don't want to see my children enmeshed in abusive relationships or abusive structures, I don't view religion as inherently abusive. I see religion as a structure that can be used for good or bad, depending on who is wielding it and what it is being used for. Recently, my six-year-old daughter suggested that if we moved we might need to go to a different denomination. I told her that I liked our Unitarian Universalist (UU) church because it is focused on doing good. "And Grandma's church is focused on God?" she asked. "Yes," I told her, "and some churches, like your Aunt Lindsay's church, are focused on doing good and on God." I want my children to understand the diversity of beliefs available to them.

Several years ago, when my daughter was around four, she declared that she believed in Jesus and Persephone. Jesus she had learned about from things she'd picked up from the wider culture, from books she'd received from relatives, and from the times we'd attended church with her grandparents. Persephone she had learned about from books we checked out from the library during her Greek mythology phase. And you know what? I let that be. I may find that combo a bit odd, but ultimately her beliefs are hers, not mine. When she asked what gods I believed in, I told her I didn't believe in any at all. She found that interesting. It presented a moment to talk about the diversity of belief.

I have a number of friends who are pagan. I could declare this "woo" and criticize or laugh at it, but after growing up with such rigidity in belief, I find I can't do that. Personally, I am not religious. I am fairly certain there is no such thing as a supernatural world. But I understand that ceremonies can have meaning, and that people draw their own purpose and values from a variety of sources. I love that my friends have the freedom to form their own beliefs—I love having that freedom myself—and I know that if I model respect for others' beliefs, my children will see that and feel their own freedom to explore.

Sometimes my children crave certainty, and to have "their" beliefs spelled out for them. Several months ago my daughter asked me what "we" believe about heaven and hell. It made me uncomfortable, because it reminded me of the expectation growing up that "we" as a family must all believe the same things. But I realized that at her age, she's still just trying to figure out where she fits in this world. And so I told her what I believe, and what her father believes, and told her that it's up to her to decide what she believes for herself. But I also told her that she absolutely doesn't have to figure that out now, and that even after she's a grown-up she may change her mind about what she believes over time.

And perhaps that is the biggest difference: I present belief as a journey, not an ultimate destination or a predetermined conclusion. I want my children to grow up comfortable with asking questions and with changing their beliefs as needed. I want them to see life, and belief, and love, and learning, as a journey. I want them to be able to embrace themselves as they are, and where they are, without having to always look backward or forward. I want them to know that they don't have to have all the answers.

In the UU church, I have found a community that supports my view of belief as a journey. UUs can be atheist, agnostic, or religious, but they are united by common progressive values such as respect for difference, a belief in equality, and deeply felt humanism. At our UU church, my daughter's religious education begins with the students repeating a simple but profound phrase: "We are the church of the open mind, the loving heart, and the helping hands." I love having a church community that embraces my children as they are and supports them in their own journeys while educating them about the diversity of belief.

Of course, raising my children with the freedom to choose their own beliefs after growing up in an evangelical home myself can cause tension with my parents. My relationship with my mother and father was extremely rocky for a time but has improved in recent years. However, they still do not know that I am not religious. They know that I am politically progressive, they know that we take the children to a UU church, and for now, that is enough.

My daughter knows that my parents do things differently in their home than we do in our home. Some differences are pretty obvious: They pray before meals and we don't. Other differences may be initially less obvious, at least to a child in the first grade. Still, I've explained to my daughter that her grandparents' church believes different things than our church does, and that she seems to get.

When we visit my parents, we go to church with them—they have family friends who like to see the children grow, and for us it's a sign of respect while visiting—and when we do so, we allow our daughter to attend Sunday school. The first time we did this (she hadn't been old enough before), I reminded her that her grandparents' church teaches different things than ours does. "That's okay, Mom," she told me, "it will be interesting to learn about what they believe."

I love her attitude and her inquisitiveness.

Currently, at age six, my daughter does not believe in God. After her Jesus and Persephone period, she decided on her own that gods and goddesses are all just stories—although she'll sometimes inform me that she doesn't know what she'll believe when she's older, and she very definitely still believes in mermaids: "They could be real, Mom! They could! We haven't explored *all* the ocean yet!"

Recently, my daughter told me that we need to tell her grandma "that God is fake," because she would probably want to know. She was very adamant and very concerned about this. And so we had a conversation, my daughter and I, about what makes beliefs "real" or "fake" and how to interact with those whose beliefs are different from ours. I told her that her grandmother believes she has seen proof of God's existence in her own life and that she already knows that some people don't think God is real. I also talked about how people draw meaning from their beliefs, and we talked about links between religion and culture, friendships, and family.

I don't want my kids to get caught up in conflict between myself and my parents. My parents know we are doing many things differently as we raise our kids and have learned to respect that in their own way, probably because I haven't exactly given them any other option. I've made it clear that they aren't to use corporal punishment with my children when they watch them while my husband and I go out for an evening, and I've made it equally clear to my mother that my children love school and that I will not be swayed to homeschool by her tears. And at this point, we've reached a sort of equilibrium. If my parents fail to respect our boundaries, or try to use our children as a weapon against us, we will make

> 66 I don't want my kids to get caught up in conflict between myself and my parents. Neither do I want my kids to think badly of my parents. 99

changes. Until then, I love taking my children to my childhood home, and they love it too.

In all this, I don't want my children to think badly of my parents. The other day I mentioned something we were doing that was different from how I was raised, and my daughter astutely noted, "Oh, so you are doing some things differently with us from how you grew up?" It was the door to an interesting conversation as I explained that, yes, I am doing some things differently, but I am also doing some things the same, and that if she has children when she grows up, she will have to decide what to do the same as how she was raised and what to do differently. I wanted her to see life as a journey, and different people as different.

And that—that right there—is important. I want my children to know that I don't expect them to grow up to parent just the way I do, or to believe just the way I do. I want to model a working out of beliefs and life choices, a negotiation between what came before and what comes next. I want my children to understand that life changes, that people change, that beliefs change, that relationships change, and that that is okay.

LIBBY ANNE grew up in a large evangelical homeschool family highly involved in the Christian Right. College turned her world upside down, and she is today an atheist, a feminist, and a progressive. Her popular blog Love, Joy, Feminism at Patheos focuses on leaving religion, her experience with the Christian Patriarchy and Quiverfull movements, the detrimental effects of the "purity culture," the contradictions of conservative politics, and the importance of feminism.

■ ■

PARENTING ACROSS
THE BELIEF GAP

DALE McGOWAN

Many nonreligious parents, especially those who were once religious, have an additional complication: a religious partner. The Pew Religious Landscape Survey found that 59 percent of the religiously unaffiliated who are married have partners who are religious.

This strikes a lot of people on both sides of the aisle as unthinkable. That's because when most people think of an atheist married to a Christian, they picture Madalyn Murray O'Hair snuggling up to televangelist Pat Robertson. No surprise that they can't imagine the marriage even getting as far as the reception.

But the great news for the religious/nonreligious marriage is that "Pat 'n' Madalyn" is a cartoon with very little to say about the people actually living these marriages. That's because most nonbelievers are nothing like Madalyn, and most believers are nothing like Pat.

Despite the culture war bullets whizzing over their heads, there's more common ground and common experience than ever before between the average religious believer and the average nonbeliever.

If you look only at the doctrines of many religious denominations, it's hard to find much common ground with nonbelievers. But look at the actual people in those denominations, and the picture brightens considerably.

Let's take three examples. Most secular Americans strongly support gay rights, women's reproductive rights, and access to birth control, but the Catholic catechism declares homosexuality a "grave depravity," abortion a "moral evil," and birth control "intrinsically evil." So you might think an atheist and a Catholic could never find common ground on these deeply felt social issues.

And you'd be wrong. Despite their church's clear doctrines, 57 percent of Catholics support gay marriage, 58 percent support abortion rights, and an amazing 82 percent believe birth control is morally acceptable. So U.S. Catholics have more common ground with the nonreligious than they do with the actual Catholic Church.

It's not just Catholics. Mainline Protestants also support gay marriage (55 percent), abortion rights (72 percent), and access to birth control (85 percent) in numbers much higher than many assume. Two-thirds of U.S. Christians accept evolution, and fewer than a third are biblical literalists, down from two-thirds in 1963.

Most telling of all, 46 percent of mainline Protestants and 49 percent of Catholics now say even an atheist can go to heaven—not to mention 100 percent of current popes.

On the atheist side, a University of Tennessee study showed that fewer than 15 percent of atheists are "antitheists" who consider all religion to be toxic and harmful. The rest, to varying degrees, are willing to coexist with people of different beliefs and are more likely to consider a mixed marriage in the first place.

When you get beyond the cartoons of belief and disbelief, it's less unthinkable that religious and nonreligious people are making strong, happy marriages together. They aren't Pat and Madalyn—they are couples so similar in values and attitudes, even as they differ in beliefs, that they're probably all around you and you can't even tell.

If joining two religions creates difficult issues, you might think that joining a religious believer and a nonbeliever would cause even more problems. In fact, there are often fewer problems in this situation. A marriage that joins a Catholic partner to a Jewish one, for example, is operating from two different rule books, each with different mandates for everything from what to do on a given calendar day to rituals, labels, and religious education related to the children. Some of these aren't just different but mutually exclusive, and working it all out can be pretty tricky.

But when one partner is nonreligious, one rule book disappears. There are still deeply felt values and preferences on both sides, but the potential for conflict on the details of parenting—do this first, then do that—is much lower. The couple is left to work out their own comfort level with the elements of the remaining religious rule book while incorporating other elements to reflect the nonreligious partner's values and identity. And as the statistics above attest, many of those who identify with religion do not ascribe to their religion's doctrines.

A lot of the issues in the religious/nonreligious marriage run through the relationship like threads. Extended family issues, church-going, communication, all of these ebb and flow over time as couples find their level and (hopefully) refine their relationship skills. But three moments stand out as exactly that—moments. Not themes, but key events that test and define the relationship.

❝ When one parent is religious and the other is not, some of their hopes and dreams for their children may take very different forms, creating a new level of conflict. ❞

One is the first discovery of the religious difference. Another is the wedding. The third, and often the most challenging, is the birth of the first child. Even when joined in marriage, two people can often agree to disagree, even about something as personal as religious beliefs. But a child manifests the relationship in an awe-inspiring way. Two people, two sets of genes, two families come together to create a single new human life. Twenty-one years after the birth of my firstborn, I still can't get over that. It's insanely beautiful.

The child is also, for better and worse, a unique vessel for the hopes and dreams of the parents. And when one parent is religious and the other is not, those hopes and dreams may take very different forms, creating a new level of conflict.

When it comes to parenting from a mixed religious/nonreligious partnership, four issues rise to the top:

1. Rituals and other celebrations
2. Identity
3. Churchgoing, prayer, holidays, and other regular practices
4. Respect, doubt, and questioning

This essay explores these issues in the lived context of couples I interviewed for my book *In Faith and in Doubt: How Religious Believers and Nonbelievers Can Create Strong Marriages and Loving Families.*

The Circumcision Decision

One morning in August 1995, I stood in a recovery room of our local hospital, exhausted from watching my wife give birth. She was also tired for some reason—maybe from watching me watch her—and was drifting in and out of sleep.

A nurse approached me through the fog and asked if we wanted our son circumcised. Her pen was poised expectantly over a clipboard. My long silence confirmed that I hadn't thought about it one bit.

"Most people do," she said. If I had been a parent for more than an hour, I might have countered, "If most people jumped off a cliff . . ." But I was new at this, so I just nodded.

The next day, the knife fell.

Circumcision was originally a religious ceremony, a gesture of faithfulness to God. Despite its near universality now, it was not at all common outside of Jewish and Muslim practice until the 1890s, when a few religious enthusiasts, including the strange character John Harvey Kellogg, recommended circumcision as a cure for "masturbatory insanity." (For girls, he recommended applying carbolic acid to the clitoris.)

Kellogg spent much of his professional effort combating the sexual impulse and helping others to do the same, claiming a plague of masturbation-related deaths in which "a victim literally dies by his own hand" and offering circumcision as a vital defense. He cited "eminent authors" in support, including the French physician Joseph-Henri Réveillé-Parise, who memorably pontificated, "Neither the plague, nor war, nor small-pox, nor similar diseases, have produced results so disastrous to humanity as this pernicious habit" of masturbation.[1]

Given all this hyperbole by well-titled professionals, the attitudes of American parents in the 1890s turned overnight from horror at the barbarity of the "un-Christian" practice of circumcision to immediate conviction that it would save their boys from short and insane lives. It was even reimagined as a symbol of Christian fidelity and membership in the church, and a number of supposed health benefits were suggested.

But organizations including the American Academy of Pediatrics and the American Academy of Family Physicians have issued statements declining to recommend the practice, suggesting that any benefits are marginal at best. The practice almost ended completely in the United Kingdom when a 1949 research paper noted that 16 to 19 infant deaths per year were attributable to complications from the procedure.[2]

Regardless of religious perspective, parents should approach the decision with all information, including the mandates of their faith (if any) and the considered opinions of the medical community. Since Becca's Christian identity did not include a circumcision mandate, our decision was not a religious one—just an unfortunate matter of going with the majority. If we had a do-over, I would decline. No invasive medical procedure should be undertaken that involves risk with few if any demonstrable benefits. It's a form of genital mutilation, after all, albeit a more familiar one.

There's also no rush. The boy can choose to go under the knife at 18 if he wishes. Knowing how unlikely that is should give parents pause.

Just a Bath, or an Indissoluble Bond?

"I always thought of the christening in salvational terms," says Sarah, an independent Christian married to Justin, a secular humanist. "My kids would be baptized to join their souls to Christ, that's how I always understood it. But when our daughter was born, my husband said he didn't want her baptized."

"I wanted her to make her own decision when she was older," Justin explains, "without having to deal with a choice that had been made for her."

"But I just couldn't imagine not having it done," says Sarah.

She talked to her pastor and learned that her church saw baptism primarily as a ritual to wash away original sin. "I was honestly taken aback. I didn't know that was the meaning. That seemed medieval to me. But I still wanted to have it done, and now I had to figure out *why* I wanted it." So she and Justin talked it through. "Eventually I realized that it wasn't even about the connection to Christ. I think that is a relationship that a person should enter into willingly, and it happens in the heart, not in a ceremony."

She tried to imagine not having their daughter baptized, just to see what feelings it brought up. "And the funny thing is, my first thought wasn't about Jesus. I probably shouldn't say that, but it's true. It was a simpler thing. My first thought was, 'But I was baptized, and my mother and daddy were baptized! She *has* to be baptized! It's what we do!' So it wasn't about salvation, or original sin, or connecting her to Christ. It was about connecting her to my family."

Justin's reaction to this news surprised even him. "I was suddenly okay with it, or at least more okay. I didn't like the idea of this supernatural ritual, and I really didn't like the original sin nonsense. But I was okay with her being welcomed into Sarah's family tradition that way, and even into their church. It's a nice church and a good community. Even if it meant something else to the church, I was fine knowing what it meant to Sarah and what it didn't."

"And I appreciated that," she said.

The experience Becca and I had at our megachurch was similar and different. I said I'd prefer not to have our son baptized. Becca said that was fine. "But would it be okay if we just had him dedicated instead?" she asked. "You know . . . for Grandma?"

It was a family thing, you see, just like Justin and Sarah. I said, "Sure, why not?" or words to that effect. Doing this meant more to her than not doing it meant to me.

What I didn't know was what a dedication actually entailed in this and many other churches. It was built around a solemn parental promise, something I only learned when the minister turned to us and said:

> In presenting this child for dedication, you are hereby witnessing to your own personal Christian faith. Dale and Rebekah, do you announce your faith in Jesus Christ, and show that you want to study Him, know Him, love Him, and serve Him as His disciple, and that you want your child to do the same? Do you pledge to teach your child, as soon as he is able to learn, the nature of this holy sacrament; watch over his education, that he may not be led astray; direct his feet to the sanctuary; restrain him from evil associates and habits; and bring him up in the nurture and admonition of the Lord?

Or words to that effect.

Becca squeezed my hand, hard. It was not a squeeze of joy at the moment we were witnessing in our child's life. I knew that. It was a squeeze that said, "Oh no, my love, I didn't know, I promise I didn't, and if you can find it in your heart to fib, just a little, I swear that I will never, ever ask you to do this again for any other children we may have, Amen."

I squeezed back, and together we turned to the minister and said, "Sure, why not?" Or words to that effect.

Becca didn't like the idea of promising such a thing any more than I did. She wanted our kids to make their own decisions regarding religious identity. She had no intention of "direct[ing] his feet to the sanctuary," nor did she agree with the implication that other choices would be the same as leading him "astray."

Had we known at the time that there were other options, including more liberal and flexible Christian denominations, we might have pursued one of those instead. Or we might have considered a Unitarian child dedication, in which parents work with the minister to create the kind of service they want. It may or may not include a religious blessing, it will usually include an expression of the parents' hopes for the child, and it often includes a promise by the congregation to support and encourage the child in his or her search for truth and spiritual enrichment. The parents are not required to be baptized nor to pledge any particular upbringing for the child. That would have been better.

There's also a growing tradition of meaningful humanist naming ceremonies conducted by humanist celebrants trained by the Humanist Society. Though Becca would become a secular humanist herself nine years later, I doubt that would have satisfied her or her family at that point. For us, the Unitarian ceremony would have been ideal. Live and learn.

Lena (Episcopalian) and her husband, Sean (agnostic/Baha'i), worked it out more intentionally, without the need for any fatherly fibs.

"There was a little bit of a discussion when we baptized our two boys," says Lena. "He was certainly not for it. My argument was, if there is no God, then it's just a bath—so what does it matter?"

Well, to be honest, it's never just a bath, and baptism has always been about more than God. In most Christian denominations, the ceremony is also meant to forge a bond between church and child and even to reaffirm the faith of the parents. Even the Episcopal church, which is far less doctrinally strict than most, calls baptism "a full initiation into Christ's body, the church," a bond that is "indissoluble."[3] And it says the ritual "is designed to deepen the Christian formation of those who will present infants and young children for baptism,"[4] and "parents promise to see that the child . . . is brought up in the Christian faith and life."[5]

So whether or not God exists, a human commitment to a particular faith is also being pledged. That's a sensible concern for many nonreligious parents, and even for many religious parents—the ones who would prefer to wait until a child can choose his or her identity.

In the end, Sean weighed these issues and agreed to the ceremony with one condition. "He didn't want to be required to say anything himself about belief in Jesus or God," says Lena. "I completely understood and was grateful that he let me baptize the boys and that he would attend. He is that kind of man, and that's why I love him."

The baptism question is less serious than circumcision in one way— no little knives in sensitive places—but it's more serious in others. Questions of honesty arise, as well as the potential for one parent to feel that the child is being formally bonded to a community in a way that excludes that parent. The first step as always is to be well informed about the purpose and meaning of the ceremony, not only to the church but to the religious partner and his or her family. Whether you forego the ceremony, modify it, find a different denomination, or go the distance, couples should come to an agreement between themselves first, then present a unified decision and reasoning to the extended family.

"Everything Became Very Real for Me When John Was Born"

The marriage of Arlene (Baptist) and Nate (atheist) exemplified the impact a child can have on a religious/nonreligious couple. For twelve years before the birth of their son John, their religious differences were mostly fodder for comic relief. "It never got too serious during those years, mostly just lighthearted ribbing, really fun," Arlene recalls. "But everything stopped being funny and became very real for me when John was born. I was a Christian; Nate was not. For Nate, the most important thing was that John grew up to be a critically thinking person who did not just believe everything he was told. But I was suddenly faced with the very real fact that I had a child with a soul. What I believed really did matter in the long run."

Their discussions got heated around the question of John's religious identity. "I found myself telling a grown man that his opinions were not good for my son—and, yes, John became 'my son' during these arguments. I was like a mama bear protecting her cub from the outside influences that did not agree with my conservative worldview."

Eventually they came to an agreement. "The religious identity would be mine to give John, but Nate would never lie to John about his differing views. When John was old enough to ask Nate how he felt, Nate was free to let loose. I promised to raise John with the open and loving religious spirit I had been raised with and not to stifle his questions."

Even though she raised John specifically as a Baptist, Arlene's approach was spot-on for best practices in the religious/nonreligious mix:

- Recognize diversity of belief.
- Point to the other parent as a positive example.
- Affirm the child's own free choice in the long run.

"When John was about eight," she says, "a Mormon friend of his told him that only Mormons go to heaven. I told John that not everyone believed that same way. When he asked me if only Christians go to heaven, I told him that it's not in my pay grade to decide who goes where. And I told him his dad didn't believe that, which opened the door for their conversation."

Fourteen years later, John identifies as Christian, "but that's about as defining as he'll go," says Arlene. "He does not follow a church. In the end, he doesn't care who believes what. He's just like me: we love who we love because of who they are and not what they believe. His best friends are a Buddhist, a Catholic, and a crystal-rubbing, humans-are-from-aliens ex-Mormon. He loves God and prays and believes but does not judge and does not limit his loved ones to those that believe like he does. It's a family tradition."

"Daddy, Did You Know You're Gonna Burn in Hell?"

Tom (atheist) and Danielle (Baptist) found a similar balance. But unlike Arlene and Nate, they talked through their approach to parenting years before the kids arrived. "We decided before we got married that I could take the kids to church at Christmas and Easter, but Tom didn't want them in Sunday school every week," Danielle says. "I didn't want that either, but I wanted them to be raised at least knowing so they could make their own choice. So that was our agreement before we even had children."

"It was, 'You get to teach them what you believe, I get to teach them what I believe, and let them make up their own mind.' It took all of five minutes."

Other discussions happened along the way as the kids grew up. At one point, after much searching, Danielle found a Methodist church she liked in Miami and wanted to take the kids. Tom agreed. "I took them to church and Sunday school every week," she says, "but I was very sensitive to what they were taught because I had such a bad experience. Tom played basketball on Sundays, and he trusted me that they weren't learning the dogma and the bigoted stuff. There wasn't a problem . . . until they started the preschool at the church."

"Yeah," Tom says, his expression darkening a bit. "Cory said two different things that made me think, 'Okay, this should stop.' One was, 'Daddy, did you know that we have to die for Jesus?' Then he came home another day and said, 'Daddy, did you know you're gonna burn in hell because you don't believe in God?' I suddenly realized he was now going to this church six days a week. We don't know if it was the teachers, the other students, who knows. But he got the message at age four that if you don't believe their way, you're going to burn in hell, and that's when I was like, 'Boom, you're done.'"

"I completely agreed," says Danielle. "I didn't want the scare tactics at all, but he picked that up in the preschool. We switched to a secular school the next year. But he kept going to Sunday school."

"Dani was totally cool about it," Tom says. "She was very upset that he would get those messages, and so we both agreed that this preschool was done, and we'll see how Sunday school goes."

A few years later they moved to another city, and Danielle was once again without a church home. "We haven't gone to church here because I can't find one that I'm comfortable with," she says.

Tom nods. "It seems that they're either too liberal for you, where you don't get the church feeling, or they're too conservative and you're like, 'Ooh boy.'"

"Exactly. Tom supports me in taking the kids when we do find one. He said he would have them go every other Sunday with me, and then the other Sundays they would stay home and have a science lesson with him. But I can't find one that's going to teach them the more moderate beliefs."

"But Then . . . What Are the Children?"

After revealing their religious difference to someone else, the most common question any mixed-belief couple will hear is, "But then . . . what are the children?"

Because a family's worldview identity has usually been placed on the kids at birth, the idea of raising a child with no specific worldview label—religious or irreligious—is as confusing to some people as raising a child without a name. But many religious/nonreligious couples do exactly that, raising a child who may participate in and learn about two or more distinct worldviews without being claimed or labeled by any until he or she is old enough to choose.

Richard Dawkins notes that referring to a child as "a Catholic child" or "a Muslim child" or "an atheist child" should sound as silly to us as saying "a Marxist child" or "a Republican child." These labels represent complex perspectives that they cannot yet claim to have examined and chosen freely. Until they can, there's no need to force the issue.

The freedom to choose or change one's religious identity is a gift of autonomy so universally valued that it's enshrined in Article 18 of the Universal Declaration of Human Rights.

Everyone has the right to freedom of thought, conscience, and religion; this right includes freedom to change a religion or belief, and freedom, either alone or in community with others and in public or private, to manifest a religion or belief in teaching, practice, worship, and observance.

This does not mean our kids shouldn't engage in religious practices or belief. It opens the door for the opposite: free exploration. Erecting a wall between the child and all religious experience isn't necessary or good. In fact, closing children off from these experiences can violate their autonomy just as much as restricting them to a single fragment of religious opinion. This issue is about resisting the urge to place a complex worldview label on a child before she is ready for it. She can go to church or Sunday school, read the Bible, and pray without being called a Christian, Muslim, or Jew, just as she can challenge religious ideas, debate religious friends, and read *The God Delusion* without being an atheist.

A child with one religious and one nonreligious parent is in a uniquely lucky position to do all of these things: Learn religious concepts and challenge them; engage in religious practices and wonder if they are meaningful; pray and question whether her prayers are heard.

My parents achieved this without even intending to. We went to a United Church of Christ church every Sunday, but we were never asked to pledge ourselves to the denomination or even to call ourselves Christians. At the same time, we were encouraged to think and question and explore ideas. As a result, I came to my current views on my own. It's the thing I value most about my worldview— that it's really mine. Why would I deprive my kids of that feeling of authenticity?

Some kids raised this way end up choosing a religious identity; others choose a nonreligious one. In both cases, the individual receives the gift of genuine autonomy in a major life decision. And in neither case does the child have to go through the guilty turmoil of deciding whether to accept or reject a label placed on him by his loving parents.

In 2013, I conducted a survey of 1,000 individuals in secular/religious mixed marriages, including both the religious and nonreligious partners. Over 400 were parents. I asked those parents to check all statements that were true about the eventual religious or nonreligious identity of their children:

▶ 63 percent said, "I am confident they will make a positive choice, even if it is not the same as mine."
▶ 78 percent said, "I will love and support my child regardless of their choice."
▶ 55 percent said, "I would prefer they end up identifying with my worldview."
▶ 9 percent said they would be "deeply disappointed" if their child chose the worldview opposite their own (religious for the nonreligious parent, or nonreligious for the religious parent).
▶ Fewer than 0.5 percent said, "Certain choices could lead me to end contact/support."

This final (terrible) answer was given by just two people out of the more than 400 parents. Though you might assume these were religiously orthodox parents, the two who suggested they might cut off contact or support from their child were both nonreligious.

Disappointment is another matter. Religious parents were twice as likely to say they would be "deeply disappointed" if their child became nonreligious compared to nonreligious partners who would be "deeply disappointed" if their child became religious.

The happy bottom line: The clear majority of parents in both categories are fine with their children making either choice, and both express confidence that those choices will be positive ones, even if different from their own.

Religious/nonreligious partners are in the ideal situation to facilitate this open process. Both parents can and should wear their own identities proudly, even as they point to each other for alternate points of view. When my daughter came to me at age eight and asked whether Jesus really came alive after he died, I gave my honest opinion. "I don't think he did," I said. "I think that's just a story to make us feel better about death. But talk to Mom. I know she thinks it really happened. And then you can make up your own mind and even change your mind back and forth a hundred times if you want." And Becca did the same for me, always sending the kids to hear my perspective after offering her own.

Both parents share the experience of their perspective, then say, "Here's what I believe with all my heart, it's very important to me and I think it's true, but these are things each person has to decide for herself, and I want you to talk to people who have different beliefs so you can make up your own mind. You can change your mind a thousand times. There's no penalty for getting it wrong, and I will love you no less if you end up believing differently from me." Imagine if that was the norm! Imagine kids growing up with an invitation to engage these profound questions freely and without fear.

Some religious leaders insist that children raised by parents with two different worldviews are subject to "confusion" and "alienation."[6] In fact, this is rarely the case. Children accept as normal the world with which they are presented. Someone raised in a one-religion home may see anything else as unthinkable and confusing. But children whose parents differ on religion see that as normal, and they tend to adapt perfectly well.

Hope had the same worries about her children being confused when her husband, David, became an atheist. "But when I asked my oldest what it was like to have mixed-religion parents, she said, 'I don't think that having parents with different religions is that much different from having same-religion parents. I think it just changed the way we think about it.'" Her answer made Hope . . . hopeful. "Even though I might sometimes feel stressed out by our difference in religion, it feels like normal to our children. They are aware that our family is a little bit different from some other families at my church or at my husband's atheist group, but it's not different to them—it's their normal."

It isn't always easy on the parents to see their kids exposed to another point of view. "Before David left the faith, we were a very committed Christian family," says Hope. "We taught our children the catechism. We watched Christian videos, sang Christian songs, and built the Christian bubble around them like 'good' Christian parents do." But since David's change, she has adopted a more balanced parenting approach—which is not always easy.

"Part of my faith is teaching my children about God, but I also think it is important to be respectful of my husband and his nonbelief. I let our children know that this is my belief, other people believe different things, and they have to make up their own minds when they are older. I admit I've had a hard time learning how to achieve this balance. We've had lots of arguments over this, especially when I've crossed the line into being dogmatic or I have felt David was being disrespectful of my faith. As a Christian, it can be heartbreaking to listen to him talk to our kids about stuff like evolution and God not being real and the Bible not being true. Before he became an atheist, we had raised our kids with Bible stories and worship songs. David had been an active part in teaching them about our faith, and now he was actively teaching them something opposite. Sometimes I don't know how to handle that. But I'm learning. It's a process."

David struggles to find the balance as well. "We did have to reach some agreements. Each of us tells the kids our honest thoughts regarding religion so long as we also encourage the kids to ask the same question to the other parent and listen to their answer."

As for the religious identity of their children, Hope and David have reached agreement on one of the essential best practices: keeping kids unlabeled and free to explore beliefs and experiences before they choose their own religious identity, if any. "Before David deconverted, I mostly just assumed our children would follow us in our faith," Hope says. "But now we do not assign a spiritual identity to our children. We both tell them that they are free to make up their own minds and to change their minds as much as they want. We say that they are too young to really make an informed decision one way or another. I take them to church with me most Sundays. Sometimes the kids want to stay home with him. Sometimes I let them, and sometimes I insist they go."

> 'Before David deconverted, I mostly just assumed our children would follow us in our faith,' Hope says. 'But now we do not assign a spiritual identity to our children. We both tell them that they are free to make up their own minds and to change their minds as much as they want.'

"Sometimes I feel like a sellout by letting my kids go to church so regularly," David admits. "I want them to enjoy their friends, but I hate the BS they are fed while there. I want to have more time with them so we can discuss my thoughts regarding religion rather than just hearing the other side at church. It is gratifying to me that they at least know that not believing is an option and that unbelievers aren't bad people as they are sometimes told at church. I hope, as they grow older, they will develop thoughtful questions of their own and I'll be able to offer my perspective more."

Hope and David's five kids are each finding their own way, knowing their parents support them. "My oldest is 12," Hope says. "She is a daddy's girl, and right away when he announced that he didn't believe anymore, she said she did not believe in God either. This has given her some trouble on the bus and with classmates, as we live in the Deep South, but she has remained steadfast in her nonbelief. Honestly, as a person of faith, my desire would be for her to one day have faith in God, and I would be disappointed if she lived her life without faith. But I love and support her no matter what."

Their second oldest is 10 and a steadfast believer. "She has always believed in God," says Hope. "I try not to put any pressure on her and try to let her know she needs to make an informed decision when she is older. This is a huge area of struggle for me because it goes against every Christian cultural instinct."

Hope describes their younger children as indifferent for the moment. "Our five-year-old son sometimes says he believes in God, because he likes the praise music and loves coming to church with me. And sometimes he says when he grows up he won't believe in God anymore."

In the end, both Hope and David say they are confident their kids will make positive choices, even if they aren't the ones they themselves have made.

Religious Literacy and Churchgoing for Kids

In 2010, the Pew Forum surveyed Americans to assess their basic religious literacy. The results confirmed that Americans, faithful as we are, don't know much about religion:

- ◆ Only 55 percent knew that the Golden Rule isn't one of the Ten Commandments.
- ◆ Just 54 percent knew that the Koran is the holy book of Islam.
- ◆ Fewer than half could name all four Gospels (Matthew, Mark, Luke, and John).
- ◆ Fewer than half knew that the Dalai Lama is Buddhist.
- ◆ Fewer than 40 percent knew that Vishnu and Shiva are Hindu deities.

◆ Just 18 percent knew that Protestants, not Catholics, teach that salvation comes through faith alone.

Our knowledge is even slim when it comes to our own religions:

◆ Forty-five percent of Catholics didn't know that their church teaches that the Communion bread and wine actually become the body and blood of Christ.
◆ Fewer than half of U.S. Protestants knew that Martin Luther founded their branch of Christianity.

If religion is mostly a matter of family inheritance, these things may not matter. But parents who want their children to make a free and informed choice—including most religious/nonreligious couples—need to help their kids encounter a wide range of religious and nonreligious ideas and practices. To make it as inclusive as possible, think of it as worldview literacy.

Most nonreligious parents support the idea of exposing their kids to a broad range of religious ideas, which might explain why they were the most religiously knowledgeable group in the Pew survey.

So how do we raise religiously literate kids? Going to church seems like an obvious answer. But as the Pew Forum study shows, a person can sit in church 52 times a year and still know very little about that religion and almost nothing about any others—an essential part of real literacy. Experiencing just one denomination is like studying haiku and thinking you know poetry.

It also doesn't require long lectures or reading volumes of religious history or scripture. Gaining religious literacy is easier and more fun. It's done by:

◆ Noticing religion in everyday life, in the culture, in the news
◆ Cultivating kids' curiosity about it
◆ Following that curiosity into knowledge
◆ Connecting the dots to create a full picture of religion

As you do all this, bit by bit, thread by thread, a more complete picture of religion as a human endeavor begins to form. It's fascinating, no matter what your perspective.

"Our kids never did get baptized, but I did manage to convince my then-nonreligious husband that the kids needed religious education," says Anna. "We started church shopping, and during that time my husband and I switched roles: he became the religious one, and I became the atheist. My son and I came to the conclusion that there is no god or other supernatural force behind the universe, while my husband accepted Jesus as his personal savior. My daughter's still undecided."

Anna and Gary's approach has always been broad and deep. "We have Sunday school at home where we learn about all the religions, not just one brand of Christianity," says Anna. "I'm lucky to have a very diverse group of friends to help me with this. They attend other services and places of worship and talk with others of different faiths whenever they can. And even though my husband and I aren't together anymore, we're still committed to letting our kids decide their own religious or nonreligious identity. I'm careful not to push my worldview on my children, so I preface everything with, 'This is what I believe.' I do notice that my kids have a confidence in their beliefs that I never had as a kid, and I still struggle with that sometimes as an adult. I think that is because we've allowed them to develop their own identity rather than force one upon them.

"That's the vital factor in almost every parenting decision related to the mixed-belief marriage: autonomy."

Keep the "Hell" Away from Your Kids

There's one major exception to all this openness that both nonreligious and liberal religious parents can agree on. If you don't want your child's exploration muddied by fear, defuse the idea of hell. Don't ignore it—as Tom and Danielle's story above illustrates, most kids in most areas of the United States will hear about hell from peers, especially if their family does not attend church or has an atheist family member. So it's important that kids have this paralyzing idea defused early on in a safe place.

Fortunately, an increasing number of fully religious homes fall into the category of safe places as well. A Pew survey in 2008 found that belief in hell as a place where the wicked are punished has declined to 59 percent in the United States.[7] Many analysts point to the increasing proximity of people of different worldviews. It's easier to hate and fear people of different religions when we don't know any. Belief in heaven is holding steady in the mid-70s.

A fine way for religious (or even nonreligious) parents to defuse hell is to get God on their side. Invite kids to picture God smacking himself on the forehead, saying, "How do they come *up* with these terrible ideas? How can they think I would punish them for honest doubts?"

And while you're exploring worldviews, don't forget the nonreligious. The history of atheism and humanism is a fascinating one and includes intellectual and ethical heroes and stories in every era.

In raising their son Will, Pete (humanist) and Joan (Catholic) methodically worked out their negotiables and nonnegotiables. "We understood that he would in time develop his own religious orientation," Pete says, "but naturally aimed for a fair balance in his exposure to our beliefs during his most formative years. It seemed reasonable for each of us to freely talk about religion from our own view, always in the context of an understood choice of beliefs, and with guidelines on how to phrase our beliefs: No attempting to convince. Any comment on a religious subject should include 'I believe.' Note the difference between 'God loves you' and 'I believe God loves you,' for example, or between 'There is no god' and 'I see no reason to believe in a god.' And Joan would often take care to add, 'You know, Dad feels differently about this.' As a beleaguered atheist in a huge extended family of Catholics, that always meant a lot to me."

They also agreed to ask extended family to respect their approach. "We asked family members to honor our compromise and not upset the hard-won balance by giving religious gifts or talking religious talk to our son."

Coming of Age

When I was about thirteen, I went through a serious bout of bar mitzvah envy. A Jewish friend had his, and I was hooked. Not with memorizing a chunk of the Torah or having to follow the 613 commandments in the Law of Moses. What attracted me was the idea of going through this formal passage from childhood to adulthood. Sure, I was going through that transition myself already, but gradually. Having a moment is different; it's a time when your community says, "Okay, you're not a child anymore. You have more privileges, but we also expect more from you."

Unless you count a particular birthday—sixteen maybe, or eighteen, or twenty-one—the transition into adulthood usually goes unmarked today. The main exceptions are in religious denominations, where a child isn't just becoming an adult but is also taking on a religious identity.

Confirmation, First Communion, and similar events mark the same kind of moment—coming of age combined with joining a community—in many Christian denominations. To avoid early labeling by a single religion, some couples choose to forego these. Others go through with them, reminding the child that the ultimate choice of identity is still his, and add exposure to other worldviews in age-appropriate ways.

Mark, a secular humanist raised in Jehovah's Witnesses, worked out a unique solution with his Catholic wife, Mary. "She feels obligated to raise the children as Catholic until they have completed confirmation," he says. "Now that my daughter has done so, I'm free to take her to religious services of other denominations, as well as nonreligious meetings. I hope to give her, and eventually my son, a broader view of what we as humans believe and how we make sense of the world. If they grow up to be Catholic, I want it to be because they choose it, not because they were born into it."

> 'If [my kids] grow up to be Catholic, I want it to be because they choose it, not because they were born into it,' says Mark, a secular humanist with a Catholic wife.

Some humanist groups around the world have created meaningful coming-of-age rituals. The trick, as always, is to keep the things religion has done well without the belief-pledging and raisin-banning bits. One of the most successful such rituals in the world is the Humanist Confirmation program in Norway. Each spring, more than 10,000 fifteen-year-old Norwegians take a course about life philosophies and world religions, ethics and human sexuality, human rights, and civic duties. At the end they receive a diploma at a moving ceremony with music, poetry, and inspirational speeches. They're confirmed not into atheism but into an adulthood grounded in the human values that underlie civil society.

UUs and the Ethical Culture movement have thoughtful, effective, coming-of-age programs that focus on the things most important in that transition—ethics, civic responsibility, sexuality—without dictating the young person's religious or nonreligious identity. And for those couples who include a Jewish identity, there are bar and bat mitzvahs.

Teaching Values

Though "values" are often conflated with "beliefs," they're not at all the same. Beliefs are opinions about what is true. Values are opinions about what is good. "Jesus is the son of God" is a belief, while "It's wrong to harm another person" is a value.

Parents have a responsibility to teach values and ethical behavior, and they will naturally frame those values in their own worldviews. But mixed-belief parents should take special care not to give their kids the message that any one frame is essential. It's the values that matter, and every major moral value can be framed in religious or nonreligious terms.

> ▸ **Jainism (non-theistic):** "A man should treat all creatures in the world as he himself would like to be treated."[8]
> ▸ **Buddhism:** "Hurt not others in ways that you yourself would find hurtful."[9]
> ▸ **Platonic philosophy (secular):** "One should never do wrong in return, nor mistreat any man, no matter how one has been mistreated by him."[10]
> ▸ **Hinduism:** "This is the sum of duty: do not do to others what would cause you pain if done to you."[11]
> ▸ **Confucianism (secular):** "Surely it is the maxim of loving-kindness: Do not unto others that you would not have them do unto you."[12]
> ▸ **Christianity:** "Do unto others as you would have them do unto you."[13]
> ▸ **Judaism:** "What is hateful to you, do not do to your fellowman. This is the entire Law; all the rest is commentary."[14]
> ▸ **Islam:** "No man is a true believer unless he desireth for his brother that which he desireth for himself."[15]
> ▸ **Taoism:** "Regard your neighbor's gain as your own gain and your neighbor's loss as your own loss."[16]
> ▸ **Baha'i:** "Lay not on any soul a load that you would not wish to be laid upon you, and desire not for anyone the things you would not desire for yourself."[17]
> ▸ **Wicca:** "Ain' it harm none, do what thou wilt."[18]

It's the heart of human morality, something people generally figure out on their own by age six. But here's a slice of humble pie for parents: Like most ethical principles, it isn't learned by teaching. As much as we would like to think we're inculcating morality into our kids, that's mostly untrue. Parents have a role; we're just not as central as we think.

Moral development research by such major figures as Joan Grusec, Larry Nucci, and Diana Baumrind has shown that moral understanding comes not from books or teaching but from experience—especially peer interactions. That's why kids start framing everything in terms of fairness around age five, right when most of them are starting to have regular, daily peer interactions—including the experience of being treated fairly and unfairly—and making choices about how they will treat others and feeling the consequences of those choices.

Parents can and should help kids process their experiences and articulate their thoughts about them, but it's the experience itself that provides the main text from which they draw moral understanding—not from a book and not from us. At least not our words: Our example still speaks volumes.

This should be a major relief to parents who are worried about the implications of a religious/nonreligious marriage for their kids' moral development. As moral development expert Larry Nucci puts it, children's understanding of morality around the world is very much the same whether they're of "one religion, another religion or no religion." There is just one major exception, one way in which parents can actually impede their children's moral growth. "If it's simply indoctrination," Nucci says, "it's worse than doing nothing. It interferes with moral development."[19]

Indoctrination isn't just a religious idea. It happens any time someone is required to accept an idea without questioning it. When a child asks why he shouldn't hit his little brother and the parent says, "Because I said so," the child gets a very weak understanding of that moral principle. He misses an opportunity to develop his own moral muscle by learning the basic principles behind right and wrong. If instead you encourage empathy ("How would it feel if he hit you?"), you build a more powerful understanding of why we should be good. "Because Mom/Dad/the law/the Bible/the parenting book says so" only teaches the ability to follow rules. If you want a moral thinker, help him think about the reasons behind the rules, regardless of your own worldview.

The Bottom Line

Whether religious or nonreligious, share both the beliefs and practices of your worldview with your kids, saying, "Here's what I believe with all my heart. It's very important to me, and I think it's true, but these are things each person has to decide for herself, and I want you to talk to people who have different beliefs, including Mom/Dad. Then you can make up your own mind and change your mind a thousand times. There's no penalty for getting it wrong, and I will love you no less if you end up believing differently from me."

Children who have the invitation to engage these profound questions freely and without fear have the best chance of choosing a meaningful and inspiring worldview that fits their vision of themselves. It's a tremendous gift for parents to give that freedom. A child with one religious and one nonreligious parent is in a uniquely lucky position to learn religious concepts and challenge them, engage in religious practices and wonder if they are meaningful, pray and question whether their prayers are heard.

> 66 Children who have the invitation to engage these profound questions freely and without fear have the best chance of choosing a meaningful and inspiring worldview that fits their vision of themselves. 99

Nonreligious partners are generally open to this approach if they are not antitheists, while the religious partner will generally be open to the idea of letting children find their own way if they themselves take a progressive approach to their religion, something that's becoming common even among traditions that are often considered conservative.

A version of this essay appeared in Dale McGowan's book In Faith and in Doubt: How Religious Believers and Nonbelievers Can Create Strong Marriages and Loving Families *(2014), a resource for marriages and other relationships between religious and nonreligious partners.*

■ ■

CHOOSING YOUR BATTLES

STU TANQUIST

Ben Franklin wisely said, "In this world, nothing is certain but death, taxes, and religious zealots." OK, so I added that last part. Were he here today, however, I suspect that Ben would add it himself.

There are many tolerant and respectful religious believers in this world, of course, and to each his or her own. By religious zealots, I mean those who feel a divinely mandated duty to assimilate everyone into their own worldview. When their tactics involve imposing their faith on others—especially by telling children that they must believe in a god in order to be good—I get a bit testy. I don't make their children eat my cooking. It seems only fair that my child shouldn't have to swallow their wafers.

Aggressive evangelical movements like the Child Evangelism Fellowship (CEF) specifically target children ages five to twelve, working to secure "decisions to accept Christ as Lord and Savior."[1] They know that they need to hook children at a young age, before they are old enough to think for themselves.

But it isn't just groups like CEF seeking religious allegiance from our children. There is also a subtler, often well-intentioned desire by mainstream religionists to share something that is meaningful to them, or to save children from some imagined divine retribution. Well meaning or not, such evangelism of children nonetheless seeks to cut off the process of independent thought before it begins. It's this aspect of religious indoctrination that is most unacceptable—the idea that doubt is bad, that unquestioning acceptance is good, that there is only one possible right answer, and that someone else has already figured out what that answer is.

> As a secular parent, I feel an obligation to help my child develop effective reasoning skills so she can form her own conclusions in all areas of life. I don't want her to blindly adopt my views.

Our kids can and must be helped to fend off these unacceptable intrusions. As a secular parent, I feel an obligation to help my child develop effective reasoning skills so she can form her own conclusions in all areas of life. I don't want her to blindly adopt my views. My hope is that her conclusions will logically follow from a careful process of critical thinking. What a concept! Imagine if all kids had that opportunity.

Of course, if that were the case, this book would not be necessary.

It's necessary to distinguish between religious believers and religious evangelists. An evangelist is a Christian who actively attempts to convert others to his or her religion. And even in a secular home (unless you raise your kids in a protective bubble), conflict with religious evangelists is inevitable. Such evangelists include teachers who impose religious views on young captive audiences, outside groups who obtain privileged access to our public schools, or our own secular government legislating that children recite a God pledge in school. The attempts are relentless and unlikely to diminish anytime soon. I for one can't wait until we are "left behind."

While some problems cannot be ignored, the challenge lies in determining where to draw the line. Some issues are too trivial to address, and others are simply insurmountable. Some would require a high investment of energy for small gain, while others entail genuine risk. The challenge is determining how to pick your battles.

A Little About Us

As a single secular parent living full-time with my sixteen-year-old daughter, I feel extremely fortunate. We have a wonderful relationship and truly enjoy each other's company. We also appreciate living in a home that is completely free from religion—except for the occasional door-to-door belief peddler.

Our home life wasn't always this way. At the impassioned request of my now ex-wife, our daughter attended Catholic school from preschool through seventh grade. At the time, I was an apathetic nonbeliever. Knowing how important religious education was to my wife and her family, I agreed to pay for several sets of snazzy blue plaid uniforms and years of private school tuition.

Our daughter initially thrived in religious school, though she grew tired of the inherent rigidity and required conformity. By the seventh grade, she was a self-professed nonbeliever, though she achieved the high score in her religion class that year. That was the year she decided enough was enough. Much to her mother's chagrin, she insisted on leaving her classmates for public school. She has never looked back— at least not fondly.

The change created new challenges in our home. Religious teaching in her Catholic school was to be expected, of course, but the promotion of religion in our public school system has been hard for both of us to swallow.

The Issue of Authority

We have two explicit "rules" posted in our home:

1. Always question authority.
2. When in doubt, see rule #1.

These two simple rules—really one, of course—are a source of pride for my daughter and an ongoing wonder for her friends. And, yes, these rules apply to my own authority as well.

This may seem counterproductive to many parents, especially to those who struggle with disciplinary issues. Quite frankly, it has not been a problem. To the contrary, this simple concept has been a wonderful and positive influence in our home.

I should note that our rules encourage her to question my comments, decisions, and rationale, to receive justifications beyond "because I said so." They do not authorize anarchy. Inviting questioning is not the same as a complete abdication of responsibility. As her parent and legal guardian, I obviously need to put my foot down from time to time. The point is that my daughter is encouraged to openly and freely challenge my views without fear of consequence for the challenge. If I am a good parent, my parenting should stand on its own merit, both in terms of her perception and the kind of person she becomes. Conversely, if I blinded myself to criticism, how would I know if I'm a good parent or not? That sounds like a recipe for self-delusion.

Our house rules are a recognition of the error in reasoning called the argument from authority. People commit this fallacy when they blindly accept statements made by people in a position of authority. It is important to remember that regardless of expertise, credential, or experience, none of us is infallible. We can all be wrong and so should not be placed above honest question or challenge.

We live in a society that values authority. Political leaders cry treason when American citizens oppose war and its related atrocities. Religious authorities expect us to sit silently and still while they tell us what to believe. In Minnesota, as in many other states, school authorities lead our children in reciting a weekly pledge to God and country—as if we don't have enough unthinking patriotism on this planet. Children who opt out risk being ostracized by teachers and classmates. This potential soon became apparent at my daughter's school.

The Nonmandatory Pledge

While attending eighth grade parent-teacher conferences, we were informed soberly that our daughter was not standing for the Pledge of Allegiance. I was unaware that she had made this choice and glowed with pride. Having children stand and recite a rote pledge to their country is something I would not expect from a free democratic nation—especially when they are further compelled to declare that nation to be "under God." If our country deserves the respect of its citizens, that respect should be earned and freely and individually expressed. If we need to bolster love of country through semicoerced oaths, something ain't right. I love my dog because she makes me happy. Imagine making up for a lousy dog by reciting a dog pledge: "I pledge allegiance, to my dog . . ."

I asked the teacher why he thought it was important to share this information about our daughter. He began squirming in his seat, then said at last that it really wasn't important—he just thought we would want to know. I retorted that it must be important to him since he felt compelled to bring it up. Again, the same awkward response. He clearly understood that our daughter was within her legal right to abstain, and it was now painfully apparent that I was unsympathetic to his concern. Recognizing that this issue was now a nonissue, I moved on to talk about things that really mattered, like our daughter's academic progress and learning needs.

Classroom Proselytizing

Things really got dicey the following year when my daughter brought home "values assessments" from her health class—a survey intended to measure a student's developing moral and ethical sense, personal assets, and social stress.

The survey consisted of a number of statements; each time the student agreed with the statement, she garnered additional points toward a high "values" score. In a cumulative assessment of this type, every "no" counts against the final total—which in the case of this survey would indicate a student whose values need some attention. Perhaps you can see why some of the statements caught my eye:

- ❑ I attend weekly religious services.
- ❑ I reach out to develop my spirituality.
- ❑ I have taught Sunday school class or have otherwise taken an active part in my church.
- ❑ I will take my children to church services regularly.
- ❑ I believe in a Supreme Being.
- ❑ I believe that it is important to support a church by giving time and/or money.
- ❑ Each day I try to set aside some time for worship.
- ❑ It is important to me that grace be said before meals.
- ❑ I believe there is life after death.
- ❑ I read the Bible or other religious writings regularly.
- ❑ I believe in the power of prayer and meditation.

The assessments were clearly skewed to show that nonreligious students have higher stress, lower values, and worse personal assets. That was enough to raise my hackles. My first step was important: I spoke with my daughter to see if she had concerns about me pursuing the matter. It quickly became apparent that she, too, found the statements insulting and wanted to see the matter addressed. I considered scheduling a meeting with the teacher—something I recommend whenever possible before escalating—but this was not the first time I had been made aware of the influence of this particular teacher's religious bias in the classroom. At an orientation earlier in the year, in a presentation reeking of religious language and influence, he had made clear his intention to focus on abstinence to the near total exclusion of birth-control education. Given his tendency toward religious proselytizing in the classroom, I was concerned that he might initially recant, then resume his underhanded tactics once my daughter moved on.

> 66 My daughter brought home "values assessments" from her health class that were clearly skewed to show that nonreligious students have higher stress, lower values, and worse personal assets. That was enough to raise my hackles. 99

To prevent this, I turned to the Freedom From Religion Foundation (FFRF) for help.

As a life member of FFRF, I called co-president Annie Laurie Gaylor to see what she might suggest. She graciously offered to write a letter on our behalf—and boy did she. Annie Laurie wrote a powerful letter to the principal and copied the superintendent. Though initially resistant, the principal eventually replied that the issue had been resolved. Ninth graders at Burnsville High can no longer substitute health class for church.

My daughter was thrilled each time a copied letter arrived from FFRF and proud to have had the courage to do the right thing. She still managed to pull an A from the class, but then the teacher didn't have much choice. Her test scores were stellar.

Surviving a Mixed Marriage—or Not

Adherents of competing religions are reasonably close in thought, especially different Christian denominations, so it doesn't seem at first glance that intermarriage should present too many problems. But after seventeen years of marriage to a devout Catholic, I now understand why Catholics seek Catholics, Mormons seek Mormons, and jocks seek cheerleaders. While liberal believers seem capable of navigating a mixed marriage, the deck is clearly stacked against disciples of moderate and especially fundamentalist sects. They generally don't mix with nonbelievers either. In our marriage, I tried to be flexible and we both compromised. However, on matters relating to religion and our daughter, opportunities offered for compromise were few and far between.

As noted earlier, I entered our marriage as an agnostic who was indifferent to religious belief. I have since come to appreciate the power that religious emotions hold over the human mind. Because religion was so important to my wife, I supported her desire to require that our daughter attend church until she was an adult. We went to church as a family when she was young, but I found that my skeptical mind could only take so much ritual and repetition. I soon learned to savor my Sunday mornings on the deck with a good freethought book and a tasty cigar, a ritual I still enjoy.

Though I tried not to intentionally influence our daughter's views on religion, she couldn't help noticing that Dad no longer attended church. Church had always been a source of conflict in our home. Our daughter rabidly objected to obediently subjecting her rear end to another hour on a hard wooden bench. Her objections gradually became more forceful, to the point where her behavior ruined the otherwise desirable experience for her mother.

I was quietly sympathetic to both sides of the conflict and strived to remain neutral, which is easier said than done. Things eventually snowballed when our daughter started questioning religious doctrine and later announced that she, too, was a nonbeliever.

I was eventually fired as a husband and found myself living fulltime with our daughter. I kept the house, the kid, and the dog. What a sweet deal. I quickly purged the house of crucifixes, ditched the artificial Christmas tree, and sent Santa packing. My daughter loves the freedom and autonomy she now enjoys in our secular home. She was recently accepted as a full-time student at a major university, which she will attend in lieu of her junior and senior high school years. The religious zealots can be found there as well—but she has the reasoning skills to find her own way now, thanks in part to the battles we chose to fight so she had a chance to develop them.

Choose Your Battles Wisely

The battle for your child's mind is real. Many religious enthusiasts—some well meaning, some certainly not—are working tirelessly to derail our children's ability to think for themselves about the big questions and to substitute the principles of one particular religious view for the plurality and freedom of belief inherent in our nation's founding principles. Their tactics are sophisticated and sometimes bold, sometimes subtle. I have tremendous respect for freethinkers and liberal believers alike who make the effort to oppose assaults on our precious liberties. It is my hope that readers of this book will do their part to protect our freedoms. As with any form of activism, one person can only do so much. As a parent, you have many demands on your time, including attending to the needs of your children—though in some cases, standing up for their right to think for themselves is an important way of attending to their needs.

It's important to consider the most appropriate course of action. For minor infractions, try to start small and give individuals the opportunity to make corrections. Consider going directly to a classroom teacher, for example, rather than escalating the issue to the principal or superintendent—though in some situations, as noted, you'll want to start at the top.

In some cases, a personal meeting is likely to be better received and therefore may be more effective than an impersonal email or letter, though the latter offers a written record of exactly what was said. If possible, solicit feedback from others before initiating contact. Bounce ideas off of trusted friends, family, or colleagues. And finally, try to maintain a positive, nonconfrontational tone. Remember that the ultimate goal is to resolve the issue in the interests of your child and other children, not to make the veins in the various adult foreheads stand out. You may find that some folks are willing to make changes if you make the effort to help them understand your concern.

Final Thoughts

Secular parenting can be a wonderful experience, even for those living in intolerant communities. We have the opportunity and responsibility to help our children develop effective reasoning skills, a trait sorely needed on our troubled planet. It is rewarding to know that our children will be empowered to think for themselves as they navigate this credulous world.

I find it especially rewarding to know that the respect I feel from my daughter is sincere and not a response to an authoritarian parenting style. I feel comfort knowing that if I were a lousy parent, she'd be the first to let me know. Better to find out now when there is time to make adjustments.

Finally, remember the two rules on authority and consider establishing them as guidelines in your home. They apply equally well to adults.

STU TANQUIST has been an emergency paramedic, a director for training and development at a large urban medical center, a national speaker, a seminar leader on critical thinking and business writing, and a published author. He holds three degrees, including an MS in management. At the time this was written, he lived near Minneapolis; he now lives in Seattle.

■ ■

WEIGHING THE OPTIONS

When thinking about whether to challenge religious intrusion in our lives, there are many factors to consider:

- Is your child concerned about the consequences?
- Could your child be negatively impacted by the challenge? Might he or she be ostracized at school by teachers or students?
- If successful, how significant would the change be? Would it positively benefit other families and children?
- Could you and your family be negatively impacted?
- What are your chances of success?
- How much time and resources are required?
- Do you risk damaging existing relationships?
- Is this likely to be a short-term or long-term fix?
- Is legal action necessary?
- Are there other parents or organizations that could assist you?
- Are you bored? Do you really need the spice this will add to your life?
- Would it feel rewarding to you and your child if you succeeded?

SECULAR SCHOOLING

ED BUCKNER, Ph.D.

To educate a child perfectly requires profounder thought, greater wisdom, than to govern a state.

—William Ellery Channing, 1838

Few tasks undertaken by parents and communities are more important than the education of our children. Several key questions arise in any discussion of the nature and purpose of that education—questions that any parent should take seriously, consider with care, and answer. Some of these are of particular interest to secular families:

♦ Why should secular parents support public schools (or oppose vouchers)?

♦ Is moral education possible in the public schools (where it would have to be taught without a religious basis of some kind)? Isn't it in fact impossible to separate religious belief or ideas from education, unless education is taken to mean nothing more than rote learning?

♦ Why should parents support the separation of church and state within public schools?

This essay explores these issues and offers some suggestions.

Supporting Public Schools

All thoughtful citizens, even those who aren't parents and never expect to become parents, should support public schools. The same goes for parents who want to homeschool their children or who pay to have them attend private schools, whether religious or secular.

Our society is more interdependent than ever. We all gain by a better-educated population and are all threatened by a less-well-educated one. Our whole economy—not just our own jobs or businesses—depends directly on workers having and maintaining complex skills. Our democratic governance will cease to be self-governance if most of us don't understand our society and its political philosophy. And our culture will be cheapened instead of enriched if we do not have

> 66 Our children need to learn firsthand that different isn't worse. All our children can gain greatly by seeing other children cope and succeed, the more so if those other children have a wide range of abilities, ethnicities, interests, geographical origins, and cultures. 99

a broadly educated citizenry, a populace able to appreciate all that life and art have to offer.

Only a public school system has any chance of educating nearly everyone, and only such a system can hope to instill a common education, language, historical knowledge, and basic moral values across the population. Public schools deserve universal support for all these reasons. That's why vouchers—grants of tax dollars to individual parents to spend at the private schools of their choice, supposedly as a way to encourage freedom and improve education—are a bad idea. Vouchers encourage, and may even guarantee, socially debilitating segregation. They certainly endanger religious liberty. Our children need to learn firsthand that different isn't worse. All our children can gain greatly by seeing other children cope and succeed, the more so if those other children have a wide range of abilities, ethnicities, interests, geographical origins, and cultures.

A major argument advanced by private-school and voucher supporters is that we have, under another very successful program, done exactly what proposed school vouchers would do, without harm to public universities or to church/state separation or liberty. Veterans since World War II have had various public funding, usually known as GI Bill educational benefits, for going to whatever institution of higher learning they wish. And Notre Dame or Bob Jones University can be chosen as easily as State University.

But the comparison of vouchers with the veterans' benefits misses a crucial set of differences: Veterans are adults making choices that are optional, including the choice to attend at all. As adults, they are full citizens, entitled to make choices that may not be deemed wise or in the best interests of the society at large. But children are generally unable to decide with any effective power of their own how much to let the beliefs of their parents affect their educational decisions—and parents deciding for their children is not the equivalent of adult veterans deciding for themselves.

An occasional argument advanced by voucher supporters against objections that church/state separation is violated is that education is a local matter, not a matter to be addressed by the federal government or the federal courts. That argument ignores the Fourteenth Amendment (and the bloody Civil War that led to it), which proclaimed in 1868 that the rights of a citizen of the United States cannot be abridged by state or local governments.

The other major basis for supporting public schools and opposing vouchers is, as already noted, that vouchers would encourage destructive segregation in our society. Taking tax dollars out of public schools and sending those dollars to private schools, even nonreligious institutions, would greatly increase the chances that students would spend most of their time with others much like themselves. Racial segregation has proven in the past to be extremely effective in undercutting justice, and voluntary segregation along racial, ethnic, class, sexual orientation, political, or religious lines would be harmful as well. Our society is strengthened by having most of our citizens educated in settings where they rub shoulders with people quite unlike themselves and where a common curriculum, with more or less consistent standards and with guaranteed access for all, prevails. Tax incentives for people to abandon this common education would unmistakably weaken it. To those who say a common curriculum with free access for all could be a condition of vouchers, the question must be, how will that be any better or any freer than what we have now? Public schools need more resources and more public support, not less. A much more fractured society, with much less practical understanding of what other people are like, would be the result of vouchers.

And as much as many secular parents might believe it would benefit our children in some ways to be educated apart from others with irrational religious beliefs, it seems likely that even our children would lose more than they would gain by being segregated—and for similar reasons.

Moral Education

All parents must of course have primary responsibility for the moral education of their children, including encouraging and supporting social institutions and organizations that have moral education as part of their purpose. While other essays in this book address moral education more generally, this essay will offer advice for secular parents on the role public schools should play in moral education. One frequent false belief is that public schools are prevented from engaging in moral education by separation of church and state. If moral education were dependent on religious beliefs, that might be true—but it isn't.

Religious believers often think morals come ultimately from God, but that ultimate basis need not be part of the education, and of course those of us without any religious beliefs don't agree about the source of morals anyway. No God is needed for—and it can even be reasonably argued that religion interferes with—moral development. How we treat each other, whether we lie or have integrity, whether we care about what is right and follow our code of right and wrong—all of this can and should be taught in public schools.

> Despite myths to the contrary, separation is not a matter of being careful not to offend either people without religion or people who follow a minority religion.

Good teachers have always helped their students develop self-respect, an understanding of justice and fair play, respect for differences, and moral understanding. Good parents should encourage and appreciate this.

Education certainly means more than making students acquire facts or information. The main goal of education should always be to learn how to learn, to become an independent thinker. While teaching students to think, any good teacher will always also teach them to treat themselves and others wisely and well. No secular parent can hope to do this alone, but every parent should consciously plan to do it.

Supporting Separation of Church and State in Public Schools

Every citizen benefits from separation of church and state or, in the case of public schools, from separation of religious education from common public education. Despite myths to the contrary, separation is not a matter of being careful not to offend either people without religion or people who follow a minority religion. Nor is separation of church and state an antireligious principle. "Secular" means "not based on religion"—it doesn't mean "hostile to religion." As every public school teacher and every parent should know, the purpose of separation is to protect religious liberty. As government becomes involved in religion, interpretations of the true meaning of "God" and "faith" inevitably drift toward one narrowly defined denominational vision. Many Christian denominations in the United States, including

Baptists and Catholics, have actively supported separation to prevent their own religious identities from being pushed aside by a different concept of God.

The Southern Baptist Convention understood the point so well that it included separation of church and state as one of its founding principles. The Southern Baptists adopted, in their statement "The Baptist Faith and Message," these words: "The church should not resort to the civil power to carry on its work. . . . The state has no right to impose penalties for religious opinions of any kind. The state has no right to impose taxes for the support of any form of religion." Only by consistently denying agents of government, including public school teachers, the right to make decisions about religion is our religious liberty secure.

> ❝ 'Secular' means 'not based on religion'—it doesn't mean 'hostile to religion.' As every public school teacher and every parent should know, the purpose of separation is to protect religious liberty. ❞

Four basic ideas form the logical underpinnings of separation of church and state:

1. Not all American citizens hold the same opinions on religion and on important matters related to religion (like whether there is a God and, if so, what his nature is; or how or when or whether to worship God; or what God says to us about how to live). Everyone thinks he or she is right when it comes to religion. But not all citizens have the same beliefs on important religious matters.

2. Human judgment is imperfect. For Catholics, the pope is sometimes considered an exception, with regard to official matters of doctrine, but even Catholics, like all the rest of us, don't believe that human voters and human legislators always know what God wants us to do. The Bible is quite clear on this point: "Judge not, that ye be not judged" (Mt 7). Most other books held sacred by followers of different religions also make this clear. The question is not whether *God's* judgment is perfect—only whether *man's* is.

3. Religious truth cannot be determined by votes or by force. In America, neither a majority of citizens nor the government acting on the majority's behalf can make religious decisions for individuals. Anyone who thinks he might disagree with this idea should

ask himself: If a nationwide vote were taken this fall and 99 percent of the U.S. voters disagreed with you on a religious matter, would that change your mind? If 99 percent of the citizens wanted this country to adopt Catholicism or Methodism or Islam or atheism as the "right" religious point of view, would you accept their decision? Would that convince you? And it's not just voting, it's the law itself, the power of government, in question here. One need only consider the poor guy in Afghanistan who was almost convicted and put to death in 2006 for the "crime" of changing his religious beliefs.

4. Freedom, especially religious liberty, is worth having and protecting.

It would seem difficult if not impossible for any citizen who understands American political philosophy to disagree with any of these four ideas, and it is equally hard to understand how anyone who agrees with all four would oppose separation of church and state. Since the fight waged in Virginia in 1784–1785 by James Madison and others—a struggle that almost certainly produced the archetype for the religious liberty established by the First Amendment—it has been clear that letting majorities or governments decide religious matters risks destroying religious liberty.

As a leader in that local battle, Madison wrote *Memorial and Remonstrance Against Religious Assessments*, a petition signed by enough people all over Virginia to defeat "A Bill Establishing a Provision for Teachers of the Christian Religion." That bill, supported by a group led by Patrick Henry, was one designed to do what some claim the First Amendment does: support Christianity without choosing among denominations. The logic and facts that caused those wanting a "multiple establishment" to lose in Virginia are the best reasons for rejecting those interpretations of the First Amendment.

What does this have to do with separation in public schools? Keep in mind that the Virginia bill was intended to support Christian teachers, and read a little of what Madison wrote:

Who does not see that the same authority that can establish Christianity in exclusion of all other religions may establish, with the same ease, any particular sect of Christians in exclusion of all other sects? That the same authority which can force a citizen to contribute threepence only of his property for the support of any one establishment may force him to conform to any other establishment in all cases whatsoever?[1]

Madison understood that governments must stay out of matters related to religion, or liberty is at peril, and this is at least as true regarding public schools as in any other case.

Many people do oppose separation of religion and public education, of course, but most do so because they lack good understanding of the principle and its purpose. The most common misunderstanding is that separation is designed to protect religious minorities, especially atheists, from being offended. Offending people without good reason isn't ever a good idea, but that isn't the point of separation. Separation is necessary to protect everyone's religious liberty.

> 66 Students can pray, including saying grace before lunch or praying that they'll pass the algebra test (though studying longer might be more effective). Students can bring a Bible or other religious book to school and can read it in free time at school. 99

Another set of misunderstandings relates to which behaviors are actually prohibited by separation, especially in public schools. Students can pray, including saying grace before lunch or praying that they'll pass the algebra test (though studying longer might be more effective).

Students can bring a Bible or other religious book to school and can read it in free time at school. Teachers can also pray if they wish. Rules that do apply, reasonably enough, include:

- Students may not disrupt classes to pray or witness about their religious or antireligious beliefs.
- Students may not proselytize others who don't want the attention.
- Teachers may not lead students in prayer or direct students to pray or not to pray.
- Teachers and administrators may not use government property or school time to promote or oppose religion.

Restrictions on teachers and administrators are the most important ones, and they are in every case intended to ensure that no one is using the power of government to impose religious decisions on students.* Secular parents owe it to their children and to their society to support public schools, to plan thoughtfully for and support the moral education of their children, and to support separation of church and state—especially the separation of religion and education in public schools.

ED BUCKNER has been a professor, a school administrator, and executive director of the Council for Secular Humanism. He and his wife, Lois Bright, have edited several books and published Oliver Halle's Taking the Harder Right *(2006). He coauthored* In Freedom We Trust: An Atheist Guide to Religious Liberty *(2012) with his son Michael. He has debated and spoken across the United States, often about the Treaty of Tripoli and other historical documents establishing the separation of church and state, and "This Is a Free Country, Not a Christian Nation." He serves on several national advisory boards and committees.*

■ ■

---

* Much more detailed information on the exact rules is available from Americans United for Separation of Church and State (www.au.org or 202-466-3234).

ADDITIONAL RESOURCES FOR "LIVING WITH RELIGION"

Books

Trooien, Chrystine. *Christian Mythology for Kids*. Mascot Books, 2016. Myths fired my imagination powerfully as a kid. Greek, Norse, Hopi, West African animist tales—I devoured them all. But the stories of the Judeo-Christian canon were an exception. The retellings were always so mired in kid-glove sacredness that all the rich drama was drained out of them. *Christian Mythology for Kids* finally restores these fantastic tales to their rightful place among the compelling stories of humanity. I want to be a kid again so I can discover Christian myth afresh. Language sometimes too advanced for the youngest kids, but perfect for middle and high school. Ages 10–18.

McKerracher, Be-Asia. *Secular Parenting in a Religious World*. CreateSpace, 2014. A well-written and thoughtful exploration of the many issues that arise for nonreligious parents in a religious culture.

Hamilton, Virginia. *In the Beginning: Creation Stories from Around the World*. Harcourt Children's Books, 1988. Probably the finest volume of comparative religion available for children, *In the Beginning* is just what is needed: a book that celebrates creation stories of all kinds as tales that are fascinating, imaginative—and mythic. The Judeo-Christian creation story is mixed among creation myths of Native American, Chinese, Tahitian, African, and Australian origin, among others. As no one story is denigrated or exalted, children can examine the concept of myth without indoctrination or objectionable overlays of punishment and reward. Heads up: The myths have (fortunately) not been scrubbed clean of antifemale or racist themes, which can and should generate even richer discussion. Exquisite watercolor illustrations by Barry Moser. Read aloud to children as young as early elementary age, or self-reading for grades four and up.

Bennett, Helen. *Humanism—What's That?: A Book for Curious Kids*. Prometheus, 2005. While learning about various religions, don't forget to learn a bit about disbelief as an authentic worldview. This book provides a good, accessible introduction to humanism for late-elementary-aged kids.

Armstrong, Karen. *A Short History of Myth*. Canongate, 2005. A lucid, accessible overview of mythic storytelling as a human response to existence. High school and up.

DVD

Jesus Christ Superstar. 1973. Music by Andrew Lloyd Webber, lyrics by Tim Rice. Directed by Norman Jewison. When it comes to family movie night, skip the indoctrination-fests in favor of the rich, conflicted, and naturalistic retelling of the story of Jesus's final days in *Jesus Christ Superstar.* If you can endure the jerky-hippie choreography, you'll find a "passion" centered on a socially conscientious Judas who accuses Jesus of getting too enamored of himself and his supposed divinity and ignoring their mission to help the poor. No miracles, no resurrection, and a balanced presentation of Christ, who is at turns wise, selfish, loving, raging, frightened, heartless, and courageous (not to mention, according to my daughter at one point, "a cutie"). Make sure kids know the basic story outline before hitting "play"—and keep a finger near "pause" for the many fabulous questions that pop up during showtime. Ages eight and up.

Websites

Patheos (www.patheos.com). The world's largest religion website and a great source for comparative religion. Home to 450 bloggers in a dozen different religious and nonreligious traditions, plus an unbeatable Religion Library. Best feature: a "Side-by-Side Comparison Lens" that allows you to compare elements of up to three traditions at once. (Full disclosure: I am on the editorial staff at Patheos.)

Beliefnet (www.beliefnet.com). Includes extensive information about all belief systems. Best feature: the Belief-O-Matic quiz. Asks 20 multiple-choice worldview questions, then spits out a list of belief systems and your percentage of overlap. I come up 100 percent secular humanist, 98 percent Unitarian Universalist, 84 percent Liberal Quaker, and more Jewish (38 percent) than Catholic (16 percent). Fun and fascinating for ages 14 and up.

Bible Gateway (www.biblegateway.com). There are times when quick access to the Bible is useful to a nonreligious person, whether self-educating, weighing or defending against religious arguments, or understanding a religious incident or event. Bible Gateway is the best searchable database, even equipped with all major versions of the Bible for comparisons. Well worth a peek and a bookmark.

CHAPTER

3

Holidays and Celebrations

INTRODUCTION

I magine life without cycles or landmarks of any kind—just birth, followed by a long, gray line of 27,941 days, then death.

I'm kidding—but even if that were true, it's a moot point. We are never without our cycles and landmarks. The religious and non-religious alike live in wheels within wheels, cycling through weeks, months, seasons, and years, each of them marked with days and events we declare to be special. Some are fixed by nature, like birthdays, solstices, equinoxes—all of which celebrate the return of the planet to a precise orbital spot—and seasons, a slower, more majestic ticking that gives a person a glimpse at the cosmic wristwatch.

The recognition of life landmarks, such as naming, rites of passage, marriage, anniversaries, and death, evolved under religious auspices— but contributor Jane Wynne Willson shows that there's no problem finding secular expressions that are every bit as meaningful and satisfying in her essay "Humanist Ceremonies."

Then there's the wheel of holidays, which more than anything else is the one by which kids measure the passing of time. That her birthday is on November 17 meant nothing to my youngest when she was five, but "just after Halloween" worked fine (until every November 1, when she would be miffed at our lack of precision). Like the celebrations of personal landmarks, most of the holidays ("holy days") have religious origins—first pagan, then Christian—and most have developed entirely secular expressions. Add to those a few special days with purely secular roots and you have a calendar of secular celebrations introduced in my essay "Losing the 'Holy,' Keeping the 'Day.'"

Next is a pair of dueling essays devoted to the eternal secular question: Isn't it better to simply skip holidays with loud religious overtones, like Christmas? This kerfuffle is the subject of "The Question of the Claus: Should the Santa Story Stay or Go in Secular Families?" Tom Flynn, editor of *Free Inquiry*, is counsel for the prosecution, and I take the side of truth and justice.

Be sure to visit the "Additional Resources" for outstanding books and links for secular family celebrations.

■ ■ ■ ■ ■ ■ ■ ■ ■ ■ ■ ■ ■

HUMANIST CEREMONIES

JANE WYNNE WILLSON

Ceremonies have always existed to mark important events in people's lives, even in quite primitive societies. Birth, puberty, marriage, and death can all be thought of as times of transition and, as such, have long been celebrated as rites of passage within families and communities all over the world.

As one would expect, the form these ceremonies take will naturally reflect the fundamental beliefs of a particular society and culture. In the Western world and beyond, Christianity has played an important role in ceremonial events, and religious procedures have come to dominate rites of passage.

For families who hold no supernatural beliefs, a religious wedding or funeral service is quite inappropriate and can be an uncomfortable and even distressing experience. Those humanists who want to mark an important event with a ceremony, to give the occasion some formality, feel the need for a secular alternative free of religious association. The growth in the popularity of humanist and nonreligious ceremonies in many countries at the present time is proof that there is a deep, though at times latent, need for such provision.

Terms and Definitions

Ceremony

Throughout this essay I have decided to distinguish between the words *ceremony* and *celebration*. I use the term *ceremony* to describe an occasion when family and friends get together to mark an event of importance, such as a birth, marriage, or death, often called *rites of passage*.

Celebration

In the United States in particular, *celebration* is often used in the same sense as *ceremony*, which can be confusing. *Celebration* originally denoted "observance" or "marking," as the corresponding verb is used in the sentence, "Do you celebrate Christmas in your family?" But in more general usage, a celebration suggests a joyful occasion for congratulation and recognition or for thanks and appreciation. Celebrations are more in the nature of parties involving friends, colleagues, and family. They could include awards for academic, artistic, or sporting achievements or special awards for bravery.

Certainly there is often a celebratory element in the major rites of passage. Parents usually like to celebrate the arrival of a new baby (or sometimes an older child in the case of adoption) and to welcome him or her into the family. They are proud to celebrate the transition of their son or daughter from childhood to adulthood. Couples who have decided to share their lives want to celebrate the event among their family and friends. Even a funeral ceremony is an opportunity to celebrate a life that has ended. But there are exceptions. Couples who are getting divorced sometimes have a ceremony to mark a new stage in their lives as joint parents rather than partners. This is likely to be a dignified and moving statement of commitment and intent rather than a celebration.

In the widest sense of the word, celebrations can contribute to happiness and well-being in family life and in society so they are of particular importance to secular families. One of the basic ideals of Humanism is to make this life as pleasant as possible for everyone alive now and for generations as yet unborn. After all, it is the only life we expect to experience. In 1876, the great American atheist and orator Robert G. Ingersoll wrote, "Happiness is the only good; the time to be happy is now, and the way to be happy is to make others so."

Ritual

Ritual is another term that is sometimes, although by no means always, used in a derogatory way. This describes a set framework and familiar series of actions that many people can find reassuring and helpful at moments of emotion or distress. The repetitive nature of church liturgy may have the same effect for religious people, but certainly not for humanists. The big difference in humanist ceremonies is that by their very nature they are personal and individual. The words are not texts from a religious book but are chosen to suit the personalities and circumstances of the people involved.

Humanist Ceremonies

For humanists, the decision to hold a ceremony is a very personal one. There is no obligation one way or the other. If parents want to investigate what is involved and to consider whether or not they would like to arrange one, the best thing to do is to meet up with other families and hear their views and experiences. National humanist, ethical, secular, and atheist organizations will furnish information about their availability in a particular country or state and will explain any legal requirements. If a humanist celebrant is not available locally, family members can usually arrange to organize a ceremony themselves. Alternatively, they can seek the help of a Unitarian or other liberal minister who is willing to conduct a nonreligious ceremony for them.

In a book about secular parenting, the most directly relevant ceremonies are those held to welcome new babies and those that mark the transition from childhood to adulthood. However, wedding ceremonies may be of interest, particularly in cases of remarriage, and funeral ceremonies are likely to occur at some time within families. The role children can play in these is important. So I shall write a brief account of all four rites of passage, stressing that this can only give a flavor of the kind of ceremonies that are already being enjoyed by humanists in many parts of the world. The beauty of our situation is that the way is wide open for any parents to create ceremonies that feel right for them and their children together as a family, if that is their wish. Humanists are not governed by convention or by church authorities.

> 66 The beauty of our situation as humanists is that the way is wide open for any parents to create ceremonies that feel right for them and their children together as a family, if that is their wish. 99

Naming and Welcoming Ceremonies

Of the main rites of passage, the naming or welcoming ceremony is usually the least formal. Often these are more in the nature of parties for close family and friends, held perhaps in a grandparent's garden or living room, or in the parents' own home. It is a happy occasion that celebrates the baby or young child's arrival in the family, whether by birth or adoption. At the same time, the parents can express their commitment to the child's well-being and their undertaking to care for him or her through the long years to adulthood, or for as long as is necessary. "Supporting adults," the equivalent of Christian godparents, are usually there, and they can pledge that they will take a special interest in the child, through good times and bad. Sometimes older siblings are included in the ceremony. The giving of a name to the baby is usually part of the proceedings, even if the ceremony is held when the baby is several weeks or even months old and the name has been registered and in use for a while. There is often some symbolic act such as the lighting of a candle or planting of a tree. Music can be played and poems read.

Coming-of-Age Ceremonies

These are essentially ceremonies to mark the transition from childhood to adulthood. It is interesting that in Norway they are by far the most popular ceremonies, whereas in most other countries they do not exist. There was already a well-established religious coming-of-age ceremony for fourteen-year-old children in Norway, preceded by courses run by the established Lutheran Church. The Norwegian Humanist Association campaigned hard to establish an alternative secular ceremony, and this was achieved some years ago. Now, in town halls throughout Norway, many hundreds of humanist "ordinands," smartly dressed and glowing with pride, take part in a magnificent and popular ceremony each year, having attended a short course in citizenship and ethical matters run by humanist teachers and counselors in the weeks leading up to the occasion.

This solemn but happy ceremony, held at a period in a young person's life that can often present difficulties, is especially valuable. The ceremony can provide a staging post on the child's road toward independence. At the same time, it can help the parents adjust to their changing role and the prospect of their child's eventual departure from the family home.

> " In town halls throughout Norway, many hundreds of humanist 'ordinands,' smartly dressed and glowing with pride, take part in a magnificent and popular ceremony each year, having attended a short course in citizenship and ethical matters run by humanist teachers. "

There is a clear challenge here for humanists in other countries to follow Norway's lead. Where one or both humanist parents have been brought up in cultures or religious traditions where ceremonies are held at puberty, this would be a natural progression. An example of such a situation might be for those from a Jewish background who would be familiar with the bar/bat mitzvah ceremony. It might be a bit more diffi-cult to introduce a secular coming-of-age ceremony from scratch where there is not already a tradition, but the benefits and beauty of such a rite would make such an effort well worth the undertaking.

Wedding Ceremonies

In most societies throughout history, weddings have taken place before the arrival of children in a family. At least that has been the theory! Nowadays, in Western societies, it is increasingly the case that children are present at, and even take part in, their parents' wedding ceremony. It is sometimes the arrival of one or more children that gives parents the idea that it might after all be sensible to establish a more stable family background than can usually be provided by two people living together without the security of marriage or an alter-native legal framework. Sometimes the wedding may be the result of pressure from the extended family or friends. More often, it is at the remarriage of one or both parents after bereavement or divorce that children are present and can play an important role. This is particu-larly the case where stepfamilies are involved, and the ceremony itself can go some way toward helping children adapt to new and at times difficult family situations.

In secular families, the form a wedding ceremony takes needs to be in keeping with the couple's deeply held beliefs. In a humanist ceremony, they can express their feelings for each other and their aspirations for their future together in their own words. They can do this in the presence of their families and friends in a place of their own choosing. The ceremony can reflect their serious commit-ment and their shared responsibility, particularly where children are involved.

In some countries and states, humanist weddings are now offi-cially recognized and include registration; in others, official regis-tration is separately performed, and the humanist ceremony that follows still has no legal status. However, for the couple involved, it is the humanist wedding ceremony rather than the formal registra-tion of their marriage that is the meaningful and memorable event, marking the start of their shared life together. This applies whether either or both have been married before and whether they are het-erosexual or gay.

Funeral Ceremonies

Humanist funeral ceremonies provide an opportunity for families and friends to meet together to celebrate the life of someone they have loved, to say their last farewells, and to help each other by remembering and grieving together. This all applies equally to adults and children.

Children need to be involved when someone close to them dies. The death and the funeral ceremony should be looked on as a family event, like other family events but this time rather a sad one. It is doing them no kindness at all to exclude them from the funeral and the preparations for the ceremony. They need something to occupy themselves during the unreal days leading up to the funeral. Even quite young children can enjoy helping in small practical ways, such as making cakes or biscuits for the wake or party afterward, or picking and arranging flowers.

If a humanist celebrant is to officiate the funeral, he or she will visit the house to meet the family, find out the kind of ceremony they would like, and, most importantly, listen and build up a picture of the deceased. Children can often help choose an appropriate poem or song; they can contribute a touching or amusing anecdote. Sometimes they are keen to write something to be read at the ceremony.

Children in secular families are likely to ask a lot of questions. They will need honest answers, particularly if well-intentioned religious friends have told them, for example, that their grandpa has gone to heaven and they will see him again one day. They will have to be told that they will be saying good-bye at the ceremony, but they will always be able to go on talking about Grandpa and remembering all the good times they had with him. They will need reassurance and comforting like anyone else.

Conclusion

Ceremonies can be seen as an important and enriching feature of life in many families throughout the world. In religious homes, they obviously follow the various religious traditions, but religions do not hold a monopoly of ceremonial practices that have existed since time immemorial. Once they have been disentangled from their religious packaging, ceremonies are as fitting in secular families as elsewhere. Humanist, ethical, and secular organizations can take pride in having gone some way toward restoring ceremonies and celebrations to their rightful place in society as a natural part of family life.

A lifelong agnostic, JANE WYNNE WILLSON became involved in the humanist movement in the United Kingdom when her oldest child met religion head-on at a state primary school. Since then she has been active at local, national, and international levels, serving as president of the London-based International Humanist and Ethical Union and vice president of the British Humanist Association. She is the author of Parenting Without God, New Arrivals, Sharing the Future, *and* Funerals Without God. *A retired special needs teacher with four children and ten grandchildren, Jane has a deep interest in bringing up children happily with a strong basis for morality but no religion.*

■■

LOSING THE "HOLY," KEEPING THE "DAY"

DALE McGOWAN

Years, decades, even seasons are abstractions to most kids. It's holidays that mark the passing of time in childhood, letting kids know where they are and what's coming. Fall began sometime in the end of September, I knew, but it wasn't until I walked into the classroom on the first of October and saw that Mrs. Mawdsley* had festooned the place with orange and black felt that I felt the rhythm of the year begin. Those pumpkins and bats would be followed like clockwork a month later with turkeys and Pilgrims, then (in olden tymes) by the Jolly Old Fat Man himself. Then came New Year's, Valentine's Day, St. Patrick's Day—in addition to the various things they celebrate, the holidays help shape the year.

---

*Has anyone ever had a schoolmarm more perfectly named than my Mrs. Mawdsley?

There's no reason for secular families to forego this lovely slow ticking of the calendar. Much to the consternation of a few fundamentalist wagon-circlers, many holidays that once had a religious overlay quickly find a nonreligious form as well, especially the fun and meaningful ones. St. Patrick's Day is said to have once been associated with a saint—can't recall which one—instead of just general Irishness. Same with St. Valentine's Day. And Easter, before it developed the admittedly weird tradition of painted chicken eggs hidden by a rabbit, supposedly had some religious tie-in as well.

Christmas, though—I'm pretty sure that one's always been ours.

Relax, believers, I kid. It's good that you've found a way to use old pagan rituals to articulate your worldview. It's what we all do, and should do: Borrow and redefine the inheritances of the past to suit our changing human needs. It's beautiful. It's fun. I wouldn't want to take away your right to do that for anything—just as I'm sure you support my right to do it my way. So we're cool, right?

Okay then. Happy holidays.

There have been many attempts to forge new holidays free of religious overtones, with mixed results. The most effective and meaningful attempts seem to be those connected to the past in some way. Something that redefines instead of creating from scratch always seems somehow more authentically grounded. On the other hand, new perspectives, especially the wonder of the universe illuminated by science, can offer new things to celebrate and contemplate, and new ways to do so.

Below is a list of holidays that lend themselves to secular celebration. If you do it right, your family can experience all the wonder, spirit, fun, and goodwill that religious holidays provide, with a little something extra thrown in.

1. Darwin Day (February 12)

Charles Darwin was born on the same afternoon as another world-shaking freethinker, Abraham Lincoln: February 12, 1809. Darwin Day events celebrate the wonder of science and the glory of human achievement. Some outstanding Darwin Day websites are listed at the end of this chapter, with games, activities, and readings for kids of all ages. Not to demean any particular other February holidays, but a little celebration of science beats the heck out of cherry trees and log cabins.

2. Easter (The first Sunday after the full moon following the vernal equinox, I kid you not. Pagan enough for ya?) and the Vernal Equinox (March 20–21, Northern Hemisphere)

Easter lends itself perfectly well to the aforementioned unholy marriage of rabbit and hen—but there's another option, and quite an intriguing one. The vernal equinox is a bona fide celestial event. Because our planet spins like a tipping top as it orbits the sun, the days grow longer and the nights shorter for half of the year, then reverse for the other half. On just two days a year, in the middle of those two cycles, day and night are balanced at 12 hours each—the equinoxes of spring and fall. The mid-March moment of equipoise, when the North Pole begins tipping back toward the sun, has been observed for thousands of years with rites of spring rejoicing in the resurrection of the natural world. The outstanding website Secular Seasons (secularseasons.org) notes that "many [Mediterranean] religions had stories of a man-god, born of a virgin, who was killed and reborn at this time each year, and this day was often connected to the worship of many fertility goddesses with names like Eostre, Ishtar, and Ostra (hence "Easter")." All the same incentives for celebration are present for secular families, as well as an additional opportunity to grasp the poetry of the top-like whirling of our planetary path through the solar system. See Secular Seasons for great family activities.

3. April Fool's Day (June 3)

Who says holidays can only be built around gratitude, introspection, and group hugs? Fine, no one says that. But if we're going to celebrate what it means to be human, why not celebrate foolishness? We are a silly species, after all, every one of us prone to self-deception, gullibility, and boneheadedness. If you exclude yourself from that company, all I can say is, "Oh, look—there's something on your shirt." I know ultrarationalists who follow a skeptical tirade with the news that their moon is ascending through Virgo. I believed for years that M&M's wouldn't melt in my hands despite daily evidence to the contrary. We are all fools. Accepting the fact that witlessness is our unanimous birthright is a fine reason to celebrate April Fool's Day in a big way. Fall for the traps your kids set for you, and set a few for them as well. Just be sure to laugh at yourself twice as much as you laugh at anyone else.

EVOLUTION AT EASTER: THE CAMOUFLAGE EGG HUNT

In the natural world, predators are always looking for something to eat. The easiest way to escape them is to blend into the background so they don't notice you. Animals that are camouflaged have the same color and patterns as the environment around them. A predator will generally notice, catch, and eat only the most easily captured prey; after its belly is full, there is no need to keep hunting. This activity will demonstrate how the principle of camouflage can help organisms survive.

What you need:

▸ 1 dozen eggs:
▸ stove and pot
▸ set of colored felt pens, or crayons
▸ pencil and paper

Boil a dozen eggs. Once the eggs have boiled for seven to eight minutes, cool them down by running cold water over them in the sink or placing them in the refrigerator.

Put all 12 eggs back in the carton and bring them outside to a natural area with grass, dirt, bushes, and other plants, like your yard or a park. Bring a set of colored felt pens or crayons, and a pencil and paper.

Look at the surrounding environment and choose pens that match the colors of the plants and other features around you. Take six eggs and draw camouflage designs on them. Use different colored pens to match the shadows and stripes and other patterns you see. Think about where you might be placing these eggs when deciding how to camouflage them. Putting them in the grass? Use greens. A bed of dried leaves? Use browns and grays. Leave six eggs plain white, completely uncamouflaged.

Once you're done coloring, ask a friend to close his or her eyes while you place all 12 eggs around the yard or park. The white and colored eggs should be placed in similar locations—for every white egg you place in the grass, place a camouflaged egg in the grass, and so on. After the eggs have been hidden, ask your friend to look around and pick up the first six eggs he or she finds. After six, have your friend stop looking and bring all six back to you.

On one half of your paper, write "Camouflaged," and on the other half write "Uncamouflaged." Make a mark under each heading for each egg found.

If the color of an egg's shell didn't make any difference to your friend, the "predator," he or she should find, on average, just as many camouflaged eggs as white eggs: three each. But how many of each kind did your friend actually find?

Retrieve the remaining six eggs, then repeat the experiment, but this time have your friend hide the eggs while you close your eyes and then search. Write down the data from the new trial. Repeat the experiment several more times until you begin to see a pattern in the totals. Did the coloring on the eggs help or hurt their chances of being detected by a predator?

4. Earth Day (date in committee)

Poor Earth Day. Organizers can't even agree on an official date and have now divided into the "Always-April 22" camp and the vernal equinoxers, with a third contingent lobbying for a move to the summer solstice. (See? Silly species.) Doesn't matter—choose your favorite date and recognize the fragility and beauty of our planet as a family by planting trees, cleaning up a park, rafting a river, climbing a tree, hiking a trail, writing an indignant letter about environmental policy to a newspaper editor or politician, working in the garden, visiting a farm or zoo or aquarium . . . the possibilities are endless.

5. Summer Solstice (around June 21 in the Northern Hemisphere)

Taking place in the middle of the traditional Midsummer observation, this is the day with the longest period of daylight. For thousands of years it has been a celebration of happiness, contentment, and security. The crops are in the ground, the snow is long gone, hunting's good, and the baseball season's in full swing. Weddings and (other) fertility rituals have traditionally been associated with Midsummer

Day, which is why June is still the biggest month for tying the knot. Call your local humanist celebrant for a secular wedding—or just have a family picnic and keep living in sin.

6. Autumnal Equinox (around September 23 in the Northern Hemisphere)

The first day of spring is a time of rebirth, so it's natural to look at the first day of autumn as a time of slowing down, of reflection on the preciousness of life as the natural world moves into dormancy. Like the vernal equinox, the autumnal is a moment when daylight and dark are balanced at 12 hours each—but this time the North Pole is beginning its tip *away* from the sun. Temperatures start their descent, and daylight begins its retreat. This, not Thanksgiving (when the harvest is generally two months in the past), is the sensible time for a dinner to celebrate the harvest and to recognize the changes associated with autumn: the first changing leaves, that first chilly wind in the evening, squirrels turning from tree-trunk tag to serious nut-gathering, geese consulting their *Lonely Planet Guide to the Southern States*. By Thanksgiving, after all, these things are done deals.

It's a natural and beautiful time to visit a cemetery to remember those who are no longer with us, or to take a nature walk to appreciate the changing leaves. Hold a fresh-food harvest potluck in your neighborhood. Find a bridge or high building and (after taking all necessary precautions, people) do a pumpkin drop. Line up an online pen pal in the Southern Hemisphere to exchange greetings and observations as they celebrate the coming of spring.

7. Thanksgiving (United States—fourth Thursday in November)

There should be no difficulty in secularly observing a holiday dedicated to gratitude. We can express to each other our thankfulness for each other, for our good fortune, and for life itself. No eavesdropping deity required. There is an additional opportunity to note that the Puritan Pilgrims were pursuing the kind of freedom of religious observance to which secularists should be devoted: fleeing harassment and religious persecution in England and heading to the New World, where they were free at last to burn witches. Okay, leave that part out.

8. Winter Solstice (December 21–22 in the Northern Hemisphere)

I wouldn't be surprised if Jamaicans were still flat-earthers. You could conceivably disbelieve the spherical earth in the low latitudes. But I lived for many years in the northern plains, where it's a whirling ball for sure, and in late December it gets to feeling like the atmosphere itself has been pared away, leaving nothing at all between our chapped, upturned faces and the brilliant stars. Downright humbling. Many traditions recognized the winter solstice—the shortest day of the year—as a time for celebration and anticipation. It was at this point each year that the sun would end its long retreat and begin moving toward us again. This "return" of the sun was good reason for celebration, for it meant that spring, though a long way off, was inevitable.

Freethought communities often adopt the winter solstice celebration as a favorite, probably to have a Hanukkah/Kwanzaa/Ramadan-esque alternative to the Christmas juggernaut. Whatever the reason, it makes a great excuse for a midwinter bash. Most of the *accoutrement* of secular Christmas celebrations transfers over just fine: gifts, cards, goodwill, peace on earth, family, even a solstice tree. The number of online resources and books is growing.

In 2001, a humanist group in New Jersey created a more specifically humanist celebration of the solstice called HumanLight. Celebrated on December 23, HumanLight is said to be a celebration of the humanist vision of a good future. Whether it will catch on in the long run comes down to the usual: Does it satisfy a widely felt human need?

9. Festivus (December 23 . . . or whenever)

The most promising new holiday in centuries, Festivus was invented (despite the stern denial of "Festivus historians") for a 1997 Christmas episode of the TV show *Seinfeld* as "a Festivus for the rest of us!"—an alternative to the commercialism and other agonies of the Christmas season. Though there is no central Festivian doctrine, typical elements include gathering around the aluminum Festivus Pole with those you *really* want to be with (as opposed to many other holiday gatherings) for such heartwarming traditions as the Airing of Grievances and the Feats of Strength.

The idea of a completely satirical holiday has taken off like a shot, with books, websites, and celebrations around the world—and around the calendar. Some celebrate Festivus on the summer solstice, the vernal equinox, or a randomly selected Thursday in July—or as many as six times a year. Why not? Unorthodoxy is the only dogma, so have a ball.

10. Christmas (December 25)

Christmas has an entirely secular persona parallel to the sacred one. No, not the excesses of buying and greed—I'm talking about the joyful humanistic spirit that sets in that time of year. It's no coincidence that holy days emphasizing family and charity and peace and goodwill are sprinkled through the shortest and latest and coldest days of the year, when we have to rely on each other to make it through. Despite the shopping and insanity, if only for a few moments, just about everyone succumbs to the best of human impulses at this time of year. The thin veneer of religion is easily stripped away to reveal natural, honest, human virtues, of which religion is just one articulation. That's why the "holy days" have so naturally and easily secularized to "holidays," these celebrations of human hope and goodness in the midst of sometimes painful realities. So have yourself a merry little Christmas, without getting too hung up on whether this or that symbol or ritual has religious roots.

11. Holidays from Other Traditions and Cultures

Why not celebrate a holiday from somewhere else? It's a great way to knock down walls of culture and nationality and especially valuable for removing our homegrown "isms" and "anities" from the center of the universe. Have a Chinese New Year party. Celebrate Boxing Day, whatever that is (the British don't even seem to know for sure). Halloween not creepy enough? Try Mexico's Day of the Dead (November 1–2). Observe X-Day on July 5, the day the world did not end in 1998, despite satirical predictions that it would, or toast Buddha on his birthday (celebrated on the full moon of the month Baisakh—sometime in April or May). For a nice exercise in comparative religion, consider joining Cubans on December 17 as they somehow celebrate both the Catholic St. Lazarus and the African god Babalú Ayé.

There's a reason this kind of cultural stewpotting drives the religious Right nuts. By recognizing the validity of the many, you make the one less and less sacred—the very sort of thing that could end us up with a more reasonable world.

Some of these holidays may seem artificial and forced at first. I'm sure the bunny-and-egg thing crossed a few eyes at the start, too, not to mention a virgin giving birth. If you want to stick with the traditional holidays, no sweat. If you want to give something else a try, as well or instead, knock yourself out. Find the right fit for your family and friends. If you find a new holiday that feels satisfying and enjoyable, do it again the next year. And there's the key to turning a new holiday into a beloved family tradition: Make it fun, make it meaningful, and do it twice. Keep it up, and who knows—20 years from now, we might all be singing Festivus carols on the White House lawn around the National Pole.

■ ■

POINT/COUNTERPOINT

■ ■ ■ ■ ■

The Question of the Claus: Should the Santa Story
Stay or Go in Secular Families?

POINT
Put the Claus Away

TOM FLYNN

Eighty-five percent of American four-year-olds believe in Santa Claus. But does the myth hurt or help in raising independent thinkers? Amazingly, science offers little guidance. Although it has become a nearly universal rite of passage for American preadolescents to discover that the most cherished belief of their childhoods was an elaborate parental lie, few researchers have studied the phenomenon—or if they have, few have opted to publish what they have found.

Hard data are so sparse that Santa's defenders still trot out a famous child psychologist's 1971 pronouncement that "the small child should be able to believe in Santa. . . . To hate reality is a likely consequence of being forced to give up fantasies too early."[1] This appeared not in a scientific publication but in the mainstream women's magazine *Ladies' Home Journal*; the famous psychologist in question was Bruno Bettelheim, who would later be discredited for concocting psychiatric principles and diagnoses out of whole cloth, allegedly causing some of his young patients enduring harm. Anyway, if you like unsubstantiated assertions, I'll go with one by Canada's George Brock Chisholm (1896–1971), first director of the World Health Organization, who warned that "any child who believes in Santa Claus has had his ability to think permanently destroyed."[2]

> There is no excuse for deceiving children. And when, as must happen in conventional families, they find that their parents have lied, they lose confidence in them and feel justified in lying to them.—BERTRAND RUSSELL

Still, when the moral arguments are weighed in light of the meager available research, the best course seems clear: "Just say no" to "ho, ho, ho." Here's why:

1. To perpetuate the Santa myth, parents must lie to their kids. We know there's no old man at the North Pole who visits all the world's households in a single night, but that's not what we tell our kids. Yes, Virginia, that's lying. Some parents rationalize it as an innocent sharing of fantasy, but a 1978 study suggested otherwise: It found that children relate to Santa as real, quite differently than they relate to, say, storybook or movie characters. Children relate to Santa as a mundane reality as prosaic—and undeniable—as a wheelbarrow in the backyard. Clearly, for parents to pass on the Santa myth isn't like passing on a Brothers Grimm fairy tale. It's lying, plain and simple. So don't be surprised if the child who caught you lying about Santa tunes out your other guidance on other issues as adolescence blooms.

2. To buoy belief, adults often stage elaborate deceptions, laying traps for the child's developing intellect. Questioning Santa is the first attempt at critical thinking many children make. Yet parents often smokescreen curious children for asking why there are so many Santas at the mall, or wondering why Santa and Aunt Nell use the same wrapping paper. Frequently, parents punish youngsters for sharing their suspicions injudiciously with schoolmates or siblings. Ambitious parents may go to enormous lengths to bamboozle an inquisitive child into believing for another few months. Whatever else we might say about such parenting strategies, clearly they represent no way to teach critical thinking.

3. The myth encourages lazy parenting and promotes unhealthy fear. Hectoring kids to be good because Santa will detect any transgression that parents may miss is equivalent to warning children to behave because God is watching. The establishment of such parental "coalitions with God" defines a parenting technique that research correlates with negative child-development outcomes. Meanwhile, a child who's "been bad" (itself a questionable concept) may dread Christmas Eve, expecting a telltale lump of coal to alert parents to some hitherto-overlooked misconduct. (A grade school classmate of mine dreaded the holiday because he expected to be exposed in a misbehavior he had up until then "gotten away

with." When Santa failed to rat him out with a stocking full of coal, that imposed further corrosive pressure on his naïve view of the world.) Some parents who recognize the danger in leaning too hard on "You better watch out, you better not cry" may strive to engender belief in Santa while avoiding the myth's Big Brother aspects. To those parents I can say only good luck; a single hearing of "Santa Claus Is Coming to Town" on the minivan radio en route to the mall can instantly undo all that careful work.

4. The myth makes kids more acquisitive, not less so. Proponents argue that belief in Santa teaches children the "spirit of giving," whatever that is. But a 1982 study, one of few to address this issue, showed conclusively that the myth actually encourages selfishness. In that study, children who in other contexts requested unselfish benefits such as health or long life for family members invariably demanded material things when writing to Santa.[3]

5. The Santa myth appears to exploit age-appropriate cognitive patterns that religious children use in forming their ideas of God. Santa—a magical being who sees all and whose judgment can be swayed by shows of good behavior—uncomfortably resembles the way theistic children understand God at the same ages. The secular parent should worry that Santa belief in early childhood might bias youngsters toward later uncritical faith.

Some parents say the opposite, arguing that unmasking Santa actually inoculates kids against supernatural beliefs. Again, the available research offers inconclusive guidance. But I can't help noticing that the relationship I suspect between belief in Santa and later religious faith—namely, that belief in the first makes belief in the second more likely—is direct and straightforward. In contrast, the proposed relationship between belief in Santa and later religious disbelief seems contrary, even tortuous. Lacking solid evidence that holding an unsupported belief now makes a child *less* likely to hold another unsupported belief later, why take the risk?

Secular parents have a choice . . . and a chance. Research shows that dissuasion works. Children whose parents explicitly, consistently discourage belief in Santa are unlikely to form the belief. So do your kids a favor. Make a conscious decision not to support irresponsible beliefs, and brick up that chimney.

TOM FLYNN is executive director of the Council for Secular Humanism and editor of Free Inquiry, *the world's largest-circulation English-language secular humanist magazine. He is also a cofounder of the newsletter* Secular Humanist Bulletin *and director of the Robert Green Ingersoll Birthplace Museum. His books include* The Trouble with Christmas *(1992) and* The New Encyclopedia of Unbelief *(2007).*

■■

COUNTERPOINT
Santa Claus: The Ultimate Dry Run

DALE McGOWAN

It's hard to even consider the possibility that Santa isn't real. Everyone seems to believe he is. As a kid, I heard his name in songs and stories and saw him in movies with very high production values. My mom and dad seemed to believe, batted down my doubts, told me he wanted me to be good and that he always knew if I wasn't. And what wonderful gifts I received! Except when they were crappy, which I always figured was my fault somehow. All in all, despite the multiple incredible improbabilities involved in believing he was real, I believed—until the day I decided I cared enough about the truth to ask serious questions, at which point the whole façade fell to pieces. Fortunately, the good things I had credited him with kept coming, but now I knew they came from the people around me, whom I could now properly thank.

Now go back and read that paragraph again, changing the ninth word from *Santa* to *God*.

Santa Claus, my secular friends, is the greatest gift a rational worldview ever had. Our culture has constructed a silly temporary myth parallel to its silly permanent one. They share a striking number of characteristics, yet the one is cast aside halfway through childhood.

And a good thing, too: A middle-aged father looking mournfully up the chimney along with his sobbing children on yet another giftless Christmas morning would be a sure candidate for a very soft room. This culturally pervasive myth is meant to be figured out, designed with an expiration date, after which consumption is universally frowned upon.

I'll admit to having stumbled backward into the issue as a parent. My wife and I defaulted into raising our kids with the same myth we'd been raised in, considering it ever so harmless and fun. Neither of us had experienced the least trauma as kids when the jig was up. On the contrary, we both recall the heady feeling of at last being in on the secret to which so many others, including our younger siblings, were still oblivious.

But as our son, Connor, began to exhibit the incipient inklings of Kringledoubt, it occurred to me that something powerful was going on. I began to see the Santa myth as an unmissable opportunity: the ultimate dry run for a developing inquiring mind.

He was eight when he started in with the classic interrogation: How does Santa get to all those houses in one night? How do the reindeer fly? How does he get in when we don't have a chimney and all the windows are locked and the alarm system is on? Why does he use the same wrapping paper as Mom? All those cookies in one night—his LDL cholesterol must be through the roof!

This is the moment, at the threshold of the question, that the natural inquiry of a child can be primed or choked off. With questions of belief, you have three choices: feed the child a confirmation, feed the child a disconfirmation—or teach the child to fish.

The "Yes, Virginia" crowd will heap implausible nonsense on the poor child, dismissing doubts with invocations of magic or mystery or the willful suspension of physical law. Only slightly less problematic is the second choice—the debunker who simply informs the child that, yes, Santa is a big fat fraud. I chose Door Number 3.

"Some people say the reindeer eat magic corn," I said. "Does that sound right to you?" Initially, boy howdy, did it ever. He wanted to believe, and so was willing to swallow any explanation, no matter how implausible or how tentatively offered. But little by little, the questions got tougher, and he started to answer that second part—"Does that sound right to you?"—a bit more agnostically.

I avoided both lying outright and setting myself up as a godlike authority, determined to let him sort this out himself. And when at last, at age nine, in the snowy parking lot of the Target store, to the sound of a Salvation Army bell ringer, he asked me point blank if Santa was real, I said, "What do you think?"

"Well," he said, his eyes huge with excitement, "I think it's all the moms and dads!" He smiled at me. "Am I right?"

I smiled back. It was the first time he'd asked me directly, and I told him he was right. "So how do you feel about that?"

He shrugged. "That's fine. Actually, it's good. The world makes sense again."

I knew just what he meant. His world was full of gravity and momentum and the water cycle and cell division—then there was this magic man at the North Pole with flying reindeer. Now that weird thing had been explained away: It was an attractive myth he had chosen to believe, then chosen to discard.

He wasn't betrayed, he wasn't angry, he wasn't bereft of hope. He was relieved. It reminded me of the feeling I had when at last I realized God was fictional. The world actually made sense again.

And when Connor started asking skeptical questions about God, I didn't debunk it for him. I told him what various people believe and asked if that sounded right to him. It all rang a bell, of course. He'd been through the ultimate dry run.

By letting our kids participate in the Santa myth and find their own way out of it through skeptical inquiry, we give them a priceless opportunity to see a mass cultural illusion first from the inside, then from the outside. A very casual line of post-Santa questioning can lead kids to recognize how we can all snow ourselves if the enticements are attractive enough.

Such a lesson, viewed from the top of the hill after leaving a belief system under their own power, can gird kids against the best efforts of the evangelists—and far better than secondhand knowledge could ever hope to do.

■ ■

ADDITIONAL RESOURCES FOR "HOLIDAYS AND CELEBRATIONS"

Books

Wing, Natasha. *The Night Before Easter; The Night Before Christmas; The Night Before Hanukkah; and so on* 1999–2015. Fun, silly, secular introductions to a wide range of holidays for preschoolers.

Aveni, Anthony. *The Book of the Year: A Brief History of Our Seasonal Holidays.* Oxford, 2004. Whether exploring the connection between ancient solstice celebrations and Fourth of July fireworks, or between the groundhog and the Virgin Mary, this accessible and impeccably re-searched book shows how humans have organized and celebrated the passage of time for millennia. It turns all of our treasured assumptions on their heads. Perfect for freethought families. Ages fourteen and up.

Willson, Jane Wynne. *Funerals Without God: A Practical Guide to Non-Religious Funerals.* British Humanist Association, 2014. A concise and practical guide to meaningful recognition of the end of life without religious symbols, rituals, or readings.

Willson, Jane Wynne. *Sharing the Future: A Practical Guide to Non-Religious Wedding Ceremonies.* British Humanist Association, 1996. Available through Amazon UK (www.amazon.co.uk).

Willson, Jane Wynne. *New Arrivals: Guide to Non-Religious Naming Ceremonies.* British Humanist Association, 1991. Also at www.amazon.co.uk.

Shragg, Karen. *A Solstice Tree for Jenny.* Prometheus, 2001. The young daughter of archaeologists wants to know if their secular family be-lieves in the "same good things" as those around them who celebrate Christmas, Hanukkah, and other holidays. Of course, her mother re-plies, though we don't believe a god created the world. "We think we can be very good people and know what is right to do" without relying on commandments supposedly handed down from a god, Mom ex-plains. Jenny continues with thoughtful questions, finally deciding she wants a celebration, too. Her family creates their own winter solstice celebration, complete with the ancient solstice tree. Ages four to eight.

Pfeffer, Wendy. *The Shortest Day: Celebrating the Winter Solstice.* Dutton Juvenile, 2003. One of many science-oriented titles by Wendy Pfeffer, this accessible and poetic book gives the history of the solstice, notes how many winter holidays derived from it, and offers several science activities and ideas for celebrating the solstice at school and at home.

Other Outstanding Solstice and Equinox Titles for Kids

Jackson, Ellen. *The Winter Solstice; The Summer Solstice; The Autumn Equinox; The Spring Equinox.* Millbrook, 1994–2003.

Conrad, Heather. *Lights of Winter: Winter Celebrations Around the World.* Lightport Books, 2001.

Haven, Kendell. *New Year's to Kwanzaa: Original Stories of Celebration.* Fulcrum, 1999. Thirty brief fictionalized tales of children celebrating everything from the Day of the Dead to April Fool's to Passover in cultures around the world. Ages four to eight.

Websites for Secular Celebrations and Holidays

Secular Seasons (www.secularseasons.org). The best of the best—a comprehensive, beautiful, and well-designed site with the names and descriptions of secular holidays organized by month, from obscure (Ingersoll Day) to the equinoxes and solstices, the National Day of Reason, April Fool's, and much more. Includes additional links and activities for each holiday.

Secular Celebrations (www.secular-celebrations.com). A good gateway site for information about secular celebrations, rituals, and holidays.

The Darwin Day Program (www.darwinday.org).

Earth Day Network (www.earthday.org).

Secular Holiday Cards

Abundant Earth (www.abundantearth.com).

Blue Mountain Arts (www.bluemountain.com).

Humanist Celebrants and Ceremonies

The Humanist Society (www.humanist-society.org).

The British Humanist Association (www.humanism.org.uk—click on Ceremonies).

N.B. Many humanist celebrants affiliate with local humanist organizations and can be found by searching online for "humanist celebrant" and the name of your city, state, or locality.

4

On Being and Doing Good

INTRODUCTION

The juvenile level of our national conversation around moral development emerges anew with every high-profile act of violence. Bob Barr, then a congressman from Georgia, captured this in June 1999, after the Columbine High School shootings, when he declared to a House hearing on gun control that if high schools were allowed to post the Ten Commandments "we would not have the tragedies that bring us here today."[1] He apparently pictured Dylan Klebold and Eric Harris running down the halls of the school, guns blazing, until they spotted the Sixth Commandment and dropped their guns in horror at the realization that murder is wrong. Millions of Americans nodded their heads in sober agreement with Barr's assessment of the problem and solution.

We act as if we have no idea where morality comes from, or worse yet, we think it comes from lists of memorized rules. In fact, we have a very solid picture of how moral development works. It works best when it is allied with critical thinking—when people are encouraged to find the reasons to be good—and worst when based on rote rule-following.

One of the leading figures in moral development research has been Dr. Larry Nucci. Nucci's cross-cultural research through the Office for Studies in Moral Development at the University of Illinois at Chicago found that children in cultures around the world tend to reach key landmarks in moral development reliably and on time, regardless of what their parents do or don't do. "Children's understanding of morality is the same whether they're of one religion, another religion or no religion," he said.[2]

But Nucci's work did point to one way in which parents can actually impede their children's moral growth. "If it's simply indoctrination," he said, "it's worse than doing nothing. It interferes with moral development."

So the one practice that conservative religious thought insists is vitally important in moral education, the one thing we are begged and urged and warned to do—to teach unquestioning obedience to rules—turns out to be the most counterproductive thing we can do for our children's moral development.

This echoes work by Joan Grusec in the 1990s that found that "parents who tend to be harshly authoritarian are less likely to be successful [as moral educators] than those who place substantial emphasis on reasoning."[3]

In one of the most powerful studies for underlining this idea of moral reasoning, Samuel and Pearl Oliner interviewed 700 survivors of Nazi-occupied Europe. Some were "rescuers" (those who actively rescued victims of Nazi persecution), while others were "non-rescuers," meaning they were either passive in the face of the persecution or actively involved in it.

The interviews focused on the survivors' moral upbringing. Though virtually all subjects said morality was a high priority in their families of origin, the two groups experienced a markedly different approach to moral education. Non-rescuers were 21 times more likely to have grown up in families that emphasized obedience—being given rules that were to be followed without question—while rescuers were over three times more likely than non-rescuers to identify reasoning as an element of their moral education. The Oliners said that parents of the group that ended up behaving most morally during the Nazi era had made an effort to explain the reasons for rules and ethical concepts.[4]

The best thing we can do for our kids is encourage them to actively engage in the expansion and refinement of their natural morality—asking questions, challenging the answers they are given, and working to understand the reasons to be good. Marvin Berkowitz, professor of character education at the University of Missouri, puts it just that clearly: "The most useful form of character education encourages children to think for themselves."[5]

Moral development is a common topic of discussion in my nonreligious parenting workshops. Few of the parents are genuinely worried that the lack of religion will hinder their children's ethical development—instead, they are looking for ways to explain to their own parents, friends, and neighbors that a lack of religion does not equate to a lack of ethics.

But there is sometimes a tiny sense of unease, especially in former religious fundamentalists, a feeling that humanity is inherently wicked and that some kind of external arbiter is required to keep the pot from boiling over. For those parents, moral-development research should be reassuring. Put kids in a prosocial family in a prosocial culture and they tend to turn out just fine. We are wired up, however imperfectly, for cooperation and fairness.

A University of Zurich study published in the journal *Nature* in 2008 underlines this. Kids three to four are almost universally selfish, after which a "strong sense of fairness" reliably develops, usually by seven or eight, except in cases where kids lack the most basic prosocial support at home.[6]

Studies like these can help us relax about the moral question.

If you think about it, it could hardly be otherwise. Imagine two Neolithic populations, one with a genetic predisposition to selfishness and mutual annihilation, the other with a tendency toward cooperation. Which of those will still be around 10 generations later?

So instead of beating back some innate depravity, we need to encourage our kids to actively engage in the refinement of their own natural morality—asking questions, challenging the answers they are given, and working to understand the reasons to be good.

So the next time a religious parent looks at you with that look—you know the one—and asks, "How are you going to raise your kids to be moral without religion?" you will calmly reply, "By avoiding moral indoctrination, of course, which research has shown to be the least effective way to encourage moral development. And what's *your* plan?"

This chapter begins with an essay on raising ethical children by Dr. Marvin Berkowitz, one of the most prominent character-education experts in the United States, which is followed by my thoughts on corporal punishment in "Spare the Rod—and Spare Me the Rest."

Next come insights on the complex concept of evil from one of the great advocates of developing reflective thinking in children, Dr.

Gareth Matthews. Dr. Jean Mercer, a developmental psychologist, then describes the process of moral development as currently understood.

This chapter introduces the first of several poems by nonbeliever and secular parent Edgar Yipsel "Yip" Harburg. Yip authored all of the lyrics and much of the screenplay of *The Wizard of Oz,* making in the process one of the greatest contributions of the past century to the imaginative landscape of modern childhood.

We conclude this diverse chapter with Shannon and Matt Cherry's thoughts on raising their young twin girls to embrace the twin virtues of pride and respect—or, you might say, self-respect and other-respect—followed by the essay "Seven Secular Virtues," which proposes a set of admirable qualities to which secularists might aspire, including a few that don't always come easy, and British philosopher Margaret Knight's argument that the deflection of questions children so often experience around religious questions is just plain "bad intellectual training."

▨ ▨ ▨ ▨ ▨ ▨ ▧ ▨ ▨ ▨ ▨ ▨ ▨

RAISING ETHICAL CHILDREN

MARVIN W. BERKOWITZ, Ph.D.

No society can flourish if it fails to take seriously the task of social-izing the next generation. This responsibility falls on the shoulders of all individuals and institutions that influence the development of youth. While there are many such influences, the two that stand at the front are families and schools. I have written about how to leverage schools to educate for ethical development elsewhere and will focus on the influence of families here. Specifically, the focus here is on optimal parenting, something that does not require a religious framework.

First, however, it is important to address what we want parents to influence. What kind of child do we hope that parents will raise? In my case, I am concerned with raising moral children. However, that is not a comfortable term for everyone, nor is it necessarily clear. What do we mean by a moral child? It is well beyond the scope of this paper to go too deeply into the nuances of morality, and there is great dis-agreement about the specifics. For this chapter, I will simply say that I am talking about human goodness.

On the extremes, there is little controversy. A child who is pred-atory, sadistic, and destructive would not fit the bill. A child who is compassionate, respectful, honest, and generous most certainly would. I want to explore what we know from social science about what par-enting strategies are more likely to produce a child whose goodness is closer to the latter. What can parents do to maximize the likelihood that they will raise children of moral character who will struggle to discern what is right and have the motivation and capacity to actually do the right thing?

Put simply, what will help us raise children who will add to rather than detract from the world?

The words we use to label this "human goodness" are imperfect and often contentious. Part of that comes from the very point of this volume: the religious-secular divide. If one is religious, then one is often concerned about whether or not the words are consistent with one's faith system. If you are not religious, you may be suspicious that words like *virtue, value, character,* and *morality* are smoke screens for religious concepts. But on a deeper level, talking about how "good" a person is can be very threatening to anyone. Hence, people often blanch at the term for fear that they may somehow be connected to a perspective they do not hold.

I see no perfect solution to this semantic quandary. I will use terms like *moral, character*, and *virtue*. I mean them simply to represent those aspects of a person that make him or her motivated and able to do the right thing. The reader may color between those lines.

I also want to take a brief but deeper look at what moral character entails. Character can be about goodness, but it can also be about effectiveness or intellectual skills. I am concerned here with the moral side of character. Character is only complete if we have the cognitive abilities to both know about goodness and to reason critically about it, the full suite of moral emotions (e.g., empathy, compassion, guilt), and the social and emotional skills necessary to navigate the sociomoral terrain that we all cross every day, even children as young as three. A shorthand for this is knowing the good, loving the good, and doing the good—or as some refer to it, the head, heart, and hand of character.

So what do we know about what actually works to foster such development? All too often people choose parenting strategies based on how they were raised, through intuition, or by chance. When I am working with teachers, they are often also parents. So I like to get them reflecting on the choices they typically make to influence the development of character in their students. I ask a series of questions about strategies they might use at home with their own children. "How many of you buy expensive posters with just one word on each, like *Honesty*, *Respect*, or *Responsibility*, and post them around your house?" "How many of you rename the spaces in your house 'Caring Kitchen' or 'Benevolent Bathroom'?" "How many of you announce which family member had the best character that month?" They routinely squirm and laugh as they realize the absurdity of the choices they make at school that they never would consider employing with their own children. And yet, the strategies at home also often fall far short of the mark, partly because they simply don't know what works and partly because they rarely reflect on and justify their parenting choices.

I am a social scientist (a developmental psychologist) and have found a niche in trying to bring the empirical wisdom of social science to educators and parents so they will choose strategies based on solid research and theory. Interestingly, I have found substantial overlap between what research tells us that parents should do and what teachers should do to nurture the development of moral character in children.

Many years ago, child clinical psychologist John Grych and I re-viewed the parenting research to see if we could identify a manageable set of "common denominator" parenting strategies related to the development of moral character in children. We discovered what I have subsequently labeled the "Fab 5." These are things that any parent (or any adult, for that matter) could do, and things that have been shown repeatedly to increase the likelihood that children will develop a wide range of moral characteristics. So let's take a look at the Fab 5.

To help remember these five strategies, I use the acronym DENIM, each letter representing one of the Fab 5. *D* is for Demandingness. *E* is for Empowerment. *N* is for Nurturance. *I* is for Induction. *M* is for Modeling. DENIM is a weave of the Fab 5, not merely a set of five discrete disconnected strategies. The five elements are woven together to make a research-based recipe for parenting for character.

Let's take them one at a time.

Demandingness

One of the great myths of parenting and teaching for goodness is that it sets low standards for your child, makes you a "soft touch." That is far from the truth. Effective parenting for character entails setting high standards or expectations for how the child will behave.

This is not as simple as it sounds. There are conditions necessary for demandingness (or high expectations) to have a positive impact on child development. First, the expectations must be high but also reasonable. Demanding that children do the impossible, or even highly unlikely, is cruel and destructive. It is fine to ask a child to do more than she thinks she can do, or even more than she might ultimately be able to do, as long as there is a reasonable chance of success. Asking children to do the impossible breeds a sense of helplessness and can lead to depression.

This is not a sink-or-swim strategy. It is not always a good idea to set high expectations and then leave the child to her own resources. Often we need to provide a scaffold for the child to climb in order to have a chance at reaching the heights of our expectations. That may entail teaching the child necessary subskills, like brainstorming ideas or preparing how to deliver a message or craft a request in advance. Sometimes it entails engaging in dialogue with children so they have a sounding board for ideas. Or it might simply be pointing them to resources that might provide information or other guidance they need:

"That's a tough question. I wonder if we know anyone who knows about crime."

"Uncle Jack! He used to be a policeman. I can ask him about it."

The bottom line: If we want our children to develop moral character, we need to expect it from them.

One final caveat is that we often in our lives have expectations of others about which they are unaware. We do that with our parents, our siblings, our spouses, our coworkers . . . and our children. And then we get angry when they fail to meet the expectations that they never even knew about. Be sure your expectations are clear, and not just to you (although that is important too), but also to your child. Ask him to repeat it back to you, or in other ways check that the message you think you have sent is the same as the message he received.

Empowerment

This is a tough one. There is a hierarchical relationship between parents and children, and for good reason. Healthy parents are wiser and more competent than their children in most respects, and they have the legal responsibility for the welfare of their children. However, in most places where this book is likely to be read, they are raising the future citizens of a democratic society. For their children to be ready to take on the responsibilities of citizenship, they need to discover their voices in public discourse. For children, the most notable public sphere after peer groups is the family. It is in this microcosm that much of citizenship development will occur. Learning that one's voice matters and can be lent to the collective search for the good is a critical part of this development.

But parenting for empowerment is important for larger reasons than simply civic socialization. It is good for children's development more broadly. Contrary to common assumptions, parents who share power have more moral children. Research has shown that parents who value, invite, and seriously listen to children's voices have children who are more moral. In large part it is because all people, including all children, have a fundamental need to feel that they are heard, that they matter, and that there is a chance they can make a difference.

Note that I said "a chance." I am not talking about parental abdication nor child veto power here. I am talking about respectful collaborative discourse. When parents invite their children's input on decisions and problem solving, and do so authentically, children need to know that the best ideas are the ones that will get adopted, and that if their ideas are the best, they will get adopted.

Empowerment is nuanced, too. The most important caveat here is that only certain categories of decisions and problems should be presented for child input. Do not ask them to chime in on issues for which the parents are not willing to alter their plans, or for which they will not be competent to help. Don't ask them about investment strategies, for example, or how to file your tax returns. Choose issues they can understand and for which you are willing to consider options. It is extraordinarily powerful for a child when their voice changes the decision or wins the day. This is just as true for each of us at work or in the community when it is our idea that resonates and solves a problem. In doing so, our very humanity is affirmed, just as it is for the child.

Nurturance

This one is a lot simpler and easier to swallow than the first two. Nurturance is simply a fancy term for love. The Beatles were wrong about this one; love is not all you need. But you do need it. We all need it, and certainly all children need it. It is like sunlight for a plant. Tragically, too many children grow up doubting they are loved, or knowing they are unloved. Make sure your children are surrounded by loving, nurturing adults, especially parents, and that they know they are loved. Usually kids are pretty good love detectors, but it is a good idea to say it out loud.

Induction

This one is a bit complex, but well worth taking the time to understand and implement. Induction is a technical term for a specific way of sending evaluative messages to children—messages telling them either how proud/pleased we are with them or how disappointed/frustrated/angry we are with them. Both are messages of evaluation of the child and/or her behavior that are either positive or negative. Certainly it is important *that* we do this, but for it to have a positive impact on character development it is crucial *how* we do it.

The first ingredient in proper induction is to give a clear and legitimate reason for your evaluative message. "I am so proud of you because . . ." "I am so angry at you because . . ." Just as for expectations, it is important that you are sure the child understands the reason. When we chastise children, they become upset. All too often, they are not upset for being reprimanded but rather because they don't understand why they are being reprimanded. Even when they are being lauded, they get little from such affirmation if they don't know the reason. So we need to explain.

The second ingredient in proper induction is the content of the explanation. In induction, the reason for the evaluative response should focus on the consequences of the child's behavior, ideally for someone else's feelings:

"I am so frustrated with you because I told you over and over to use your words and not your hands. Now you hit your little brother, and what is he doing?"

"He's crying."

"That's right. He is crying because you hurt him and you scared him."

Or, "I am so proud of you because I know you don't like the present Aunt Margie gave you, but you hugged her and thanked her, and look how happy she looks. You made her so happy."

Induction has been found over and over in research to generate a host of positive character outcomes.

Modeling

The last ingredient in the Fab 5 is both simple and challenging: simple to understand and challenging to implement. Gandhi once said, "Be the change you want to see in the world." I am challenging you to be the character you want to see in your children. I periodically ask people to think of one of their character strengths and then to consider how they ended up being that kind of person. The answer is almost always that one of their parents embodied that same characteristic. Try that question out on yourself. See? So if most of us think that our character strengths came from parents who modeled those same characteristics, then it should not be surprising that research tells us that children who develop empathy had empathic parents, altruistic children had altruistic parents, and so on.

It takes some courage to change. When my son was born, I asked myself what I do that I didn't want him to replicate. I was able to make a list. It is not horrendous, but I found plenty. Stop swearing, stop watching violent TV, and so on. And I did. It wasn't easy, but it was necessary. Parents need to clean up their acts and to use as a guide the dictate to be the character they want to see in their children.

If we want our children to grow up to be prosocial, ethical people who add to the world and not antisocial hedonistic predators who drain the value out of the world, we need to be deliberate and consistent in using the Fab 5 of DENIM. Research tells us that this set of strategies results in increased moral reasoning capacities, greater altruism and empathy, stronger consciences, and a general orientation to have healthy relationships with others, among many other desirable character strengths.

MARVIN BERKOWITZ is the former Coors Professor of Character Development at the Air Force Academy and professor of psychology and director of the Center for Ethics Studies at Marquette University. He is currently the Sanford McDonnell Professor of Character Education at the University of Missouri–Saint Louis.

■ ■

SPARE THE ROD—
AND SPARE ME THE REST

DALE McGOWAN

Secular parenting should not be motivated primarily by disbelief in God. My religious doubts sprang from thinking for myself, not the other way around. So it's freethought down at the roots of my parenting, not atheism. When someone asks for the foundations of my parenting, I paraphrase the Bertrand Russell quote that begins this book: Good parenting is inspired by love and guided by knowledge. Next to the love of my children, my parenting philosophy is motivated primarily by confidence in reason—and there's no reason this should apply any less to discipline and moral development than any other aspect of parenting.

I don't spank my kids. Many religious fundamentalists spank in earnest, convinced it is an essential element of moral development. For support, they often cite the biblical injunction "Spare the rod and spoil the child."

There's something doubly funny about the invocation of that scripture. First of all, it isn't scripture. Second is its actual source: a raunchy poem by Samuel Butler that skewers the fundamentalists of his time, the English Puritans:

> What med'cine else can cure the fits
> Of lovers when they lose their wits?
> Love is a boy by poets styl'd;
> Then spare the rod, and spoil the child.
> —Samuel Butler, *Hudibras,* Part 2 (1664)

He's lampooning the Puritan obsession with sexual abstinence as the cure for passion, using "the rod" in this case as a wickedly clever double entendre while making sly reference to an actual passage from Proverbs: "He that spares his rod hates his son: but he that loves him disciplines him promptly" (Prv 13:24).

It's amusing to hear sex-averse fundamentalists quoting from a bawdy satire that was aimed at them, and invoking a penis in the bargain. It's almost as much fun as watching my homophobic aunts happily shouting along with the refrain to "YMCA" like it's a song about recreation facilities.

Though most strong advocates of corporal punishment are religious, not all religious people support corporal punishment. Christian child-development expert Dr. William Sears strongly opposes the practice. In the process, though, he and other religious progressives have suggested that the rod mentioned frequently in the Bible is a tool meant to guide, not to smite. Though this is true on occasion ("Thy rod and thy staff, they comfort me," Ps 23), in far more cases it's a tool for smiting, beating, whipping, chastening:

> *And if a man smite his servant, or his maid, with a rod.*
> *(Ex 21:20)*
> *If he commit iniquity, I will chasten him with the rod.(2 Sm*
> *7:14)*
> *Their houses are safe from fear, neither is the rod of God*
> *upon them. (Jb 21:9)*
> *He that spareth his rod hateth his son: but he that loveth*
> *him chasteneth him betimes. (Prv 13:24)*
> *Withhold not correction from the child: for if thou beatest*
> *him with the rod, he shall not die. Thou shalt beat him with*
> *the rod, and shalt deliver his soul from hell. (Prv 23:13–14)*
> *A whip for the horse, a bridle for the ass, and a rod for the*
> *fool's back. (Prv 26:3)*
> *For thou hast broken the yoke of his burden, and the staff*
> *of his shoulder, the rod of his oppressor. (Is 9:4)*
> *Rejoice not thou, whole Palestina, because the rod of him*
> *that smote thee is broken. (Is 14:29)*
> *I am the man that hath seen affliction by the rod of his*
> *wrath. (Lm 3:1)*

So the Bible clearly sees the rod primarily as an instrument of interpersonal violence, including violence against children. These are verses cited by many conservative Christian leaders in their strong advocacy of corporal punishment—advocacy that continues to encourage a practice that should have died out long ago.

Perhaps the most enthusiastic advocate of corporal punishment has been Dr. James Dobson, founder of Focus on the Family. In his influential book *The New Dare to Discipline*, Dobson turns parenting into a contest of wills:

You have drawn a line in the dirt, and the child has deliberately flopped his bony little toe across it. Who is going to win? Who has the most courage? Who is in charge here? If you do not conclusively answer these questions for your strong-willed children, they will precipitate other battles designed to ask them again and again.

He says "spanking should be of sufficient magnitude to cause genuine tears" and recommends painful squeezing of the trapezius muscle on the neck to obtain "instant obedience." Dobson recommends employing switches and paddles to hit children, whipping as early as 15 months, and hitting a toddler whenever he "hits his friends." And if a child cries more than a few minutes after being spanked, he says: hit him some more.[1]

But I shouldn't refrain from spanking just because religious fundamentalists spank—I should refrain because our accumulated knowledge says it's the wrong thing to do.

Before I go further, let me confess that I spanked my kids in the early going, before I had my parental wings. I had been spanked as a child, and in moments of frustration, I simply and stupidly turned to what I knew. I'm ashamed to admit it. I stopped on a dime when I realized that it represented a serious failure in my parenting—most of all, a twofold failure in my confidence in reason.

Every time a parent raises a hand to a child, that parent is saying, "You cannot be reasoned with." In the process, the child learns that force is an acceptable substitute for reason, and that Mom and Dad have more confidence in the former than in the latter.

I eventually learned to correct behaviors by having my children recognize and name the problem themselves. Replace "Don't pull the dog's ears" with "Why is pulling the dog's ears a bad idea?" Very young kids can grapple with that, and you've required them to reason, not just to obey. Good practice.

The second failure is equally damning. Spanking doesn't work. In fact, it makes things worse. The research is compelling. A meta-analysis of 88 corporal punishment studies compiled by Elizabeth Thompson Gershoff at Columbia University found 11 outcomes strongly correlated with corporal punishment. Ten of those were negative, including a damaged parent-child relationship, increased antisocial and aggressive behaviors, and the increased likelihood that the spanked child will physically abuse his or her own children.

The study revealed just one positive correlation: immediate compliance.[2] A much larger study in 2016 underlined every one of those findings and added a kicker: that the more kids are spanked, the more they tend to defy their parents, which quickly undercuts the compliance benefit.[3]

So parents with a view longer than 30 seconds can and should make use of the many other techniques that get their attention equally well or better without the terrible long-term legacy of corporal punishment. A discipline plan that is both inspired by love and guided by knowledge finds the most loving option that works, and spanking fails on both counts.

If our ultimate goal is creating autonomous adults, we should raise children who are not merely disciplined but self-disciplined. So if your parenting is grounded in reason, skip the spankings and teach them to find the reasons to be good. We all have an investment in a future less saddled by aggression, abuse, and all the other antisocial maladies to which spanking is known to contribute.

Discipline and moral development are also related to freethought in a way that might not be obvious. I don't care if my kids end up identifying with religion as long as it's a choice, not a need. And the best way I can ensure that is by giving them not just knowledge but also confidence and security.

As it turns out, we know how to give them confidence and security—and it's not by beating them. You start with a sensitive, responsive, and consistent home life. Build a strong attachment with parents and other significant adults. Don't hit or humiliate them or let others do so. Encourage them to challenge authority, including your own. Make them comfortable with difference. Use knowledge to drive out fear. Build a sense of curiosity and wonder that will keep them self-educating for life. Let them know that your love and support are unconditional. Teach and expect responsibility and maturity. Encourage self-reliance. Help them find and develop "flow" activities and lose themselves in them. These practices are straight out of the best child-development research, which strongly supports attachment theory and authoritative parenting.

Just as the best practices for being a humanist are in sync with the best practices for being human, the best practices for humanist parenting are in sync with the best practices for . . . parenting.

■ ■

MORALITY AND EVIL

GARETH B. MATTHEWS, Ph.D.

Secular parents may feel that they have a special advantage over religious parents in not having to discuss the problem of evil with their children. That is, since they do not believe there is such a thing as a divine being who is both all good and all powerful, they do not have to try to explain to their children why terrible things sometimes happen to innocent or even good people: tsunamis that kill thousands of innocent victims, or terrible illnesses that make babies and small children suffer unbearable pain before they then die. These parents, like most all parents, may want to shield their children from news about the horrors of the world. But if the children see something heartbreaking on TV, at least they do not have the burden of explaining how a loving and all-powerful being could allow such a thing to happen.

On the other hand, religious parents may feel that they have an advantage over secular parents when it comes to moral upbringing. These parents may be upset at the moral relativism they and their children see in the movies or hear in their favorite music, but they may feel confident that they have an answer to all moral relativism: Morality, they believe, rests on the unshakable commands of God.

In fact, I shall argue, both assumed advantages are illusory. The idea that it is God's commands that justify morality is not as much of an advantage in helping our children to become morally good people as one might think. And the idea that the problem of evil is only a problem for religious believers is mistaken. But my counsel is not a counsel of despair. It is rather that parents, whether religious or secular, should have open discussions with their children, including discussions about morality and about evil. Children need to work out their own answers to the fascinatingly difficult questions of life. With encouragement from their elders, they will do this. I begin with the problem of evil.

My grandson Julian has always loved trucks. When he was barely fifteen months old and just learning to talk, he would take my hand and lead me to one of his father's trucks, most likely to his father's dump truck, which was then his favorite. He would stand by the dump truck in an almost ecstatic trance, quiver all over, and pronounce, very carefully, perhaps several times, those magic words, "dump truck."

Julian continued to like dump trucks through early childhood. But his primary allegiance shifted from dump trucks to bucket-loaders. I remember seeing him at two and a half, in the same trancelike state, literally shaking all over, as he watched the magical actions of a bucket-loader.

Julian was also, and remains so to this day, an ardent nature lover. Even at age three he could recognize a large number of bird varieties, more than many of us adults. He also knew much, much more about frogs and turtles than I have ever dreamt of knowing. He was especially passionate about frogs. While he was still two, he and his mother, my daughter, Sarah, had heard wood frogs quacking in the wetlands across the street from their house. So, in the following spring, just as Julian was turning three, Sarah took Julian and his older sister, Pearl, onto the land across the street in the hopes of hearing wood frogs again and maybe getting a look at one.

Unfortunately, a developer had recently cleared a huge tract of land adjacent to the wetlands and had filled in some of the wetlands. Julian had enjoyed watching the big trucks do this work. But now, when Julian and his sister and mother went to look for wood frogs, none could be found. Instead of the quacking sound of wood frogs, which Julian could clearly distinguish from the call of tree frogs, they heard nothing but the sound of bucket-loaders. Without thinking about what effect her words might have on Julian, Sarah blurted out, "The bucket-loaders have killed the wood frogs."

Sarah's remark stunned Julian. He kept repeating, "Oh my God! You're kidding, Mama! The bucket-loaders have killed the wood frogs?" Sarah tried to console Julian, but nothing helped.

In that experience, Julian encountered the problem of evil. It is not that he wondered how it is possible that God, who is all good and all powerful, could allow evil to exist in the world. He was relatively innocent of any explicitly theological framework for thought. But he had to face the shattering realization that one preeminent good in life, a bucket-loader, could destroy another preeminent good in life, a colony of wood frogs.

Later on, in a move somewhat reminiscent of Immanuel Kant's argument from justice for human immortality, Julian developed the conviction that mother wood frogs have babies, then die, and then later come to life again. In this way he reassured himself that his beloved wood frogs had not, after all, been completely obliterated by his equally beloved bucket-loaders. They would be born again.

Evil does come from good. This is a metaphysical problem. This is also, as it was for Julian, an existential problem. There is no particular age, or stage in life, when we have to confront the problem of evil. It may hit us when we first read David Hume in a philosophy class. It may hit us when we read the Book of Job in church or temple. It may hit us when we read about the torture of prisoners in Iraq or Guantánamo. Or it may hit us when we have seen what a bucket-loader, or perhaps a developer, who may, of course, be a very good person, has done to the wetlands, and to the wood frogs that had inhabited it.

The religious parent who teaches her children about God's love and unlimited power should be prepared to think freshly with her children about the problem of evil. It is not easy for anyone to do that. Yet, I maintain, it is part of the responsibility of a religious parent to have an honest discussion with her children about the problem of evil.

Surprisingly, perhaps, the challenge for secular parents is not entirely different. They might hope to avoid having to deal with any form of the problem of evil with their children. But for parents who have a genuine respect for their children and for the hard questions their children ask, the hope of evading the problem of evil may well be frustrated. After all, evil does sometimes come from good.

Parents may not want their children to think of either frogs or bucket-loaders as inherently good things. Yet, one could argue, it is an impoverished childhood in which nothing seems to be unqualifiedly good. Julian's consuming love of nature, and of trucks, gave his childhood an especially magical quality. But it also gave him the problem of evil.

I turn now to my second topic, the issue of whether the idea of morality as something commanded by God can help ward off the threats of nihilism and moral relativism so pervasive in our society. No doubt many religious parents feel they have a distinct advantage over their secular counterparts when it comes to moral education. After all, they can teach their children that it is God, no less, who commands us not to kill, lie, or steal, and it is God who commands us to love our neighbors as ourselves.

> 66 For parents who have a genuine respect for their children and for the hard questions their children ask, the hope of evading the problem of evil may well be frustrated. After all, evil does sometimes come from good. 99

Secular parents who are conscientious about raising their children to be morally good people may also wish they had an easy way to ground morality and protect their children from cynicism and moral relativism. They may even harbor the secret wish that they could pull out the divine trump card to fend off the attractions of immorality their children will have to face.

Yet the divine trump card is not fully effective in the way religious parents may expect. This was shown a long time ago by Plato in his dialogue *Euthyphro*. In that dialogue, Socrates asks what the holy is. After several failed efforts to answer the question, Euthyphro offers the suggestion that the holy is doing what the gods love. Socrates then asks, "Is it holy because the gods love it, or do the gods love it because it is holy?"

We can translate Socrates's famous question into the theology of monotheism by asking, "Is it morally right

> 66 The religious parent and the secular parent are in much the same boat when it comes to raising their children to be morally good people. 99

(for example) to tell the truth simply because God commands it ('Do not bear false witness'), or does God command us to tell the truth because that is the morally right thing to do?" If we say it is right simply because God commands it, we leave open the possibility that moral rightness could be a mere matter of divine whim. For most religious believers, that doesn't seem right. But, if we say that God commands us to be truthful because that is the morally right thing to do, then it seems we should be able to understand what is morally required of us independently of the fact that God commands it.

I once discussed the Euthyphro problem with two classes of seventh graders in a Hebrew day school. We were discussing whether the things God commands in Leviticus 19 are holy because God commands them or whether instead God commands them because they are holy. One student said this: "God wants us to do these things because they are holy. If God [had] told us to kill, steal, and commit adultery, would [those] be holy thing[s] to do? I don't think so. I think these things are holy, and God wants us to do them *because* they are holy."

If what this seventh grader said is right, and I am inclined to agree that the religious person should say this, then the religious parent and the secular parent are in much the same boat when it comes to raising their children to be morally good people. Moral development will have to include cultivating moral feelings, such as empathy and a sense of fairness; developing habits of telling the truth and keeping promises; nurturing attitudes of generosity and loyalty; and reflecting on how to resolve moral dilemmas when, for example, the duty to tell the truth or keep a promise conflicts with the duty to help someone in need, or under threat of assault.

Whether the ideal of a moral life has a divine sanction is not a trivial question. But once one sees the implications of the Euthyphro problem, the question of divine sanction does not offer much enlightenment about what morality requires, or about how to become a moral person. Unless what God commands us to do is what we morally ought to do anyway, then the very idea of a divine sanction for the moral law seems to threaten the rationality of trying to be moral.

So where does this leave thoughtful secular parents with respect to issues about the problem of evil and the nature of morality? It seems to leave them in roughly the same situation as thoughtful religious parents. Children cannot be shielded from the problem of evil, even by trying to keep them innocent of theology. Evil does come from good. And as for helping one's children to become caring, fair-minded, responsible moral agents, the primary resources open to religious parents are much the same as those open to secular ones.

If one believes that God is supremely just, merciful, and good, then it will follow that God also wants us to be just, merciful, and good. But we will have the very same reasons for being just, merciful, and good as God has, even if, as the religious among us may suppose, we don't understand those reasons as well as we think God does, or even as well as we ourselves would like to.

GARETH MATTHEWS (1929–2011) was a renowned scholar in the philosophy of children and professor of philosophy at the University of Massachusetts at Amherst, the University of Virginia, and the University of Minnesota. He authored many articles and three books on philosophy and childhood: Philosophy and the Young Child (1980), Dialogues with Children (1984), and The Philosophy of Childhood (1994). Sadly, Gary passed away a few years after the first edition of this book was published. He was the father of three and grandfather of seven.

■ ■

BEHAVING YOURSELF: MORAL DEVELOPMENT IN THE SECULAR FAMILY

JEAN MERCER, Ph.D.

A five-year-old boy swipes the coins his mother has left on her desk. As it happens, the mother knows exactly how much she has put there in preparation for a trip to the Laundromat. She confronts the little boy, who says he didn't take the money—but there lies the exact amount of the missing money right on his pillow. The mother gives him a serious talking-to, then sends him to his room, telling him to come out only when he can say why he should not have taken the coins. After some minutes, he emerges in tears, but is able to state what was wrong with what he did: "Ya get in trouble!"

This vignette contains many elements common to the moral instruction of secular and religious families alike. The child did not plan to break any rules, but he was not able to resist temptation when it occurred. The offense was only a minor inconvenience to the mother at the time, but she wanted to respond appropriately because she was concerned that the child not take other people's property in the future. She was influenced by what she feared was the development of an undesirable pattern of behavior and so was unwilling to let the incident pass. She believed the child was old enough to think through the situation, but she was also willing to accept a very simple rationale when the child offered it.

The early development of moral thinking and moral behavior choices is largely based on brief interactions like this one. Children do childish wrong things, and parents provide ad hoc corrections. In early and middle childhood, parents are quite unlikely to instruct children on major moral issues, because the children are unlikely to do things that obviously involve major issues in a direct way. It is probably safe to say that no parent gives direct training on avoiding the most serious moral lapses—"Sally, when you go out to play, I don't want you to murder anybody. And, Timmy, no raping—I don't care what the other boys do, it's not nice to rape people." Nevertheless, few adults commit murder or rape, in part because they received direct instruction about related minor matters like hitting or pulling another child's pants down—instruction from which abstract moral principles may be derived as the child's reasoning ability matures. The whole process is a gradual one involving repeated experiences, rather than memorization of a list of "right things" and "wrong things," or the early mastery of universal principles.

Whether a family is secular or religious in beliefs, the basic processes of moral training and development are probably pretty similar. One college student, brought up in a devout Catholic family, responded to this idea with a disbelieving exclamation: "How can they develop morally if they're brought up without any values!" Of course, every family has a set of values, although the parents might have trouble stating just what they are, and every family has an interest in passing on a value system to the next generation. Although some families admire criminal or simply underhanded behavior and encourage it in their children, most families in a cultural group want to foster socially desirable behaviors: some degree of truthfulness; some willingness to sacrifice for others; some concern with others' property rights; and, later on, some caution about sexual activity. Background values are different, however. In nonsecular families, supernatural entities and events are presented as reasons for complying with rules about behavior; in secular families, compliance is connected with overarching principles related to human needs and experiences, such as individual autonomy, equal rights of human beings, and freedom of conscience.[1] Religious families may find it easier to state the connection between values and behavior than do secular families, who are generally thinking in terms of highly abstract principles rather than of nonhuman entities who can be presented as having personal wishes and emotions. But all families function to help establish children's ways of thinking about moral issues, emotions connected with morality, and behavior patterns related to value judgments.

The Development of Moral Reasoning

The term *moral development* describes the fact that children's moral behavior and thinking change with age in predictable ways. Developmental changes of all kinds can be studied empirically, and many aspects of development have proven to follow systematic pathways, so that most human beings go through the same developmental steps, often at similar ages. Empirical studies of moral development have most often focused on changes in moral reasoning, the kind of thinking that underlies decisions about moral issues. The best-known theory of developmental change in moral reasoning comes from the work of Lawrence Kohlberg, who studied the process by presenting children with moral dilemmas—problems where two decisions seemed equally desirable—and asking them to explain why they made the choice they did.[2] Kohlberg felt that the development of moral reasoning could be described as involving six stages. (Because Kohlberg's method involved talking about a problem, the first stage could not be identified until the child could talk well, which would not occur until at least age three for most children.)

The earliest stage Kohlberg described was one in which right and wrong are defined by punishment rather than by any larger principle. If something is followed by punishment, it was wrong; if it is not, it was right. The light-fingered five-year-old mentioned before was at this stage. A second stage considers reward as an important indication that something is right. The stress in these early stages is on works, not faith: Rightness or wrongness is identified in terms of what a person actually does, not what he or she intended but was unable to perform.

A third stage described by Kohlberg involves social approval and disapproval. By this point, the child separates moral correctness from specific punishment or reward. The moral choice is instead the one that makes other people consider someone a nice boy or a good girl. Continuing with the stress on community approval, a fourth stage emphasizes the existence of laws or rules that are valuable in themselves; breaking a rule is morally wrong simply because it is a rule, not because of the possible consequences for the rule breaker or for others.

Very few individuals would move beyond this fourth stage during childhood, but in adolescence or afterward a number of people will achieve a "social contract" level of moral reasoning, in which laws and rules are seen as desirable for the comfort of the community but potentially changeable if they do not work well. Moral decisions can involve complying with rules or working to change them. A final stage, not likely to be reached before late adolescence, involves thinking in terms of universal ethical principles such as the value of human life; decisions to support a universal principle could be made in spite of others' finding one "not nice" or even in the face of certain punishment under the laws.

Most descriptions of developmental change involve steps that are typical of all human beings. Kohlberg's theory is somewhat different, however. This approach suggests everyone follows moral development in the same sequence, but people do not necessarily arrive at the same step at the same age, and some may never reach the higher stages. Certainly, a number of adults do not appear ever to go beyond the second stage posited by Kohlberg, and the "official morality" of the United States appears to be somewhere between the fourth ("law and order") and the fifth ("social contract") stages. These facts raise a question about advanced development in moral reasoning: Are there experiences that help people achieve these higher stages?

> Contrary to traditional beliefs, frequent punishment and the assertion of parental authority are not factors that facilitate growth in moral reasoning.

Family actions do seem to be related to the development of moral reasoning. Contrary to traditional beliefs, frequent punishment and the assertion of parental authority are not factors that facilitate growth in moral reasoning. Parents of children with advanced moral reasoning are more likely to be authoritative (taking charge, but without an overly strict or punitive approach) than authoritarian. Authoritative parenting fosters cognitive development in general, so it is not surprising that moral reasoning, a type of cognitive skill, is also facilitated.

Advances in moral reasoning are also associated with exposure to parental discussion of moral uncertainties and to equal sharing of power between parents, which leads to frequent negotiation and compromise.[3]

Intriguing as it is, Kohlberg's theory is far from a complete description of moral development; for example, women and girls are not usually assessed as highly advanced moral reasoners in Kohlberg's model. And, of course, moral reasoning is not the whole story of moral development. Decisions about moral behavior involve motivation to do what is right as well as the ability to apply moral principles in thought.

Emotion and Moral Development

Looking at moral development from the viewpoint of moral reasoning showed us stages of morality beginning in the nursery school years. When we consider the emotional aspects of morality, however, we must go back to an astonishingly early period of development—even as far back as early infancy, when the first social relationships begin to form. This statement is particularly true of values based on human needs and rights, because events during infancy provide the foundation for our understanding of others' feelings and our wish to comfort and help them.

Infants in the first few months of life have little ability to understand facial expressions or other indications of emotion, but they already react very differently to human beings than they do to inanimate objects, even moving ones. If they have frequent experiences with sensitive, responsive adult caregivers, infants soon begin to notice emotional cues. For example, an infant responds by beginning to cry if an adult simply turns a blank face toward the baby and does not respond to smiles or vocal sounds. By seven or eight months, an infant confronted with some surprising new object turns to look at a familiar caregiver's face; if the caregiver looks frightened, the baby backs away from the object, but if the caregiver looks happy, the baby goes on to investigate. The baby is beginning to develop an essential set of skills, sometimes categorized as theory of mind.[4] Theory of mind allows each person to be aware that behind every human face is an individual set of experiences, wishes, beliefs, and thoughts; that each of these sets is in some ways similar to and in other ways different from one's own set; and that facial expressions and other cues can enable each of us to know something of how others feel and what they are going to do. The development of theory of mind has already begun by 9 or 10 months, when a well-developed baby can already show the important step of joint attention. In this behavior, the child uses eye contact and movement of the gaze to get an adult to look at some sight that interests the baby and then to look back again, to gaze at each other and smile with mutual pleasure. Importantly, not only *can* the child do this, but he or she *wants* to do it, demonstrating the very early motivation to share our happiness with others—surely the foundation of empathic responses. Without this early development, it would hardly be possible to achieve secular values such as a concern with equal rights, a principle based on the understanding that all human beings have similar experiences of pleasure and pain.

How does this complex and early developmental process occur? Does it simply unfold, or does experience with others play an important role? This question is more complicated than it appears because some individuals, often characterized as autistic, do not seem to develop theory of mind, even though they have normal experiences.[5] For most infants, however, there seems to be an initial component of being especially interested in human beings, and this is followed by many experiences of predictable interactions with caregivers, so that a facial expression or tone of voice becomes a signal that the adult is about to do certain things. Ideally, the caregiver also responds in a predictable way to the baby's signals of smiling or reaching or turning the eyes away. Unfortunately, many babies are exposed to the much less responsive and predictable demeanor of a mother who suffers from a perinatal mood disorder or who is involved with drugs or alcohol. They may also spend many hours in poor-quality child-care arrangements, with repeated changes of foster family so that no one learns to "read" the baby's expression, or with caregivers who mistakenly believe that responding to the baby's emotional expressions will cause "spoiling." Theory of mind is facilitated by responsive nurturing and the devoted care of adults who value infants as members of the human species.

Early steps in theory of mind seem to be essential to the growth of the empathic attitudes that are a basic part of humanistic values. However, the first steps are not the end of the process. Experiences in the toddler and early preschool period provide a watershed for the development of empathic behavior. It is important to realize that the distress of another person does not provide a simple signal calling for a simple response. Distress causes complex facial expressions and behavior patterns that call out ambivalent reactions in young children and in adults. People who like clowns find their sad faces funny; many of us have horrified ourselves by laughing quite inappropriately at a funeral; a common trigger for child abuse is the child's crying. The appearance of distress can call out an impulse to help but can also create amusement or even the wish to attack the troubled person. What makes some human beings more likely to respond compassionately to distress, others more likely to laugh or attack? This is a difficult topic to study systematically, but it is thought that experience with caregivers helps to establish an individual's compassionate or aggressive response to distress signals. When the young child is distressed, a caregiver's kind or hostile response models the appropriate way to act when others are uncomfortable. Nurturing, responsive caregivers are likely to help children become compassionate, and unsympathetic caregivers guide children toward an aggressive response to others' distress. Perhaps the worst model is the adult who teases and torments a child into a tearful rage and then dismisses or even punishes the distressed child as "a big baby."

Guidance, Discipline, and Moral Development

As a child develops theory of mind and the capacity for emotional empathy, and as moral reasoning progresses to more advanced stages, parental guidance provides specific information about right and wrong behavior. (Incidentally, the actions that are considered right or wrong will change as the child gets older—for example, a toddler might be punished for trying to pick up a crying infant, but a ten-year-old praised.) Such guidance helps to establish knowledge about specific behaviors that can eventually be used to derive abstract principles of morality.

Although the behavior of parents serves as an important role model for children, few families rely on modeling alone as a way to shape children's behavior. And, although parents may prefer to praise and reward approved behavior, few manage to raise children without some use of punishment. For secular families, this fact may be problematic, because the use of punishment by persons in authority appears to be in conflict with humanistic principles such as the autonomy of the individual. Nevertheless, it is clear that when a parent is dealing with a young, relatively nonverbal child who is doing something dangerous to himself or painful to others, punishment may be the quickest, most effective way to stop the behavior, and thus to work toward understanding of related moral issues.

Punishment need not be physical in nature, although physical restraint or removal of the child from the scene may be part of the parent's action. Punishment may simply involve the parent's communication of anger or sadness and interruption of the behavior (which the child presumably wanted to carry out). To be effective, punishment must be highly consistent—if there is a rule, it always applies. The timing of punishment is critical, and it is by far the most effective if it occurs just as the undesirable behavior begins. If punishment is swift and sure, it need not be severe, and in fact milder forms of punishment, which do not trigger an intense emotional reaction, are more likely to teach effectively. These points about punishment suggest that the most effective parents will be those who plan their use of guidance techniques, who are consistently attentive to the child's behavior, and who respond predictably even when they find it inconvenient or boring to do so.

Parental guidance techniques are also associated with moral development as factors in the establishment of the social emotions. These emotions occur in response to the child's awareness of others' evaluation of her, and they appear in the late toddler/early preschool period. One approach to the social emotions classifies these feelings as either positive or negative, and as either global or specific, yielding four basic social emotions that occur in response to awareness of others' opinions.[6] The child may experience guilt, an unpleasant feeling of having failed in some specific way; shame, an unpleasant feeling of having been judged as globally bad or wrong; pride, a pleasant sense of having received approval for a specific action or characteristic; and hubris, a pleasant but unrealistic feeling of global approval by others. Of these emotions, guilt and pride are useful guides to good behavior because they involve specific acts that can be avoided or repeated in the future. Shame and hubris are far less useful because the individual has no control over the nature of the self and cannot change the basic self to gain approval or avoid disapproval. In fact, the response to shame may be one of helpless terror and rage, as destruction of the self seems to be the only way of escape from the judgment. In older children and adults, shame experiences may be triggered easily by events that imply "disrespect," and extreme antisocial reactions may result.

This view of the social emotions suggests that moral development would be fostered best by parenting that stresses pride and guilt rather than hubris and shame. Such parenting involves mild punishment that does not overwhelm the child with fear and anger, and careful verbal communication that clarifies for the child exactly what was bad or good in his behavior. Parents who work toward desirable social emotions need to have insight into their own reactions of approval or disapproval. Parental reactions of contempt or disgust toward the child are difficult for the child to process as connected with specific actions, and they may pass unexplained if the parent is only vaguely aware of their attitude; a pervasive sense of shame is a likely outcome if there are many experiences of this type.

As a general rule, parenting practices seem to support desirable behavior and moral development best when they involve mild emotion that does not threaten the child's autonomy. Messages to the child are most effective when they are understandable but indirect and have some humorous component.[7] Parenting practices are less successful when they involve a high degree of psychological intrusiveness or attempts to control the child's beliefs and emotions through psychological means such as threatened withdrawal of love. Although effective parental control of children's behavior (like demanding mature behavior) has positive outcomes, psychological intrusiveness results in a higher number of emotional and behavior problems, and this is, surprisingly, particularly true when a high level of parental affection is also present.[8]

Advantages and Disadvantages of a Secular Approach to Moral Development

Are there differences between secular and nonsecular families in the fostering of children's moral development? There is no recent evidence that seems to support the superiority of one group or the other. The development of emotional components of morality, such as empathy, begins so early that it is doubtful that family beliefs play a significant role. As for discipline and guidance practices, these are probably similar in families with various beliefs, except that a small number of religious fundamentalists stress "breaking the child's will" and try to establish complete obedience from the age of a few months.[9] It is possible that secular humanist principles such as individual autonomy and equal rights may reduce secular families' use of punishment, or at least point up the need for reasoning and discussion of behavior issues in addition to reward and punishment.

The major difference that might be expected to result from contrasting beliefs has to do with moral reasoning. Whereas nonsecular families may choose to stress reasoning in terms of the punishments or rewards available from supernatural entities or their agents (which they do not necessarily do), such ploys would be most unlikely among secular parents. Secular families base their standards on overarching ethical principles that may be highly abstract and that are connected to specific behaviors through extensive reasoning. Because discussion of moral issues in the family encourages advanced moral development, it is possible that children of secular families have an advantage here.

Are there disadvantages in a secular approach to moral development? The one obvious problem has to do with

> 66 Secular families base their standards on overarching ethical principles . . . that are connected to specific behaviors through extensive reasoning. Because discussion of moral issues in the family encourages advanced moral development, it is possible that children of secular families have an advantage. 99

the need for a community that shares and reinforces the family's values. Although the earliest steps in moral development occur within the family, older children and adolescents come into increasing contact with the standards of the surrounding community. The issue here is not so much that the children will abandon the family's values as that family members may feel isolated or even beleaguered by value conflicts with neighbors. Nevertheless, if this situation is handled well by secular parents, value disagreements may be turned to advantage through family discussion and opportunities to model advanced moral reasoning.

JEAN MERCER is a developmental psychologist with a doctorate from Brandeis University, professor emerita at Richard Stockton College, and a founding fellow of the Institute for Science in Medicine. Her book Alternative Psychotherapies: Evaluating Unconventional Mental Health Treatments *(2014) is her latest contribution in the fight against attachment therapy, a cultlike belief system that encourages intrusive and harmful physical practices in the guise of child psychotherapy.*

■ ■

TAKE TWO TABLETS AND CALL ME IN THE MORNING

YIP HARBURG

If the Lord, who could surely afford it,
Were a little bit more democratic,
That is, if the Lord didn't lord it
And weren't so doggone dogmatic,
The world would be one bed of roses,
Sweet psyches and better digestions
If the tablets he handed to Moses
Were inscribed not commands but suggestions.[1]

EDGAR YIPSEL "YIP" HARBURG, *among the greatest and most beloved lyricists of the 20th century, was also a nonbeliever and a secular parent. Author of such classics as "Somewhere Over the Rainbow," "Brother, Can You Spare a Dime?," "April in Paris," and "Paper Moon," Yip created lyrics and poems that were brilliant and unbearably clever. He often addressed serious social issues, such as war, intolerance, and injustice, with incisive and devastating wit.*

The five poems appearing in this book are excerpted from Rhymes for the Irreverent, *a collaboration between the Harburg Foundation and the Freedom From Religion Foundation, and are reprinted with their kind permission.*

■ ■

DOUBLE VISION: TEACHING OUR TWINS PRIDE AND RESPECT

SHANNON and MATTHEW CHERRY

We will build a home that is compassionate to all,
full of respect and honor for others and each other.
May our home be forever filled with peace, love, and happiness.

When we said these words at our humanist wedding ceremony thirteen years ago, we didn't even know if we would have children. Now that we have twin daughters, this vow has taken on a whole new importance.

Yes, Lyra and Sophia have changed our lives, but not our values.

We are raising our children in an explicitly humanist family. Chambers Pocket Dictionary defines humanism as "seeking, without religion, the best in, and for, human beings." That's really how we see our job as parents: seeking to bring out the best in our children so that they can have the best in life.

The humanist tradition in the West has its roots in the ancient Greek ideal of cultivating human excellence. There are many principles needed to bring out the best in people. But there is one value mentioned in our wedding vows that keeps coming up in our discussions of how to raise good kids: respect.

R-E-S-P-E-C-T is more than an Aretha Franklin song. It means treating the world around us—and everyone in it—as valuable. It also means self-respect, or pride. We want to raise our girls to respect themselves, their surroundings, their pets; to value families, friends, and neighbors. And we don't just mean an attitude of respect, but respectful behavior; we see too many people who boast all the tolerant opinions required in liberal society but don't actually accomplish much with their lives.

Perhaps most challenging of all will be teaching respect for people who have different values—even people with beliefs we think are daft and behaviors we fear as dangerous.

Philosophically, respect is at the heart of the major systems of morality: from the Golden Rule (treating others with the same respect with which we would want them to treat us) to Kant's categorical imperative (that we must always treat people as ends in themselves and not merely as means to our own ends). But philosophy won't cut it with our infant girls. Even though they can't speak a word yet, their big blue eyes are constantly watching and learning from us. What matters to them is not the philosophy we preach but how we practice those lofty principles.

To teach them respect, we need to model the right behavior. "Do what I say, not what I do" is not only unfair but just doesn't work. Sooner or later, children see through hypocrisy and will lose their respect for you or copy your hypocrisy—or both.

All of this sounds good on paper, but in reality it can be hard. That's why as parents we work on respect every day. It's in the little things. It's when we volunteer for social justice groups or do the shopping for an elderly neighbor. It's when we're waiting in line and see an opening to cut ahead of others. Even though the girls may be too young to realize it, we do the right thing and wait our turn—though waiting in line with twins gives you both motive and excuse to jump ahead.

And it's in the big things. It's having their mother create a successful public relations business that allows her to work at home while helping other women pursue their business goals. This shows the girls that with hard work, women have choices—many choices. And they can choose the options that work for them.

It's making the choice to live in an urban—not suburban—neighborhood, where diversity reigns and people of all races, beliefs, classes, and sexual preferences live together. When we sit on our stoop with our girls—along with the cats and dog—we talk with everyone, including the men living in the halfway house, the politicians, the families, the old, the young, and the homeless.

The girls will realize early on that living downtown isn't always an episode from *Sesame Street*. Seeing disrespect out in public will open the door to interesting conversations around the dinner table about how we feel it was wrong and what we can do. And, yes, having dinner together, with conversation, is another of our family goals.

Modeling respect means that we need to set a high standard for ourselves as parents. But we're only human, not saints or superheroes. So when we screw up, we will need to admit it, apologize to everyone affected by it, and correct the situation to the best of our ability.

Sure, God Isn't Watching Us—but Our Children Certainly Are

We believe that the best foundation for respecting others is respect for oneself. Once the girls value themselves, it's easier to teach them to respect their possessions, family, friends, and the world around them. We want our daughters to have compassion, courage, and creativity, but to do that the girls need to develop a fourth c: confidence.

The ancient Greeks taught that pride was a virtue; indeed, Aristotle said it was the crown of all the virtues. Yet many religions treat pride as a sin—especially for women and girls—and this attitude has seeped deep into our everyday culture. Maybe that's why educators and parenting books use long-winded synonyms for *pride*, such as *self-confidence* and *self-esteem*. Pride may be the virtue that dare not speak its name, but all the children's experts agree that self-esteem has been grievously neglected in our society.

Raising confident girls means encouraging them to explore their potential. Fulfilling their potential will take ambition, hard work, and deferred gratification; it requires self-discipline. We expect confident children to enjoy their accomplishments; they will have earned it. This kind of justified pride is very different from hubris or arrogance, with its overconfidence and disrespect for others.

The recipe for instilling self-confidence is well known. Every day we give our girls opportunities for success and then praise them when they achieve it—though it's important to respond with genuine appreciation, rather than just rote flattery. When they struggle, we help them face their challenges. When they fail, we help them cope with their defeats and learn from them.

In reading about how to raise children with strong self-esteem, we've noticed that humanist values are emphasized again and again. For example, teaching children to critically examine their options, and giving them the freedom and responsibility to act on their choices, are among the best ways to build self-esteem.

Again, modeling plays a role as well; as parents, we celebrate our individual successes and when faced with a problem help each other find a way to get through it. After all, it's what a family is really about.

We also model both independence and collaboration. While pursuing separate careers we try to find ways to work together—like writing this essay.

We have been focusing on the positive, but we know we will face some tough issues as a secular family in a predominantly religious society.

Perhaps one of the first situations our girls will face is how to deal with the Pledge of Allegiance when they go to school. If they are not comfortable using the phrase "under God," how will they deal with the ever-present peer pressure when their classmates say it and they don't? And if they do say it, will we (perhaps unconsciously) pressure them not to?

While we want to raise our children to have the courage of their convictions, it's a lot to ask from a five-year-old.

One of the biggest challenges we will face as the girls get older is teaching respect for those who not only have different beliefs but actually hold opposing values. Unlike most other nonreligious families, our beliefs are at the forefront of our lives, since one of us runs an international humanist organization, the Institute for Humanist Studies. We cannot hide this—nor should we, because that would teach our girls that we don't respect our own beliefs and values.

Fortunately, we live in a very diverse and liberal neighborhood in one of the most progressive corners of the country. Still, our children are going to meet a lot of people who don't like their father's work. Even in the most friendly of environments, they are likely to find themselves explaining what humanism is far more than most kids. So they will find themselves discussing why their parents don't believe in God and other charged issues—like the interesting news that Lyra is named after a fictional hero who overthrows God to establish a Republic of Heaven.*

Let's be honest here. We want our daughters to be intelligent, discerning individuals who are willing to demand answers to their questions and not afraid to criticize bad ideas.

We don't believe that all ideas have equal merit. Some are right, some are wrong. Some are good and some are bad. So we cannot say that we want our children to respect all beliefs equally.

And yet we do want them to treat all believers with respect and dignity, just as we want everyone to treat our daughters with respect, even if they disagree with our family values. How do we teach our children to respect others whose values they disagree with?

---

* See James Herrick's essay "Parenting and the Arts" at the end of chapter 6 for more on the character Lyra.

We don't claim to have the perfect, pat answer to this. We do know, however, that we are able to do this, for the most part, in our own lives.

The girls' mother has parents who consciously brought their children to different religious events—from a Jewish seder to a Muslim wedding, as well as the family's own Catholic ceremonies—to help them appreciate diversity. We hope to be able to involve our daughters in such events as well, so they can appreciate others' traditions and points of view.

> 66 We don't believe that all ideas have equal merit . . . so we cannot say that we want our children to respect all beliefs equally. And yet we do want them to treat all believers with respect and dignity . . . even if they disagree with our family values. 99

Their father serves as the president of the United Nations NGO Committee on Freedom of Religion or Belief, which works with hundreds of groups, both religious and secular, to defend the United Nations' agreements on freedom of conscience. This models the idea that even when you disagree profoundly on major issues, you can still find common ground to work together respectfully.

It won't always be easy, especially as humanists in such a religious society. We want our children to respect others, but we won't let our daughters' self-esteem be damaged by asking them to defer to people who openly disrespect them or their family's values.

These issues may not arise until the girls are older. We hope the foundation of pride and respect that we're building will empower our daughters to rise to these challenges.

We started this essay with vows and are ending it with uncertain hopes and unanswered questions. Yet as humanists, we relish questions to which we haven't worked out all the answers. If we do a decent job raising Sophia and Lyra, we expect they will work out answers for themselves, as well as pose questions that never occurred to us. We can respect that. In fact, it would make us proud.

MATT CHERRY is the executive director of Death Penalty Focus. He served three terms as president of the United Nations NGO Committee on Freedom of Religion or Belief, five years as executive director of the Council for Secular Humanism, and eight years as executive director of the Institute for Humanist Studies.

SHANNON CHERRY, APR, MA, is the founder of ShannonCherry. com—Savvy Strategies for Smart Entrepreneurs and coauthor of Trust Your Heart: Building Relationships That Build Your Business. *She lives with her partner, Matt, and daughters, Sophia and Lyra.*

■ ■

SEVEN SECULAR VIRTUES:
Humility, Empathy, Courage, Honesty, Openness, Generosity, and Gratitude

DALE McGOWAN

The idea of virtue is a noble one: Identify those qualities that make for an admirable person; then work hard to attain them and encourage others to do the same. Identifying virtues and building a collective desire to achieve them can go a long way toward making a better world. And it's a good idea for parents of any stripe to have a solid idea of the qualities they want to encourage in their children.

The trick, of course, is naming the right virtues. The early Christian church named seven (faith, hope, charity, courage, justice, temperance, and wisdom), placing them in opposition to seven deadly sins (pride, avarice, lust, anger, gluttony, envy, and sloth) for command of the human soul. Once Thomas Aquinas weighed in, the list of virtues was set in stone.

Freethinkers don't take kindly to stone-carved lists. We know that the best possible rules, principles, ideas, and theories result when we continually reconsider, rethink, and challenge them.

This is not some comprehensive list of human virtues, nor a list that applies only to secularists. Nor do they represent qualities that always come easy to secularists. This helps explain the absence of things like critical thinking from the list. It's an absolutely indispensible skill and value, but one that doesn't require much convincing on our side of the aisle. This particular list is reserved for the things we sometimes think less about. Sometimes that's because we take them for granted, and (in at least one case) it's something we seldom even think of as a virtue.

In that case, I'll make my case for these seven qualities, and you can obviously disagree.

Like traditional virtues, these are qualities to which we can aspire, often with difficulty. But unlike traditional virtues, their value is something we can choose to accept or reject. This list is carved not in stone but in butter, meant to stimulate your own thinking about secular virtue rather than to dictate an immutable set of commandments.

Humility

Yes, I know. To secular ears, humility can sound awfully Christian, and not even like much of a virtue. But despite the lip service to humility, the Christian worldview makes it nearly impossible. Humans are said to be the specially created repositories of the divine spark, molded in the image of the creator, granted dominion over "mere beasts," and promised eternal life in a heaven made just for us.

It's hard to be humble when you think the universe was made for you.

By contrast, one of the greatest ongoing contributions of science has been its humbling reassessment of our place in the scheme of things. Instead of the main event in a young, small universe, we have come to realize that we are a blink in time and a speck in space. Instead of having dominion over the animals, we find that we are simply one of them, special only in the development of one organ (which we too often underuse). We've done some pretty amazing things, but genetically we're still less than 2 percent away from our fellow chimps.

> Everything about [the scientifically informed] worldview cries out for . . . humility. We are trousered apes, yet many nonbelievers arrogantly strut and crow about having figured out that we *are* apes. [That's] pretty hilarious if you think about it.

Everything about this worldview cries out for genuine humility—but atheists forget that as often as theists do. We are trousered apes, yet many nonbelievers arrogantly strut and crow about having figured out that we *are* apes—which is pretty hilarious if you think about it. Arrogance is something for secular parents to watch for in their kids. It can be pretty awesome to feel that you've figured out the biggest thing in the universe when most of your peers (not to mention most adults) are still getting it wrong. But left unchecked, it can lead to an overconfidence that stops listening, learning, and empathy. That in turn builds walls between us and those around us. We've all known that person, and most of us have been that person at one time or another. Helping our kids and ourselves avoid it is both justified and worthwhile.

Like so many of these virtues, humility is partly about considering what others think and feel, seeing things from another point of view, and accepting the demotion that comes with such a practice. The best way for parents to teach this is to model humility ourselves. How often do I say or imply, "I may be wrong about that," and how often do my kids hear me saying it? A skeptic knows that everything includes an element of doubt. How often do I invite someone else's opinion and genuinely listen to it? Do I spend at least half of the conversation asking about the other person, or am I mostly yakking about myself? Do I find something to validate in the other person's thoughts, or is it wall-to-wall corrections?

Empathy

Empathy is the ability to understand how someone else feels and, by implication, to care. It's the ultimate sign of maturity. Infants are, for their own adaptive good, entirely self-centered. But as we grow, our circle of concern and understanding enlarges, including first the primary caregiver, then family, then one's community. But after developing empathy for those who are most like us, we too often stop, leaving the empathy boundary at the edge of our nation, race, or creed. That's a recipe for disaster. Statements of concern for "the loss of American lives" in armed conflict, for example, carry an unspoken judgment that American lives are more precious than others—a serious failure of empathy.

Continually pushing out the empathy boundary is a life's work. We can help our kids begin that critical work as early as possible not by preaching it but by embodying it. Allow your children to see poverty up close. Travel to other countries if you can, staying as long as possible until our shared humanity becomes unmistakable, and get outside of whatever bubbles of social and economic privilege contain your family here at home. Engage people of other cultures and races, not just to value difference but to recognize sameness. It's difficult to hate when you begin to see yourself in the other.

And why stop at the species? Knowing that we are just one part of the incredible interwoven network of life on earth should engender a profound empathy for those who just happen to be across the (relatively arbitrary) boundary of species.

Secular parents must be on guard against a particular failure of empathy: the failure to recognize and understand the religious impulse. Too many nonbelievers shake their heads contemptuously at the very idea of religious belief, failing to recognize religion for what it is: an understandable response to the human condition. And if not for some unearned privileges, I could easily have ended up a believer myself.

I've been very fortunate. I grew up in a stable home, never at serious risk of starvation, violence, or death. I had a world-class education and parents who encouraged me to develop my mind and refused to dictate my beliefs. My life expectancy is in the late 70s, and I'll probably make it. Those circumstances, and a few dozen others, have given me the freedom—the luxury—of seeing my way out of superstition. But it would be pigheaded of me to fail to understand why others who are more directly in the shadow of death or without access to education or freedom to question ideas would find comfort in religious belief. That doesn't mean I can't challenge the many ill effects of that belief—I can and I do, without apology—but we must begin by understanding the realities that gave birth to religion and keep it alive. The best thing we can do is work hard to remedy those realities, to give everyone the benefits for which we should be grateful. Until then, we must give ourselves a good hard mental swat every time we feel inclined to mock, sneer, or roll our eyes at those whose beliefs differ from our own. You'll know you've failed at this the first time you see your kids mocking or sneering at religious belief—something they most likely learned from watching you. Fess up and fix it on the spot, not just because it's "not nice," but because a lack of empathy is literal ignorance.

> " We must give ourselves a good hard mental swat every time we feel inclined to mock, sneer, or roll our eyes at those whose beliefs differ from our own. You'll know you've failed at this the first time you see your kids mocking or sneering at religious belief. "

Courage

The philosopher Paul Kurtz called courage "the first humanistic virtue." Secularists need courage for two main reasons: to live in a religious world that marginalizes and demonizes disbelief, and to face the realities of human existence honestly.

It takes little courage to live in the mainstream. As long as you embrace the norms and beliefs of the majority, you'll encounter little difficulty, little resistance. Go with the flow and the world will pat you on the head and coo. Protest what is "normal"—dress differently, believe differently, speak differently—and you'll create problems for the Machine. And the Machine, in return, will create problems for you.

Kids need to know that nonconformity requires courage. There are plenty of nonconformists to draw upon as examples, secular and religious people alike, from Socrates to Martin Luther King to Ayaan Hirsi Ali to Malala Yousafzai—people whose strength of conviction led them to face with dignity and courage the consequences of stepping outside of the norm in the name of heartfelt principles. It isn't easy, but doing what's right can be well worth it.

The second reason secularists need courage is even more daunting. As noted earlier, religion primarily evolved not to provide answers but to console fears. The idea of death is terrifying to a living being. Evolution has made sure of that; the more indifferent an animal is to death, the more quickly it will achieve it, and the less such unwise indifference will appear in the next generation. An afterlife illusion addresses the fear of death by simply denying it really happens. Not much integrity in such a plan, but if you can get yourself to believe it, the comfort would be undeniable.

Secularists, God bless us, have opted for the truth. In doing so, we face the ultimate terror of existence: our eventual nonexistence. Philosophy has its consolations, but I'm not convinced they do the whole job. If you've come happily to terms with oblivion, bully for you. You're way ahead of me and 99.8 percent of the species. For the rest of us, courage, in the face of mortality and the other genuinely challenging aspects of being human, is a virtue well worth cultivating.

Honesty

Honesty is the essence of secularism. It is a willingness to set aside any and every comfort in order to know the truth that allowed us to see our way out of religious belief. Somewhat more difficult is ensuring that we practice the same level of honesty in all other aspects of our lives. I say "somewhat more difficult" because in truth most of the humanists and atheists I know are relentlessly, exhaustively honest, sometimes to a comical extent. We are often paralyzed by our obsession with honesty—yet in one of the greatest ironies I know, nonbelievers consistently rate as the least trustworthy minority in America.

Yet in one aspect of honesty, we too often fall flat. How many of us have stuttered or stammered when a pollster asked our religious preference, or when a new neighbor asked what church we attend? It may not be surprising that we blanch at revealing our disbelief to someone who may have heard once a week for 800 consecutive weeks that disbelief is the ultimate, unforgivably hell-bound sin. But what better way to overturn culturally ingrained misconceptions about nonbelievers than by revealing that, hey, this person you've known and liked for years, your friend, neighbor, sister, or brother, is a nonbeliever? What is accomplished by continuing to "pass"?

Teach your children to choose their beliefs honestly, whatever they are, and then to honestly and proudly own them.

Openness

Openness has several facets, but all are rooted in the same two principles: embracing your own fallibility and embracing diversity.

Secularists, being human, are as prone as anyone to cling stubbornly to our opinions once they're established. Openness includes recognizing our own fallibility: No matter how thoroughly we have examined a question, we could still be wrong. The best way to avoid being wrong is to keep our opinions and ideas open to challenge and potential disconfirmation.

The other principle—which often goes by the awful name of "tolerance"—is the very fundament of liberal philosophy. A student in an honors seminar once asked me to define the difference between liberalism and conservatism in a few words—one of the best questions I'd heard in my years as a professor. I stared at the floor for what seemed like an hour, then was struck by what I still think is the right answer: The key distinction is the attitude toward difference.

Conservative social philosophy tends to believe that there is one "best way" to be, and that our job as individuals and as a society is to find that one way and to unify around it—united we stand, you're with us or you're against us, join the saved and to hell with the damned. Liberal philosophy holds that there are many "good ways" to be, and that our job as individuals and as a society is to embrace that diversity of approaches to life. Different strokes for different folks.

One student raised the usual concern that the liberal view looks like an anything-goes position. But it isn't, of course—it embraces *many* ways, but not *all* ways. Someone whose choices harm others would not be permitted by the society to make that choice. So liberals have tended to oppose war, which invariably inflicts harm on innocents, and were prominent in the fight for same-sex marriage rights, which harms no one and makes many people happy.

My concern with the conservative position is that we humans tend to each define *our* way as the "one true way" and quickly end up facing each other in armed camps, coalesced around our various "best ways," determined to eradicate the others, with God on our side.

A conservative secularist might declare nonreligious beliefs the "one true way," dreaming of a day without religion. That would be as boring and undesirable a world to me as a Planet Evangelical. We shouldn't even wish for everyone to be like us—and fortunately, few secularists do. Our worldview is inherently liberal philosophically. We should therefore look toward a world in which our view is one legitimate voice among many and teach our kids openness of spirit and embrace of diversity as a fundamental virtue.

Generosity

If you hear enough deconversion stories, you'll begin to see a pattern. Many people feel sadness and confusion as their faith begins to flag, only to describe peaceful relief once it is finally gone, followed by a sense of personal freedom. But then (despite the dire warnings of the evangelists) instead of rampaging through the streets with guns blazing, we are hit with what I'll call the humanist epiphany: In the absence of a god, we are all we've got. Freedom is joined by an awesome sense of responsibility.

If they wanted to, Christians could justify an entirely hands-off approach to charity. God is all just, after all. He will provide for the needy, if not in this world, then in the next. Yet plenty of Christians are out there doing good works for others as a direct and visible expression of their values. Good for them.

Atheists have no excuse to sit passively. Charity without church is not a stretch but a mandate, a logical outgrowth of a nontheistic worldview.

> 66 Atheists have no excuse to sit passively. Charity without church is not a stretch but . . . a logical outgrowth of a nontheistic worldview. 99

We know there's no divine safety net, no universal justice, no Great Caretaker, no afterlife reward. We have the full responsibility to create a just world and care for the less fortunate because there's no one else to do so.

Studies continue to show that churchgoers give two to three times as much discretionary income to charity as nonchurchgoers. Conservative commentator Arthur Brooks called this a "gap in virtue," implying churchgoers are just better people. That's nonsense, of course. The fact that such studies are framed in terms of churchgoing instead of belief points to the real reason behind the gap: When a shiny plate passes in front of you 52 times a year, full of the generous donations of your friends and neighbors, it serves as a pretty effective prompt for generosity.

The humanist charity Foundation Beyond Belief was founded in part to provide that regular, systematic means of giving for the nonreligious through automatic monthly donations to a changing slate of featured charities. After the first full year, many of the members reported that their discretionary donations had risen two to three times since joining.

How about that.

Clearly it's not that they suddenly became virtuous. They just needed the regular nudge that benefits everyone to increase charitable engagement.

Generosity goes far beyond organized charity, of course. We should also model the kind of generosity of spirit that improves everyone's experience of daily life. Giving a compliment is an act of generosity. Allowing a car to merge in front of you; spending time with an isolated person; expressing love, interest, concern, or support; allowing someone else to take credit for something done together—these acts of generosity are all better modeled than "taught" to our children, and they represent a virtue that fits hand in glove with the nonreligious worldview.

Gratitude

The most terrible moment for an atheist, someone once said, is when he feels grateful and has no one to thank. That's pretty silly. Nonbelievers of all stripes should and do indeed feel enormously grateful for many things, and I'm not aware of any terrible moments. Whereas religious folks teach their children to funnel their gratitude skyward, humanists and atheists can thank the actual sources of the good things we experience, those who actually deserve praise but too often see it deflected past them and on to an imaginary being.

We have no difficulty reminding the four-year-old to "say thank you" when Grandma hands her an ice cream cone, but in other situations—especially when a religious turn of phrase is generally used—we often pass up the chance to teach our kids to express gratitude in naturalistic terms. Instead of thanking God for the food on your table, thank those who really put it there: the farmers, the truckers, the produce workers, and Mom or Dad or Aunt Diane. They deserve it. Maybe you'd like to honor the animals for the sacrifice of their lives—a nice way to underline our connection to them. You can give thanks to those around the table for being present, and for their health, and for family, and friendship itself. There is no limit. Even when abstract, like gratitude for health, the simple expression of gratitude is all that is needed. No divine ear is necessary when we are surrounded by real ears and real hearers.

I read once about a woman who had lost her husband unexpectedly. She was devastated and bereft of hope—until her neighbors and friends began to arrive. Over the course of several days, they brought food, kept her company, laughed and cried, hugged her, and reassured her that the pain would ease with time and that they would be there every step of the way. "I was so grateful for their love and kindness during those dark days," she said. "Through them, I could feel the loving embrace of God."

She was most comfortable expressing her gratitude to God, but the love and kindness came entirely from those generous and caring human beings. Humanists and atheists are not impoverished by the lack of that god idea; they are simply better able to notice who truly deserves thanks.

■ ■

EXCERPT FROM "MORALS WITHOUT RELIGION"

MARGARET KNIGHT

If [a child] is brought up in the orthodox way, he will accept what he is told happily enough to begin with. But if he is normally intelligent, he is almost bound to get the impression that there is something odd about religious statements. If he is taken to church, for example, he hears that death is the gateway to eternal life, and should be welcomed rather than shunned; yet outside he sees death regarded as the greatest of all evils, and everything possible done to postpone it. In church he hears precepts like "resist not evil," and "Take no thought for the morrow"; but he soon realizes that these are not really meant to be practiced outside. If he asks questions, he gets embarrassed, evasive answers: "Well, dear, you're not quite old enough to understand yet, but some of these things are true in a deeper sense"; and so on. The child soon gets the idea that there are two kinds of truth—the ordinary kind, and another, rather confusing and embarrassing kind, into which it is best not to inquire too closely.

Now all this is bad intellectual training. It tends to produce a certain intellectual timidity—a distrust of reason—a feeling that it is perhaps rather bad taste to pursue an argument to its logical conclusion, or to refuse to accept a belief on inadequate evidence.

ADDITIONAL RESOURCES FOR "ON BEING AND DOING GOOD"

Kohn, Alfie. *Unconditional Parenting: Moving from Rewards and Punishments to Love and Reason.* Atria Books, 2006. A hugely influential book that deserves its accolades, this is an essential counterpoint to conservative notions of authority, punishment, and "because I said so" rules. More than anything, this book can help parents relax around moral and behavioral questions, casting aside the idea, rooted in traditional religion, that our children are boiling pots of depravity in need of a lid.

Medhus, Elisa, MD. *Raising Children Who Think for Themselves.* Beyond Words, 2001. Recipient of numerous awards, this book encourages the eponymous value of freethought: thinking for one's self. Medhus offers suggestions for raising children who are inner directed by self-defined values rather than externally driven by peer pressure, pop culture influences, and authority.

———. *Raising Everyday Heroes: Parenting Children to Be Self-Reliant.* Beyond Words, 2003.

Humphrey, Sandra McLeod. *If You Had to Choose, What Would You Do?* Prometheus, 1995. A well-conceived attempt to present the youngest children with situations requiring moral decision-making. Twenty-five short scenarios are presented in which a child grapples with questions of right and wrong in a commonplace setting. Each parable is followed by the basic question "What would you do?" along with a few corollary questions. Parents should scan the stories to find those best matched to their child's level. Some are eye-rollingly simple, others more complex and interesting—including some that can even get a parent head-scratching. Do you turn in a good friend for petty shoplifting? At the age of six, my son had a quick answer—"yup"—until I suggested the shoplifter was Sean, his dearest friend in the world. He offered to rat out half a dozen less-precious acquaintances, but not Sean. The ensuing discussion was rich and rewarding, finally resulting in a nuanced solution of his own making (Sean gets one last warning before my boy drops a dime)—followed by an insistence that we read another of the stories, then another, then another.

In another story, two sisters gather pledges to participate in a walk for the World Hunger Drive. Niki sprains her ankle halfway through and pleads with Leslie to go with her to the doctor. Leslie must decide whether to refund the money she collected from her friends and neighbors or to send it on to the World Hunger Drive, even though she hadn't finished.

Now that's a brow knitter worth pondering, a wonderfully complex, multidimensional, real-world situation that demonstrates the ineffectiveness of a commandments approach to morality. Ages 6–12.

Barker, Dan. *Maybe Right, Maybe Wrong: A Guide for Young Thinkers.* Prometheus, 1992. A good, well-presented introduction to principles-based morality for kids. Ages 8–12.

Borba, Michele, Ph.D. *Building Moral Intelligence.* Jossey-Bass, 2002.

Grayling, A. C. *Meditations for the Humanist: Ethics for a Secular Age.* Oxford, 2003. A beautifully written and thought-provoking set of reflections on values and ethics without religion.

Mather, Anne, and Louise Weldon. *Character Building Day by Day: 180 Quick Read-Alouds for Elementary School and Home.* Free Spirit, 2006.

Wykoff, Jerry. *20 Teachable Virtues.* Perigee Trade, 1995. Twenty chapters, each offering parents tips for teaching a single virtue—and more importantly, a warning that what you don't model yourself will not be learned. The spotlighted virtues—including empathy, fairness, tolerance, caring, courage, humor, respect, and self-reliance—should warm the secular heart. The title says it all. "Faith" and "reverence" are blissfully absent from the list of virtues.

Espeland, Pamela, with Elizabeth Verdick. *Knowing and Doing What's Right: The Positive Values Assets.* The Free Spirit Adding Assets Series for Kids, 2006. One of a large series of excellent books by Espeland for parents and children, this focuses on six positive values assets: caring, equality and social justice, integrity, honesty, responsibility, and healthy lifestyle.

Great Introductions to Freethinking Heroes

Allen, Norm R. *African-American Humanism: An Anthology,* Prometheus Books, 1991.

Gaylor, Annie Laurie, ed. *Women Without Superstition: "No Gods— No Masters": The Collected Writings of Women Freethinkers of the*

Nineteenth and Twentieth Centuries. Freedom From Religion Foundation, 1997.

Haught, James A. *2000 Years of Disbelief: Famous People with the Courage to Doubt.* Prometheus Books, 1996.

5

Death and Consolation

INTRODUCTION

We are going to die, and that makes us the lucky ones. Most people are never going to die because they are never going to be born. The potential people who could have been here in my place but who will in fact never see the light of day outnumber the sand grains of Arabia. Certainly those unborn ghosts include greater poets than Keats, scientists greater than Newton. We know this because the set of possible people allowed by our DNA so massively exceeds the set of actual people. In the teeth of these stupefying odds it is you and I, in our ordinariness, that are here.

—Richard Dawkins, *Unweaving the Rainbow*

When I told *New York Times* science writer Natalie Angier that I was working on this book, she offered a little advice. Sure, religions give their members rites of passage and structure and all that, she said—but the afterlife myth is the big prize. "Unless you tackle the subject of death head-on," she said, "you'll be leaving your readers in the lurch at what are likely to be some of the darkest moments of their unchurched parenthood."

She was right, of course. So—how are you doing with the idea of death?

Forgive me for asking. But since you are reading this, I assume you've set aside the consolations of theology and are asking your children to do the same. Nonbelievers tend to focus on how and what we know without spending much time acknowledging the gaping existential questions that are, after all, the real reasons religion was born and persists. We are, each and every one of us, going to die. There is every reason to believe our consciousnesses will vanish into nothingness. We live a very short while, then are dead forever.

So how *are* you doing with that? And if the answer is "not too well," how are you going to help your kids with it, without turning to the usual comforting illusions?

Let's not pretend this is an easy question. I often wonder what it really means to cease to exist. I can't imagine it myself. It is beyond our ability to form a conscious notion of our own utter nonexistence. Hence the alternative so many choose: to simply deny it. We don't really die after all; we ascend to a higher reality.

It works! Try it. You'll feel ever so much better. And you won't find out that you're mistaken until . . . well, you'll never find out! That's the beauty.

But most of us became nonbelievers once we decided honesty was better than comfort. We fell in love with the idea of knowing what is and learning to deal with that rather than hiding our eyes behind comfortable myths. Seems the grown-up way to be a conscious thing, doesn't it? But that doesn't make it easy.

So how can we turn away from the consolations of religion in the face of death?

After his beloved four-year-old son succumbed to scarlet fever, the 19th-century biologist and agnostic Thomas Huxley asked himself much the same question. The Reverend Canon Kingsley had urged Huxley to renounce his agnosticism in the face of his loss and to embrace the consolations of faith. Huxley politely declined, replying with moving candor in a letter that many consider the single greatest and most profoundly moving testament to intellectual integrity:

> My convictions, positive and negative, on all the matters of which you speak, are of long and slow growth and are firmly rooted. But the great blow which fell upon me seemed to stir them to their foundation, and had I lived a couple of centuries earlier I could have fancied a devil scoffing at me and them and asking me what profit it was to have stripped myself of the hopes and consolations of the mass of mankind? To which my only reply was and is *Oh devil!* Truth is better than much profit. I

have searched over the grounds of my belief, and if wife and child and name and fame were all to be lost to me one after the other as the penalty, still I will not lie.[1]

Huxley is among my greatest heroes. But even Huxley, turning from false consolations in the midst of his grief, offered little in the way of compensation other than a picture of breathtaking intellectual courage. Yes, I want to reject the false consolations of theology—but might there be true consolations out there somewhere?

Yes, indeed. They are the consolations of philosophy.

Science has worked wonders in recent centuries when it comes to replacing superstition with reason. But when it comes to setting aside superstition in less concrete areas—such as morality, attitudes toward death, and the like—progress has taken place not in the bright light of scientific inquiry but in the quiet, reflective works of philosophy. And it is to these works we can turn for true consolation.

The Greek philosopher Epicurus thought that we are afraid of death mainly because we fail to really grasp nonexistence. Creatures of consciousness, we can only picture it as "me-floating-in-darkness-forever." Is it really surprising that that horrific idea sends people racing to the kneelers to pray to someone who is said to have conquered it for us? Heck, if the darkness was really the thing, I'd be wearing out my own knees. But it isn't. The key, Epicurus says, is to really get that death is the end of experience. One can only experience life up to its final moment, not beyond. "As long as I exist," he said, "death does not. Once death exists, I will not. Why should I fear something I will never experience?"

Thinking hard about that simple fact can make for real consolation—and give parents one more small way to help children deal with death without immersing them in dishonest fables.

Epicurus also offered the symmetry argument. If you fear death, he said, consider the expanse of time before you were conceived. The past infinity of nonexistence before your conception is just the same as the future infinity of nonexistence after death. You have already been there, in other words—though that is really just exactly the wrong way to phrase it. We don't consider having not existed for an eternity before our conception to be a terrible thing, so we shouldn't think of not existing for an eternity after our deaths as a terrible thing. There is literally no difference in the two other than our ability to contemplate and anticipate the future. (See Yip

Harburg's "Before and After," coming up next, for a poetic take on the idea.)

Though it may take a lifetime to grasp, it should be possible to come peacefully to terms with our mortality by fully understanding it. And it never hurts to recall that life is made immeasurably more precious by the fact that it ends. Life as a preamble to afterlife would be just a warm-up. But understanding this existence as an unimaginably lucky shot at consciousness—in the teeth of these stupefying odds, it is you and I, in our ordinariness, who are here—has the power to make every moment unspeakably precious. We should wake up every morning laughing with amazed delight that we are here at all, not weeping because it won't last forever. Easier said than done, I know. Believe me, I know.

After Yip Harburg giving death a philosophical raspberry in "Before and After" comes Rebecca Hensler's "Helping Your Child Live with Grief without Religion." Since the death of her young son in 2009, Hensler has devoted herself to creating and maintaining Grief Beyond Belief, the first comprehensive support network for addressing grief and loss in a nontheistic context. I offer a snapshot of the first difficult conversation in which my daughters grappled with the idea of death ("Where All Roads Lead"), followed by my older daughter's first painful loss in "The First Really, Really Hard Good-Bye."

Yip Harburg lightens the mood once again with "Small Comforts"; then we end with a returning essay by the Reverend Dr. Kendyl Gibbons, "Dealing with Death in the Secular Family."

Gibbons is among the most articulate and thoughtful of a very articulate and thoughtful breed: Unitarian humanists. If the idea of a minister who doesn't believe in God is new to you, she is a marvelous introduction to the concept.

The modern Unitarian Universalist movement is a fascinating post-Christian institution consisting almost entirely of nontheists. Despite having set aside traditional belief in God, they still seek the other benefits of religious institutions: the shared search for meaning, a sense of community, the consolation of others in time of need, and dedication to the good. Among her many gifts, Gibbons brings the wisdom of a counselor who has provided solace in time of loss to countless secularists without benefit of the easy answers available in traditional religion.

■ ■ ■ ■ ■ ■ ■ ■ ■ ■ ■ ■ ■

BEFORE AND AFTER

YIP HARBURG

I cannot for the life of me
Recall at all, at all
The life I led
Before I tread
This small terrestrial ball.

Why then should I ponder
On the mystery of my kind?
Why bother with my great beyond
Without my great behind?

HELPING YOUR CHILD LIVE WITH GRIEF WITHOUT RELIGION

REBECCA HENSLER

Loss enters every child's life eventually. Many children experience some sort of death during their youth: a pet, a relative, a classmate. Some even lose someone integral to their lives—a parent or guardian, a sibling, a cherished grandparent, a close friend or teacher—before they reach adulthood. As a parent, you want to both comfort your child through the early months of bereavement and help them learn to live with their grief as they grow up. My goal in this essay is to provide you with guidance in this area, one that often seems overwhelming to even the most confident parent.

I had supported families through this process as a school counselor, but it was not until I founded the secular grief-support network Grief Beyond Belief that I became familiar with the particular challenges secular families face when their young ones are grieving.

Like every adult, every child grieves differently. A young person's grief depends on so many factors: their relationship to the deceased, their developmental age, the nature of the death itself, and the surrounding family and community before and after the loss. Beyond this, there is simply the child: the personality, resilience, and internal resources and challenges that shape his individual needs.

That said, certain themes permeate both professional advice and the experience shared by parents: Be honest, be open, listen, and validate.

Honesty begins with being truthful with the child about the death itself: when, how, and why the death occurred, and what death means. Avoid euphemisms when informing a child, especially a young child, of the death of a loved one. Expressions like "gone away" or "gone to sleep" can confuse or even scare a child. Instead, be very clear that death is the complete end of all processes of life, such as thinking, feeling, eating, and moving, as well as of any sort of pain or suffering, and that death is final and irreversible.[1]

Rachel, whose children have experienced multiple losses, writes, "What worked for my children was being honest with them about what happened and how. Yes, the truth can be scary, but so can the unknown or what they might make up in their head. We let them ask any questions they have and give honest answers."

You may worry that you are not offering the comfort that a believer would by softening the information with religious platitudes. Keep in mind that many of the euphemisms believers offer young children can actually frighten them more than the truth. The idea that God wanted the child's sibling with him or "needed another angel" can make a child wonder whether God will next want them or another beloved family member.[2] By telling the truth, you free your child from these fears.

Secular parents sometimes voice a related concern that they are depriving their child of the solace of an afterlife belief. When explaining the death of a loved one, it may seem like heaven is the kindest lie you could ever tell your child; it is difficult to tell a child that someone is gone forever. As Erin, whose sons were 5 and 12 when they lost their grandfather, writes, "You want to fix everything for your children. . . . Many times I thought, 'This would be so much easier if we were religious because I could just say, "They're in heaven."' But that is ultimately the denial of death. You cannot avoid death, and that is a hard reality to face at a young age." The key to supporting a grieving child as a secular parent is to provide comfort that is based in reality, as well as healthy ways to process their grief.

In addition, remember that by being honest with your children, you are sparing them the cognitive dissonance that can result when a rational child attempts to digest the idea of heaven. Imagine the obvious questions in your child's mind: "I know that space is above me so where is heaven? If my uncle is in heaven, does he miss me? If Grandma is watching over me, does she see me peeing?" To a logical child, particularly one who has observed the natural world, the truth about death fits what they already know about life without inducing unnecessary anxieties.

If your child will be interacting with grieving peers or adults who are believers—and most do eventually—you will need to have a frank talk about other people's beliefs. Help your child decide ahead of time how they want to respond to religious condolences. Discuss the difference between how they will respond to a person expressing their own beliefs, especially another child, and a person pushing belief on them.

None of this is to say that you must correct a child who imagines an afterlife for their loved one. It is up to you whether to correct these notions as you would any other incorrect idea your child acquired about how the world works—being careful not to shame your child for having been comforted by the belief. The alternative is simply to listen to the child's afterlife idea with respect and compassion. Many children will let go of their imagined comforts when ready, particularly those raised with critical thinking skills. There is no need to push this process.

In our group, Crystal shared her thoughts on the topic: "My daughter believes my parents are in heaven. She knows I don't believe in that and why, but more importantly she knows that she doesn't have to believe what I believe. She has a choice."

The exception to this is if your child's belief is frightening rather than comforting them. In this case, allow the child to explain their ideas, but then explain the reality of death to your child. Assure them that you know that their loved one cannot feel any pain or fear and that their mind and body have completely stopped.

Regardless of whether you choose to correct any mistaken beliefs your child has about death, a conversation about this sort of belief might provide a good opportunity to talk with a child about the comforts of imagination memory. Help your child identify ways in which they could use their imagination to enjoy the continued presence of the deceased in their mind, perhaps by imagining a conversation they might have, or envisioning how their loved one would react to a current event in their life. Make sure they know that this kind of daydreaming is normal for grieving people.

With older teenagers, you can even help them understand the ways the brain responds to grief and loss—for example, the confusing denial and grief hallucinations some people experience immediately after a death. Amy describes the conversations she and her eighteen-year-old daughter, Sydney, shared following her seventeen-year-old son Jake's death. "It is the brain doing what the brain does, and feelings, however convincing, are not always an appropriate tool for determining the most logical next step. I encourage and practice critical thinking and an objective point of view."

The second piece of advice parents in our group agreed on was the importance of being open with their children about their own grief. Rachel explains, "I believe [seeing me cry] has made my boys more empathetic and reassures them that even well after someone is gone, it is okay to be sad and that they can talk to me about it." Erin agrees: "We need to show them that we grieve, too, and that it is okay. To teach them that while it hurts to have someone die, memories are invaluable and the joy of living with them is worth the pain when we lose them."

Professionals and parents agree that perhaps the most important thing you can do for a grieving child is listen. Amber shares how much just listening to her nieces seemed to make a difference when they were grieving their great-uncle: "They talked about things he did for them, but mostly just how sad they were. It seemed like being given that space to just express their sadness made them feel better overall."

Some children may struggle to express emotions verbally. Genevieve, whose son was only 18 months old when his father died, describes this well: "He couldn't tell me what he felt—but he told me what he wanted. He often asked to see pictures and videos of Eric, and I obliged. I found it hard, but I thought if it can help him through this and strengthen his memory of his dad, let's do this." You may want to offer less verbal children metaphorical ways of expressing their feelings, such as asking them to describe feelings as a color or a kind of weather, or let them pick from a selection of pictures of facial expressions.

As a counselor to grieving youth, I have observed that even with these supports, not all children are able to process their grief verbally. Grief manifests differently in different children and teenagers; they aren't all ready to share memories and loving feelings about their loved ones. They may be experiencing conflicted emotions, including anger, guilt, and shame, that they are not necessarily comfortable disclosing to a parent or caregiver. Particularly for teenagers, grief can be complicated, entangled with negative as well as positive feelings they have about the deceased, about themselves, and about those who have survived and remain while the deceased is no longer there for them.

Listening becomes all the more important in this context—respecting your teenager's limits and requests while remaining available and making accessible other adults with whom the adolescent may feel more comfortable talking. This can be difficult for parents, particularly when they themselves are grieving.

The final consensus among group members regards the importance of validating your child's individual emotions. Children often suffer from what is known as disenfranchised grief simply because many adults have so little understanding of the internal emotional lives of children. Hilda, whose daughter was 15 when her little brother died, recalls: "I never minimized her suffering. Some would say, 'It's her brother, it's not like he was her child.' I defended her from statements like that and always validated her feelings. She owns her grief, and nobody is allowed to take it from her." Amy says of her daughter, "I validate her pain, her unsteady footing, her confusion, her fear, her determination, her tenacity, her love, all of it. I tell her I'm proud of her."

Children and teens who have lost a brother or sister will require particular validation of their concerns as the surviving sibling. "I remember when Jake died," says Amy's daughter Sydney, "I said, 'I don't want this to come across as selfish, but I don't want to be the forgotten child.'" Veronica describes a different fear: "Considering we lost another child, my son was terrified that he might die too. I wanted to give him a place to express those fears without feeling silly."

Honesty, openness, listening, validation: These acts alone go a long way to support a young person through grief without resorting to myths and mysticism. Beyond these basics, there are two types of help that parents can offer grieving children and adolescents: the things we can do for them and the things we can support them in doing for themselves.

Among the former, providing comfort in whatever way feels right to you and your child is primary. Erin illustrates with a story:

One night my five-year-old was in bed and just started crying because he was thinking about "Paw." I climbed in bed and just hugged him close and let him cry, and I joined in on the tears. My twelve-year-old heard us and sheepishly looked in the room with tears in his eyes. I opened my arms and he ran into the bed to join, and we all just hugged and cried. And that was okay, there was no shame in being sad.

Another form of comfort you can offer is sharing stories of your child's loved one with them, encouraging them to focus on the lasting influence that the deceased has had on them and the way it shapes their own identity and abilities. Engaging your child in these conversations periodically over time—demonstrating that there is no deadline after which they will be expected to stop talking about their loved one—assists your child in learning to live with grief in a healthy way.

Provide additional relief by asking trusted adults who are not themselves grieving to aid in supporting your children emotionally—or simply to provide periodic breaks from grief with favorite activities.

Once an adult has agreed to furnish this kind of assistance, identify them to your child and practice how the child can seek comfort or distraction from them—a phone call, a text, a note—when they need it.

Rachel reminds us of the importance of communication with the other adults with whom your child will be interacting. "I informed their teacher. Not because they should be treated differently, but just so the teacher is more aware of what is going on because anything could trigger them or they might do poorly on a test because they are distracted. If the teacher sees a change at school, the line of communication will already be open so concerns can be addressed." School counselors can also do regular check-ins with grieving students and provide other resources.

It isn't always predictable what an adolescent will want or need from you when grieving. As Carol wrote, "My daughters, 13 and 10 when my husband died in a plane crash, say the best thing I did for them to help with their grief was to get them a dog. They tell me that dragging them to counselors hurt more than it helped." Jennifer, whose daughter was in her first year of high school when a beloved mentor died, suggests: "Even as your kid might seem to be falling apart, it can be very helpful to project a confidence that they will find a way to organize themselves, that they will find their own resilience. And for them to do that, you have to give them a little space. This is sometimes particularly difficult when your instinct might be to smother them with protective embraces." Amy agrees. "I respect her, even when it means she needs space while in the throes of anguish, as she did the moment we found out he was gone. I don't take her need for space personally."

Not taking your grieving teenager's angry, erratic, or rejecting behavior personally is one of the challenges of caring for a grieving adolescent. The key seems to be—as in so many situations—to be infinitely kind and patient on an emotional level while maintaining dependable and consistent structure and limits.

Structure—knowing what can be depended upon—becomes very important to a child at a time when the world seems unpredictable, with a loved one gone and usually reliable adults acting differently. Whether the loss has just occurred or your family is in the process of adjusting to a new reality, to the best of your ability, let them know what is going to happen in the coming hours, days, and weeks and who will support them through it.[3] This includes setting limits for their behavior as well. The fact that grief and sadness often manifest as anger for teenagers can make this extra challenging. Teaching your child that their pain does not justify abusing others can be hard, but it is such an important lesson for a humanist adulthood that it is worth both explaining and modeling even at this difficult time.

You may begin to wonder whether and when to seek grief counseling or therapy for your child or adolescent. In *Healing the Bereaved Child*, Dr. Alan Wolfelt delineates signs that a grieving child may need counseling. They include "total denial of the reality of the death"; "prolonged physical complaints without organic finding"; "chronic hostility, acting-out towards others or self"; and "consistent withdrawal from friends and family members."[4] Note that Wolfelt uses terms like *total, prolonged, chronic,* and *consistent* in describing these signs, differentiating them from behaviors you might observe in a grieving but healthy and resilient child.

As Erin noted, as a parent your instinct is to "fix everything." But in supporting your grieving child, much of what you will find yourself doing is helping your child identify and engage in activities that help them live with grief. This may be particularly true with young children, who have a more difficult time with abstract concepts and therefore with abstract comfort. To an older teenager, the idea that a beloved elder has taught them a skill or knowledge that they can use in the future to help others—allowing the deceased a sort of immortality—might be very comforting. To the toddler or school-aged child, the concrete act of baking Grandpa's favorite cookies and sharing them with people who also loved Grandpa provides the same sense of continuity without requiring abstract thought.

Regardless of age and development, the very humanist consolation of acts of kindness and creativity in memory of a loved one are comforting to children. The key is to match the activity to the developmental level. For a young child, drawing pictures of their loved one, or of things that person liked, can be an excellent way of processing grief. (Don't worry if the pictures seem disturbing or morbid; children often lack the filters of social niceties regarding death and can be quite literal.) Art is also a great outlet for a preteen or adolescent, while journaling or writing a letter to their loved one provides an additional opportunity to express their emotions.

As the young person moves forward in their life, the task of grieving becomes a matter of finding ways to enfold their love and grief into their own sense of self as it develops. This sort of meaning-making is as important to a grieving child as to an adult. Volunteer work and philanthropy in memory of a loved one can be matched to any developmental level. Even a young child can put aside a bit of their allowance over the year to donate in memory of a grandparent or buy an item for a holiday toy drive in honor of a friend who has died. When the child engages in this activity, talk with them about how proud or happy the person they are grieving would be. An older child can participate in fundraising activities and volunteer for causes or organizations important to their loved one; a teenager may even choose to engage in activist causes.

It may seem counterintuitive, but one other way we can help the children we love is to support them in engaging in non-grief activity as well as in processing their emotions. Rachel seems to have come to this intuitively. "We ask them what they would like to do. If not sure, we would suggest drawing a picture or having some quiet time. We also say that if they want to cry, that is okay. If they want to go back to playing their video game, that is okay, too. Because, just like some adults, kids may not want to focus on their grief right away but instead be distracted till they are ready to process."

This parent's instinct to both give her children time to process grief and to offer them ways to distract themselves from their sorrow is remarkably consistent with grief researcher George Bonanno's findings that suggest that resilience in grief correlates with flexibility and context-appropriate expression of emotion.[5] There is no reason to think this applies any less to children. Make sure your children know it is okay to laugh and play and enjoy life as well as to grieve; encouraging them to balance happiness with sadness will help them incorporate the loss into their lives and emerge healthy and happy from the early period of intense sorrow.

Which, of course, raises the question, "How long will my child be hurting so much?" There is no easy answer, in part because the impact of the loss is so dependent on the degree of attachment and reliance the child felt for the deceased. The death of a parent, for example, will be grieved in an ongoing way through the course of the child's development. The impact of other losses will differ. Do not worry if your child seems to become "their old self" quite quickly. But also don't be surprised if waves of grief hit periodically—particularly at holidays, birthdays, death anniversaries, and special occasions such as graduation, big games, and performances—and you need to pull out a reliable comfort all over again. Help your child find ways to incorporate their love and memories into these difficult moments.

This essay is only a beginning. I encourage you to seek out some of the excellent writing done on this subject, including books to read with young children and evidence-based advice from clinical psychologists and researchers. Journal prompts and therapeutic art projects abound. Numerous camps and groups provide support for thousands of grieving kids and teenagers every day—just make sure to communicate clearly with organizers and counselors that your family is secular and confirm that all activities will be appropriate for a child grieving without faith in a deity or afterlife.

I want to end with this message: You've got this. When you are loving, honest, and listening to your grieving child—and ready to seek professional help if needed—you are raising a child who will live with grief in a healthy way, both now and in the future.

I'll close with the words from secular teenager Sydney to her mother, Amy, who has supported her through the terrible first year following the death of her brother Jake:

> Our relationship is stronger than ever. Going through this loss together, as mother and daughter who have lost a son and brother, grieving with as rational minds as we can have is so important to me. You bring me up from my lowest lows, something Jake once did. I love you, Mama.

REBECCA HENSLER founded Grief Beyond Belief, a support group for grieving people who do not believe in God or an afterlife, in 2011. Hensler's own son Jude died at three months of age in 2009. She works as a middle school counselor and lives in the San Francisco Bay Area with her wife.

■ ■

WHERE ALL ROADS LEAD

DALE McGOWAN

My two daughters and I were lying on my bed, looking at the ceiling.

"Dad, I have to tell you a thing. Promise you won't get mad," said Delaney (6), with very serious eyes.

"Oh jeez, Laney, so dramatic," said Erin (9).

"I plan to be furious," I said. "Out with it."

"I . . . I kind of got into a God fight in the cafeteria yesterday."

I pictured kids barricaded behind overturned cafeteria tables lobbing Buddha-shaped meatballs, Flying Spaghetti Monsters, and Jesus tortillas at each other.

"What's a 'God fight'?"

"Well, I asked Courtney if she could come over on Sunday, and she said, 'No, my family will be in church of course.' And I said, 'Oh, what church do you go to?' And she said she didn't know, and she asked what church we go to. And I said, 'We don't go to church,' and she said, 'Don't you believe in God?' And I said, 'No, but I'm still thinking about it,' and she said, 'But you *have* to go to church and you *have* to believe in God,' and I said, 'No you don't, different people can believe different things.'"

I asked if the two of them were yelling or getting upset with each other.

"No," she said, "we were just talking."

"Then I wouldn't call it a fight. You were having a conversation about cool and interesting things."

"Then Courtney said, 'But if there isn't a God, then how did the whole world and trees and people get made so perfect?'"

"Ooo, good question. What'd you say?"

"I said, 'But why did he make the murderers? And the bees with stingers? And the scorpions?'"

I don't know about you, but my first-grade table banter never rose to this level. Courtney had opened with teleology, the argument from design. Delaney countered with theodicy, the argument from evil.

"But then," Delaney said, "I started wondering about how the world did get made. Do the scientists know?"

I described the Big Bang theory to her, something we had somehow never covered. Erin filled in the gaps with what she remembered from our own talk, that "gravity made the stars start burning," and "the earth used to be all lava, and it cooled down."

Laney was nodding, but her eyes were distant. "That's cool," she said at last. "But what made the bang happen in the first place?"

I told Laney that we don't know what caused the whole thing to start. "But some people think God did it," I added.

She nodded.

"The only problem with that," I said, "is that if God made everything, then who . . ."

"Oh my gosh!" Erin interrupted. "Who made God?! I never thought of that!"

"Maybe another God made *that* God," Laney offered.

"Maybe so, bu—"

"Oh wait!" she said. "Wait! But then who made *that* God? Omigosh!"

They giggled with excitement at their abilities. I can't begin to describe how these moments move me. At ages six and nine my girls had heard and rejected the cosmological, or first cause, argument within 30 seconds, using the same reasoning Bertrand Russell described in *Why I Am Not a Christian:*

> I for a long time accepted the argument of the First Cause, until one day, at the age of eighteen, I read John Stuart Mill's *Autobiography,* and I there found this sentence: "My father taught me that the question 'Who made me?' cannot be answered, since it immediately suggests the further question 'Who made god?'" That very simple sentence showed me, as I still think, the fallacy in the argument of the First Cause. If everything must have a cause, then God must have a cause.

Incredible what an unfettered young mind can work out with or without a parental boost. I doubt that Mill's father was less moved than I am by the realization that confident claims of "obviousness," even when swathed in polysyllables and Latin, often have foundations so rotten that they can be neutered by thoughtful children.

There was more to come. Both girls sat up and barked excited questions and answers. We somehow ended up on Buddha, then reincarnation, then evolution, and the fact that we are literally related to trees, grass, squirrels, mosses, butterflies, and blue whales.

It was an incredible freewheeling conversation I will never, ever forget. It led, as all honest roads eventually do, to the fact that everything that lives also dies. We'd had the conversation before, but this time a new dawning crossed Laney's face.

"Sweetie, what is it?" I asked.

She began the deep, aching cry that accompanies her saddest realizations, and sobbed,

"I don't want to die."

Now let's freeze this tableau for a moment and make a few things clear. The first is that I love this child so much I would throw myself under Pat Robertson for her. She's one of just four people whose health and happiness are vital to my own. When she is sad, I want to make her happy. It's one of the simplest equations in my life.

I say such obvious things because it is often assumed that nonreligious parents respond to their children's fears of death by saying, in essence, "Suck it up, worm food." When one early reviewer of *Parenting Beyond Belief* implied that that was the book's approach, I (shall we say) corrected him. I am convinced that there are real comforts to be found in a naturalistic view of death, that our mortality lends a new preciousness to life, and that it is not just more truthful but more humane and more loving to introduce the concept of a life that truly ends than it is to proffer an immortality that inquiring minds will have to painfully discard later.

But all my smiling confidence threatens to dissolve under the tears of my children.

"I know, punkin," I said, cradling her head as she convulsed with sobs. "Nobody wants to die. I sure don't. But you know what? First you get to live for a hundred years. Think about that. You'll be older than Great-Grandma Huey!"

It's a cheap opening gambit. It worked the last time we had this conversation, when Laney was four.

Not this time.

"But it *will* come," she said, sniffling. "Even if it's a long way away, it will come, and I don't want it to! I want to stay alive!"

"Well, a lot of people think you do get to stay alive, in heaven."

Her expression told me that she was already past that one. She had told me before that it seemed like something people only believed to make themselves feel better.

I took a deep breath. "It's such a strange thing to think about, being dead. Sometimes it scares me, too. That's normal. But then I realize I'm not thinking about it exactly right."

She stopped sniffling and looked at me. "I don't get it."

"Well, what do you think being dead is like?"

She thought for a minute. "It's like you're all still and it's dark forever."

A chill went down my spine. She had described my childhood image of death precisely. When I pictured myself dead, it was me-floating-in-darkness-forever. It's the most awful thing I can imagine. Hell would be better than an eternal, mute, insensate limbo.

"That's how I think of it sometimes, too! And it frrrrreaks me out! But that's not how it is."

"But how do you *know*?" she asked, pleadingly. "How do you know what it's like?"

"Because I've already been there."

"What? Ha-ha! No you haven't!"

"Yes I have, and so have you."

"What? No I haven't."

"After I die, I will be nowhere. I won't be floating in darkness. There will be no Dale McGowan, right?"

"And millions of worms will eat your body!" chirped Erin, unhelpfully.

"..."

"Well, they will."

"Uh . . . yeah. But I won't care because I won't be there."

She shrugged. "Still."

I turned back to her sister. "So a hundred years from now, I won't be anywhere, right?"

"I guess so."

"Okay. Now where was I a hundred years ago? Before I was born?"

"What do you mean, where were you? You weren't anywhere!"

"And was I afraid?"

"No, because . . ."

It hit both girls at the same instant. They bolted upright with looks of astonishment.

"Omigosh," said Laney, "it's the same!"

"Yes. It's exactly the same. There's no difference at all between not existing before you were born and not existing after you die. None. So if you weren't scared then, you shouldn't be scared about the next time. I still get scared sometimes because I forget that. But then I try to really understand what it means to not be anywhere, and I feel better."

The crisis was over, but they clearly wanted to keep going.

"You know something else I like to think about?" I asked. "I think about the egg that came down into my mom's tummy right before me. And the one before that, and before that. All of those people never even got a chance to exist, and they never will. There are billions and trillions of people who never even got a chance to be here. But I made it! I get a chance to be alive and playing and laughing and dancing and burping and farting . . ."

(Brief intermission for laughter and sound effects.)

"I could have just not existed forever—but instead, I get to be alive for a hundred years! And you too! Woohoo! We made it!"

"Omigosh," Laney said, staring into space. "I'm like . . . the luckiest thing."

"Exactly. So sometimes when I start to complain because it doesn't last forever, I picture all those people who never existed telling me, 'Oh, come *on*. At least you got a chance. Don't be piggy.'"

More sound effects, more laughter.

Coming to grips with mortality is a lifelong process, one that ebbs and flows for me, as I know it will for them, and I doubt we ever really achieve it. Delaney was perfectly fine going to sleep that night, and fine the next morning, and the morning after that. It will catch up to her again, but every time it comes it will be more familiar and potentially less frightening. We'll talk about the other consolations—that every bit of you came from the stars and will return to the stars, the peaceful symphony of endorphins that usually accompanies dying, and so on. If all goes well, her head start may help her come up with new consolations to share with the rest of us.

In his brilliant classic *The Tangled Wing*, Emory psychologist Melvin Konner notes that "from age three to five [children] consider [death] reversible, resembling a journey or sleep. After six they view it as a fact of life but a very remote one." Though rates of development vary, Konner places children's first true grasp of the finality and universality of death around age ten—a realization that includes the first dawning deep awareness that it applies to them as well. So grappling with the concept early, before we are paralyzed by the fear of it, can go a long way toward mitigating that fear in the long run and maybe even replacing some of it with wonder and gratitude.

Laney is ahead of the curve. All I can do is keep reminding her, and myself, that knowing and understanding something helps tame our fears. It may not completely feed the bulldog—the fear of our mortality is too deeply ingrained to ever go away completely—but it's a bigger, better Milk-Bone than anything else we have.

■ ■

THE FIRST REALLY, REALLY HARD GOOD-BYE

DALE McGOWAN

"Daddy! Something's wrong with Max!" Erin (10) was upset, her face a mask of anguish. "He's making sounds I've never heard before . . . and he's laying wrong!"

Her guinea pig Max, the first pet that was all her own, was clearly not okay. The vet confirmed an upper respiratory infection the next morning, dispensing a little medicine and not much hope.

"Guinea pigs are prey items," he said, introducing me to a colorful new term I was glad Erin didn't hear. "They don't handle stress well. But sometimes the medicine works. He'll either get better quickly . . . or he won't."

Erin held him all evening, cooing and stroking and sobbing. In the morning, he was gone.

When Erin's heart breaks, it takes every other heart in the room with it—and her heart was as broken then as I'd ever seen it.

I know the loss of Max was an important experience for her. Pets can contribute, however unwillingly, to our lifelong education in mortality. Though we don't buy pets in order for kids to experience death (with the possible exception of aquariums, oh my word), most every pet short of a giant land tortoise will predecease its owner.

The deaths of my own various guinea pigs, dogs, fish, and rabbits were my first introductions to irretrievable loss. At their passings, I learned two things Erin learned with Max: how to grieve and just how deeply we can love. They certainly helped prepare me for the sudden loss of my father. It didn't shorten my grief, which continues to this day. But the grief didn't blindside me in quite the way it would have if my father's death had been my first experience of profound loss.

When we looked into the cage Thursday morning and saw that Max was still, Erin screamed, then did the precise opposite of what I would have done: She flung open the cage, grabbed him, hugged him to her, and wailed.

I've never had that kind of equanimity with the dead. I recoil from lifelessness. When my dog Opie died, I was in my late thirties and still seriously considered paying someone $300 to remove his body from the yard. When (for lack of $300, and no other reason) I did it myself, it took all of my personal steel. Ever since I stared at my dead father, I just can't bear the recognition of what's no longer there. But Erin sprints toward it, even in abject grief.

She hugged Max's little body to her for an hour and keened. She stroked his fur and touched his teeth and gently rolled his tiny paws between her fingers, all the time whispering, "Maxie, Maxie. Please wake up."

Then came a monologue both stunning and familiar—that ancient litany of regret, guilt, and helplessness:

"I wish I had given him a funner life. He didn't have enough fun."

"Do you think he knew I loved him?"

"I should have played with him more."

"I wanted to watch him grow up!"

"Do you think I did something wrong? I must have done something wrong!"

"I want to hear his little noises again."

"It isn't fair at all. It isn't fair. Things should be fair."

She sang in a concert at the end of the day and was all smiles for two full hours—then lost it again when we returned home. So it was for two days.

We buried Max in the backyard under a metaphor of falling yellow leaves. Erin placed him in the shoebox on a layer of soft bedding. She put his water bottle to his lips once, twice, three times, convulsing with tears. She added food pellets near his head, like an ancient Egyptian preparing a pharaoh for the journey to the next life. Flower petals, followed by Max's favorite toy, and at last—this nearly did me in—Erin carefully dried her tears and placed the tissue in with him.

We talked over the grave about what a lucky guy he'd been to be born at all, that a trillion other guinea pigs never got the chance to exist, to be loved and cuddled like he was. She liked that.

Experiencing loss and regret has one undeniable payoff: It can make us appreciate what we still have. And our dog Gowser was lavished with more love and attention in the following days than ever before.

A year later almost to the day, her sister, Delaney (7), got a guinea pig of her own. Erin asked to go with us to the pet store to help Laney pick out the toys, the food, the bedding. She knowledgeably led her sister up and down the aisles. "Max really liked timothy hay," she said. "You'll want to get some of that. Ooh, and look, there's that little wooden thing he liked to chew on!"

As we stood in line at the register, Erin looked up at me. "I'm surprised I'm so okay with all this," she said. "I mean, I still miss him a lot, but it's not so, . . . you know . . ." She pressed a palm to her chest and closed her eyes, then looked up again. "You know?"

I knew. I reminded her of something she said a few days after he died. "You thought it would never stop hurting, remember?"

She nodded. "But it did. Time is amazing."

And there it is. In addition to learning how much she could love and how much she could grieve, she learned that no matter how much a loss hurts, it will eventually hurt less. So next time—and there is always a next time—she'll have a comfort she didn't have before.

■ ■

SMALL COMFORTS

YIP HARBURG

Before I was born, I seemed to be
Content with being non-be-able;
So after I'm gone, it seems to me
My lot should be not less agreeable.

DEALING WITH DEATH IN THE SECULAR FAMILY

REV. DR. KENDYL GIBBONS

The human impulse to deny the reality of death is deep and ancient. It affects us all, including our children. One of the challenges of parenting is to introduce this subject and help them respond to it in developmentally appropriate ways.

There is a great deal of helpful literature about how children deal with death, and both secular and religious children have the same needs for reassurance and support when they begin to confront mortality. The challenge for secular families is the absence of the comforting answers supplied by various faith traditions. Yet by telling the truth, providing emotional comfort, and validating the child's own experiences, secular parents can give their children the tools to understand and accept death as a natural part of life and to find meaning in their grief.

> The challenge for secular families is the absence of the comforting answers supplied by various faith traditions. Yet by telling the truth, providing emotional comfort, and validating the child's own experiences, secular parents can give their children the tools to understand and accept death as a natural part of life and to find meaning in their grief.

The reality of death touches our lives in at least two distinct ways. The most obvious is when someone important to us dies. A second way is through the realization that we and those we love must someday die.

Dealing with Ordinary Death

Natural death is still challenging for children, as it is for all of us. That grandparents and older relatives may die while a child is young is always a possibility, and the death of shorter-lived pets is inevitable. In such situations, secular parents will want to emphasize the naturalness of such deaths and how they are part of the cycle of life. But no matter how expected such a loss may be, it still requires all of us, children and adults alike, to move through the process of grieving.

Grief is a journey without shortcuts, and if it is approached with acceptance, it leaves us wiser, more mature, and more loving than we were before.

One of the important gifts that parents can give their children is the knowledge that adults also grieve and that it is painful and hard work for everyone. At the same time, parents know what children do not: that healing and growth will come, and something precious will be gained through the process. We can help our children to grieve in a healthy way by assuring them that the process does move forward, even when it feels endless.

> 66 One of the important gifts that parents can give their children is the knowledge that adults also grieve and that it is painful and hard work for everyone. 99

> *It's okay to feel sad. I'm sad too. But I know that after a while we will feel better again. We will be able to think about Blue and be happy while we remember him. It just takes time.*

It is also important to acknowledge that grief takes many forms and is changeable. A child may experience obvious sadness and withdrawal, but at times may also exhibit manic energy, regressive behavior, anger, fear, or denial. All of these are normal feelings and coping strategies that adults may have as well.

> *It can be harder to go to sleep when you are thinking how much you miss Grandma. I miss her, too. Would you like a nightlight or your old blankie for a while?*

Children are paradoxically both concrete and magical thinkers. On the one hand, they will make visible, tangible realities out of abstract concepts; on the other hand, they often think themselves responsible for events that are out of their control. The child may imagine, for example, that her momentary feeling of anger toward the deceased brought about the death. It is important to assure her that she is not responsible for a person or a pet dying. Children may not speak of these apprehensions, so it is wise to offer the affirmation unasked.

Grandmother died because she was old and ill. We all took the best care of her that we could. It wasn't anybody's fault.

Ceremony and ritual may be helpful to children and adults. Ceremony is a formal act that is thoughtfully planned, even though it may be done only once. Ritual is usually an act that gathers meaning through repetition. While both can be associated with religious beliefs, they do not have to be. They can be public, or private, or personal. A formal memorial service in a church would be a public ceremony; going alone to visit your grandfather's favorite park every year on his birthday would be a personal ritual. Ceremonies help to structure the time of grieving, which can feel amorphous and hard to define. Working with children to make a plan so they have something to anticipate can give them a sense of landmarks, as well as permission to move forward in their mourning.

> 66 Children are paradoxically both concrete and magical thinkers. On the one hand, they will make visible, tangible realities out of abstract concepts; on the other hand, they often think themselves responsible for events that are out of their control. 99

Tomorrow afternoon, let's bring all of Tuffy's toys and dishes and put them in a special box to give to the animal shelter. If you want, you can choose something to keep. We can take turns saying things that we remember about him.

•

Why don't you come to the store with me in the morning and pick out some flowers? We can take them to the retirement home where Uncle Gordon lived and sit on his special bench for a few minutes.

Rituals help to reassure children that the world is still dependable and that the person or pet they have lost will continue to be part of their lives through memory.

Each year at Thanksgiving, we'll have a toast to Grandma and remember the time she dropped the turkey.

•

Before you go to sleep each night this week, let's write down one thing that you liked about your teacher Mr. Gonzales.

Once a child adopts a ritual, he may find comfort in it long after the adults have moved on. Be patient with a child's attachment to whatever comforts her, and help children develop personal rituals that they can maintain as long as they need to without placing unreasonable demands on the rest of the family.

Five Affirmations in the Face of Death

There are five affirmations that everyone needs to hear when confronted with the death of a loved one. They may be part of public ceremonies like a memorial service, or we may need to work through them in our own ways as a family or as individuals. Parents can help their children by making sure that each of these statements is clearly made, and some of them may need to be repeated.

1. Acknowledge the reality.

The first affirmation is that death has actually taken place; it is the antidote to denial. This is why most cultural traditions arrange for wakes, viewings, funeral services, and burials; it helps the reality of loss to sink in. Even fairly young children can be consulted about whether they wish to view the body or attend public ceremonies. On the one hand, children may find seeing the body of their grandparent or pet reassuring, since it may be far less terrible than their imaginings. Being denied this opportunity may create a lack of closure. On the other hand, being pressured to do so if they do not wish to can make a difficult moment more traumatic. A sensitively attentive parent will listen carefully to the child's preferences and help him make a choice based on the child's wishes rather than the parent's expectations.

The wishful impulse of denial can be powerful in a child's thinking, so that the fact of death may need to be repeated. The idea of impermanence, that something may vanish without being able to reappear, is something that develops over time in the mind, and a young child may struggle with it. Though it may be difficult for a grieving parent, the reality of a death should be calmly restated whenever the child questions it. She is not being silly or uncaring but trying to understand how the world works.

2. Validate sadness.

The second affirmation is that loss is painful and sadness is appropriate. It is important to acknowledge the reality of powerful feelings that we do not control. Telling anyone "Don't cry" or "Don't feel bad" is not helpful at the time of bereavement. It is especially confusing to children, who may take this as a cue that there is something wrong with their emotional responses. When we have loved someone or something, our sorrow is a function and measure of that love. Loss would not be painful if there had not been a profound attachment, and in the end, our capacity for such connections makes our lives fulfilling and meaningful.

3. Acknowledge the unknown.

Secular families in particular can emphasize the unknown aspect of death. Whatever we think happens to people after they die is speculation. One of the most powerful lessons parents can teach is that adults don't know everything. This does not mean that we cannot communicate our convictions to our children, but in this realm, as in others, it is important to leave room for them to explore their own ideas. Avoid telling children that death is like sleep, as this has often been observed to disrupt their sense of safety in falling asleep themselves or allowing others to sleep. In their concrete thinking process, children may want to know where the dead person "goes." It is all but inevitable in our culture that their peers or others will talk about the idea of heaven, and perhaps even hell. Children may also have fears about the dissolution of the body, thinking this process will be painful for their loved one.

Secular parents can affirm their own conviction that death is the end of all personal experience, that there are no places where the spirits of the dead "go," and that no pain or suffering is possible for the deceased. It may be helpful to present these as "I" statements—"This is what I believe"—and to acknowledge that there are many other ideas, including those that the child may have heard or may be exploring in their own mind. It can be comforting even for adults, who have no actual belief in such ideas, to imagine the kind of next world or existence that would be particularly gratifying for the deceased; such pleasant fantasies may have a healing effect as long as they are acknowledged as wishes rather than realities. Such imaginings on the part of children can be treated as part of the grieving process and affirmed as feelings rather than facts.

Dog heaven is a lovely idea. I think Blue would like a place where he could run through the grass and chase sticks all day long and never get tired.

•

People have lots of different ideas about what might happen after someone dies, but no one knows for sure. What do you like to think Aunt Chandra might be doing?

•

Before you were born, you didn't exist—you didn't feel anything at all. I think that's what it's like for Gramps now; he isn't there anymore, so he can't think or feel, and certainly nothing can hurt him. What do you think?

4. Celebrate individuality.

Each individual is unique and irreplaceable; this is what makes our memories precious. It is also the reason for allowing an appropriate period of mourning to pass before seeking another pet. Children need permission to remember their loved one in ways that are meaningful to them. This may involve quietly looking at pictures or visiting a grave; it may take the form of talking about or wanting to hear stories about the deceased; it may be more active, such as drawing or writing about what they remember. Parents can affirm the child's perception of what was irreplaceable about the lost one. It is seldom helpful to argue that other people can take the dead person's place, or that other pets will be equally loved. At the same time, the child may need to be reassured that their life will go on in a safe way; there will be change, but the change will be manageable. Children may cling to artifacts of the deceased—clothing, a stray key, a pet's bowl—for a long time as a tangible vessel for their memories. If possible, parents should not interfere in this, but indicate that the child will know inside themselves when the time comes to put the object away.

Blue did some funny things, didn't he? Remember how he always loved to lie in the sun? And how he could always hear you coming?

•

We can still go fishing together, but it won't be quite the same without Uncle Miguel to dig our worms for us, will it? He was really good at that.

5. Affirm the continuity of life.

The final affirmation tells us that the universe remains dependable; life goes on, and what we trusted in before the loss can still be trusted: love, integrity, family and friends, the world of nature. This assurance is communicated by parents more by how they speak and behave than by most of what they say, particularly by how honestly reflective they can be about acknowledging their own feelings. "It's kind of scary sometimes to think about living in a world without my mom, but then I remember all the other people who care about me, and what a brave person she was, and I think we'll all be okay"—this tells the child that feelings are both real in the moment and changeable, and can be faced. The most basic affirmation of all, that the opportunity to share love is worth the pain of grief, is as important to children as it is to the rest of us.

> I'm glad we had Kitty as part of our family, even though I'm sad she died.

Particularly Difficult Situations

It is also possible that death may touch a child's life in a more traumatic and difficult way. When someone is killed by violence or in a sudden accident, it is not a normal part of the cycle of life. When a sibling or friend near the child's own age dies, it often feels more tragic and wasteful to the adults, and bewildering to the child, because such things are not "supposed" to happen. The same is true when a pet is hit by a car, or runs away and disappears. Despite the extra tragedy of such situations, children need much the same sort of reassurance, honesty, and permission to grieve as they do in more ordinary bereavement. The advice of psychological professionals can be very helpful and should be seen as an ordinary resource. Just as one would consult a doctor to be sure of healing properly from a physical trauma, checking in with a knowledgeable counselor is a routine aspect of handling emotional upheaval.

When confronted with a death by violence, children need to know that everything possible is being done to keep them safe and that it is very unlikely that anything like this will happen to them. The specifics will depend upon the situation, but it may help to emphasize that even adults do not always understand why people make the choices they make and do what they do. Children usually take comfort from the knowledge that the authorities are trying to catch and punish the perpetrator, because this communicates a sense of moral order in the world. Yet it is not helpful for them to displace all of their anger about death onto that individual because in the long run this will make healing more difficult for them.

When a young person dies of a disease, it is also important to assure children that they do not have the disease themselves and are likely to live for a very long time. This is another time when it must be confessed that adults don't know everything, even though they try as hard as they can. Secular parents generally reject the explanations that god has a plan, or wanted the person in heaven, and so on. Children are able to grasp that random events sometimes happen for no good reason and that bodies do not always work the way they are supposed to.

> Dying's part of the wheel [of life], right there next to being born. You can't pick out the pieces you like and leave the rest.
> —From *Tuck Everlasting*, by NATALIE BABBITT

When death is the result of an accident, parents may be tempted to drive home the moral of the story with reference to the child's own potential behavior. Not only does it seem like a relevant object lesson, but assigning responsibility for carelessness is often a mechanism by which adults attempt to cope with random tragedy. However, a child may interpret such explanations as meaning that death is a punishment for something wrong that the deceased did, and that sorrow is therefore unjustified. To whatever extent an accidental death may be someone's fault, it is important to emphasize that death is a disproportionately severe consequence.

Care must also be taken not to make the child unduly fearful. Secular parents cannot offer their children guardian angels; instead, we want them to assess risks rationally and to respond with courage as well as good sense. The child may be sensitive to particular circumstances, such as riding in a car following a bereavement by car accident, or going into the water after someone has drowned. This kind of hesitation should be treated with gentle respect, but at the same time parents can express their confidence that fatal mishaps are very rare, assuring the child that appropriate safety precautions—seat belts, lifeguards, etc.—can minimize risks.

Confronting Mortality

It is entirely possible in 21st-century Western culture for an individual to be well into middle age before a loved one dies. Children may not be confronted with the process of grieving for a person or pet they care about during childhood. Nevertheless, it is an inevitable part of the developmental process that they will be exposed to the idea of death and the dawning realization that they and those they love and depend upon will die.

The secular parent will wish to respond to this growing awareness with realism and reassurance. The younger the child, the more important it is on every occasion to announce that neither parent nor child should expect to die for a very long time. It is always good to explore a little when such questions are raised to see if there is some particular incident or comment in the child's mind before embarking upon a philosophical discussion. But the moment will come when the child sincerely wants to know how parents have reconciled themselves to the thought of dying and how to make sense of this unwelcome news about the human condition.

It may be helpful to begin with the recognition that our evolutionary history has built into our species a very powerful instinct to want to live and has made our bodies very good at continuing to live. The desire to live helps us measure risks carefully and do what is necessary to take care of ourselves.

It is natural to think that we would like to live forever and for those we care about to live forever. But that's not the way the world works. Rather, new life keeps popping up, and old life at some point dies. Nobody deliberately made it that way; that's just how evolution turned out. For a child old enough to understand the outlines of the scientific origins of life, parents can emphasize how delicate and fragile was the first coming together of chemicals that resulted in living organisms, and how essentially unstable a process life is; any given individual is such a complex set of functions that it could not possibly operate correctly in all regards forever. Everything wears out eventually—even machines, even rocks.

Many people, including most of you reading this book, believe that death is the final end of all personal experience and do not expect to continue their existence in some other life or other world. In this view, it is precisely the fact that our lives are limited that makes them precious.

How we choose to use our time is all the more important when we know that we won't have the opportunity to do everything. The fact that we can lose the ones we love makes it urgent for us to resolve our quarrels, forgive our injuries, be as thoughtful and kind as we can, and

> 66 Many people . . . believe that death is the final end of all personal experience. . . . It is precisely the fact that our lives are limited that makes them precious. 99

be sure to let those we love know about it. If we were immortal, it would not matter if we chose to spend our time being bored, cranky, or spiteful; as it is, we don't have time to waste with such unproductive and unpleasant attitudes.

Secularism at its best can turn negative appraisals of death into affirmations of life. For a secular person, the question is not, "Why did a universe designed for our benefit have to include death?" but, "Isn't it amazing that we have the matter of the world arranged in such a way that we find ourselves with this incredible opportunity to be awake and alive?" What is surprising is not that our awareness must cease to be at some point in the unknown future but that it has arisen now in the first place. That we are able to think and feel, to learn things and to love people, is a gift. It might just as easily not have happened.

There is a certain existential heroism and tragedy about living in the shadow of mortality that teens in particular sometimes find quite romantic. A sympathetic parent can acknowledge how trivial many mundane concerns may appear in this light and still insist that they be attended to. In general, what secular parents can most helpfully do for their children is to demonstrate that a full, happy, satisfying life can be lived even in the awareness that death comes at the end— perhaps even because of that awareness. Paradoxically, although many popular religious cults focus on attaining an afterlife and escaping the reality of death, in their origins, many of the world's highest spiritual and philosophical teachings summon people to live with a clear awareness of death. Such practices are meant to lead to maturity, serenity, and an enhanced capacity for deep happiness. I know from personal experience that it is possible to grow from a secure childhood into a well-balanced adult without ever supposing that death is anything other than the absolute end of personal consciousness. Because of this conviction, I know how urgently precious my life and the lives of those around me are. I find that awareness to be life-giving.

There is evolutionary value in the fear of dying; it makes us take action when necessary and precautions when appropriate. A person with no fear of dying might be too careless or daring to survive for long. So it is normal to feel afraid when we think of dying. Secular parents can assure their children that everyone has these feelings to some degree. They are appropriate and even useful. When children express fears related to death, it is helpful to discover something about the content of that fear. Are they afraid that those they depend on will die and leave them without protection? Are they afraid that the process of dying will be painful? Are they troubled to think of not existing anymore, or think that it would hurt to be dead? The more specifically the issue is identified, the more effective a parent's reassurance can be. In the end, the child will have confidence in the parents' honesty if they calmly acknowledge that the same fears affect them.

Responding to Religious Doctrines and Cultural Images

It is all but inevitable that children will encounter ideas about death and what happens to the dead that will differ from those of their secular parents. Such alternative images may be appealing because they are more dramatic, colorful, or certain than what secular parents have offered. These may include ideas about heaven, hell, ghosts, reincarnation, and communication with the dead. It is certainly true that many people have experienced some sense of presence of loved ones who have died; a naturalistic explanation of these sensations need not deny that they can be comforting and healing or, alternatively, frightening. With older children it is possible to explore both the psychological reasons why people who are grieving might have such sensations and the ways unscrupulous others might try to take advantage of them. In some of the same ways, the ideas of heaven and hell can be discussed as present states of mind rather than future states of existence. With younger children, for whom the line between fantasy and reality is more permeable, it may be best to help them identify such concepts as stories that can be pleasant to think about, either for themselves or others. Endorsing the child's capacity for imaginative comfort does not require the parent to affirm false realities.

The kind of heaven your friend is talking about seems like a nice idea, even though I don't think it really exists. It's nice to think we could see Grandma again someday; what would you like to say to her if that could happen?

Death confronts the secular family both as a challenge and an opportunity to clarify and communicate our convictions. It is part of the larger world that children encounter as they grow, a world that parents must help them understand. Ever since the origins of our kind, humans have pondered death as one of the ultimate mysteries and sought to soften its great shadow over us. Perhaps none of us is ever fully reconciled to the loss of those we love or to the inevitability of our own demise, but we learn to live as fully as possible within the unknown limits of the time we have. Living in the secular world gives us freedom from the dogmas and superstitions of the past, but it does not eliminate the mystery and power of life's endings. When parents share those essentially human feelings with their children, they are engaged in the profound task of making meaning together, which is one of the great privileges of parenthood, or indeed of any human relationship.

Kendyl Gibbons is the senior minister at All Souls Unitarian Universalist Church of Kansas City. A graduate of the College of William and Mary, she holds a master's degree from the University of Chicago Divinity School and a doctorate of ministry from Meadville/Lombard Theological School. In 2015 she was named Religious Humanist of the Year by the UU Humanist Association.

■ ■

ADDITIONAL RESOURCES FOR "DEATH AND CONSOLATION"

Books

Miller, Matt. *Facing Cancer Without God.* Forward Publishing, 2014. An extraordinary personal memoir by a pioneering computer scientist who faced his impending death with the humor and intelligence that had characterized his life and without religious comforts. High school and adult readers.

Emswiler, James and Mary Ann. *Guiding Your Child Through Grief.* Bantam, 2000. Thorough, thoughtful, loving, well informed. This is a powerful resource for secular parents helping a child who is dealing with loss and grief. The Emswilers confront the questions head-on and in detail, offering specific advice for dealing with holidays, helping grieving teens, even helping grieving stepchildren. The only mention of religious beliefs is an excellent one. Parents are invited to "share whatever beliefs your religious tradition holds about death and the afterlife" but are also cautioned not to say, "God took Mommy because she was so good," or, "God took Daddy because He wanted him to be with Him." Think about the implications of those two statements for about 10 seconds and you'll see why the Emswilers label them no-nos. "Don't use God or religion as a pacifier to make grieving children feel better. It probably won't work," they note. "Do not explain death as a punishment or a reward from God." So much for the single greatest alleged advantage of the religious view of death. For secularists, there is even more to be grateful for in this terrific book: "It is also acceptable to say you're not sure what happens after death. . . . It is always okay to say, 'I don't know.'"

Arent, Ruth P., MA, MSW. *Helping Children Grieve.* Champion Press, 2005. If a loss comes suddenly, parents might not have the time or freedom to read *Guiding Your Child Through Grief.* In that case, *Helping Children Grieve* is a thoughtful, concise resource achieving much the same. Once again, the issues children face are separated by age, and once again, religious traditions are provided as potential resources but not as answers to the problems grief presents.

Thomas, Pat. *I Miss You: A First Look at Death.* Barron's, 2000. Secular parents in search of ways to help the youngest children deal with death and loss can hardly do better than this lovely little book. In a scant 29 pages of colorfully illustrated kid-lit format, it seems to anticipate most everything likely to go through the mind of a young one upon the death of someone special. Once again, religious ideas get a nod but are denied a pedestal: "There is a lot we don't know about death. Every culture has different beliefs about what happens after a person dies. Most cultures . . . share . . . the idea that when a person dies their soul—the part of them that made them special—takes a journey to join the souls of other people who have passed away. It's not an easy idea to understand." It's true, of course: Most cultures do share some form of that belief. But instead of following this acknowledgment with a hallelujah, Thomas chooses a Taoist metaphor, one that I have always found deeply moving: "Sometimes it helps if you think of the soul as a single raindrop, joining a great big ocean." Ages three to eight.

Rothman, Juliet Cassuto. *A Birthday Present for Daniel: A Child's Story of Loss.* Prometheus, 2001. A heartbreaking and beautiful story narrated by a girl whose brother has died and whose family struggles over how to observe his approaching birthday. Ages seven–ten.

Trozzi, Maria, M.Ed. *Talking with Children About Loss.* Perigee Trade, 1999. One of the premiere references in the field of child bereavement.

Dougy Center. *35 Ways to Help a Grieving Child.* Dougy Center, 1999. A practical, accessible resource.

White, E. B. *Charlotte's Web.* HarperCollins, 1952, renewed 1980. In his book *The Philosophy of Childhood*, contributor Gareth Matthews calls special attention to two works of fiction for their substantive treatment of mortality: *Charlotte's Web* and *Tuck Everlasting*. Children in the terminal wards of hospitals request and read *Charlotte's Web* over and over, especially after one among them dies. Death is not avoided or sugarcoated—it is the book's pervasive theme, from Fern staying her uncle's ax from Wilbur's neck to Charlotte weaving "SOME PIG" to prevent him becoming the Christmas ham to Charlotte's own demise and symbolic rebirth through the springtime hatching of her egg sac. Unnatural death is something to protest, goes the message—but natural death is to be accepted with grace and courage. A stunning work of American literature, to be enjoyed repeatedly. Special treat: Look for the audiobook of E. B. White reading *Charlotte's Web*. Considered by many to be the finest children's audiobook ever. If your public library does not own a copy, suggest it buy two. Ages four to adult.

Babbitt, Natalie. *Tuck Everlasting.* Farrar, Straus, & Giroux, 1985. The Tuck family has happened on the secret of eternal life—much to their dismay. In the absence of death, the Tucks discover that life loses much of its meaning and preciousness. A truly original book and a worthy follow-up movie (2002). Book ages nine–twelve; movie for all ages.

Websites/Organizations

Grief Beyond Belief (www.griefbeyondbelief.org). An online community created to facilitate peer-to-peer grief support for the nonreligious. A space free of religion, spiritualism, mysticism, and evangelism in which to share sorrow and offer the comfort of rational compassion.

The Dougy Center for Grieving Children & Families (www.dougy.org). An organization founded in 1982 to "provide support in a safe place where children, teens and their families grieving a death can share their experiences as they move through their grief process." Website includes a search function to locate grief counseling centers across the United States and around the world.

The Good Grief Program at Boston Medical Center (http://www.bmc. org/pediatrics-goodgrief.htm). One of the top childhood grief counseling and research centers in the United States. Led by Maria Trozzi, M.Ed., author of *Talking with Children About Loss* (see above).

■ ■ ■ ■ ■ ■ ■ ■ ■ ■ ■ ■ ■

6

Wondering and Questioning

INTRODUCTION

What we need is not the will to believe, but the will to find out.

—Bertrand Russell

One of the most astonishing experiences for a parent is watching a human mind develop before your eyes. From the moment of birth, babies are sponges, soaking in everything they can lay their senses on. Wonder is pretty obviously present from the beginning—just look at the eyes of a newborn. Light, motion, temperature, shape, noise, and a million other novelties rain down on the little brain in the first few minutes, and the eyes register a mix of dismay, confusion, and wondering.

So there's wondering. But for *questioning* we'll need words. By the first birthday, kids will often have a few useable ones; by eighteen months they are generally learning a new word or two per day. At age four, they're up to twelve new words a day, with amazing syntax and a sense of how to generalize the rules of grammar (like plural "s" and past tense "ed," as evident in sentences like, "We goed to the farm and seed the sheeps"). At age six, the average child has a vocabulary in excess of 21,000 words. And we're pretty much in the dark about just exactly how that happens.[1]

Which brings us back to wonder.

Wondering and questioning are the essence of childhood. Many of us bemoan the loss of wonder and the ever-greater difficulty of finding experiences and subjects that are truly untapped enough, and still interesting enough, for our minds to feel the inrushing flood of question after question that we remember from childhood.

Children have the daunting task of changing from helpless newborns into fully functioning adults in just over 6,000 days. Think of that. A certain degree of gullibility necessarily follows. Children are believing machines, and for good reason: When we are children, the tendency to believe it when we are told that fire is dangerous, two and two are four, cliffs are not to be dangled from, and so on helps us, in the words of Richard Dawkins, "to pack, with extraordinary rapidity, our skulls full of the wisdom of our parents and our ancestors" in order to accomplish the unthinkably complex feat of becoming adults.[2] The immensity of the task requires children to be suckers for whatever it is adults tell them. It is our job as parents to be certain not to abuse this period of relative intellectual dependency and trust.

The pivotal moment is the question. How we respond to the estimated 427,050 questions a child will ask between her second and fifth birthdays will surely have a greater impact on her orientation to the world outside her head than the thirteen years of school that follow.* Do we always respond with an answer—or sometimes with another question? Do we say, "What a great question!" or do we just fill in the blank? How often do we utter that fabulous phrase, "You know what . . . I don't know!" followed by, "Let's Google it together," or, "I'll bet Aunt Sarah would know that; let's call her"? When it comes to wondering and questioning, these are the things that make all the difference. We have 427,050 chances to get it right, or 427,050 chances to say "because I said so," "because God says so," "Don't concern yourself with that stuff," or something similarly fatal to the child's "will to find out." This chapter, you won't be surprised to hear, opts for the former.

Though you wouldn't know it from your high school English class, Mark Twain was a passionate nonbeliever and a heartfelt critic of religious thinking. Many of his late works were devoted to skewering, needling, and puncturing religious belief by way of satire—the

---

*The figure 427,050 is an unscientific estimate of my own, based on the 78 questions I once counted from my daughter in a 2-hour period, times 5 (for a 10-hour day), times 365 days, times 3 years. Told you it was unscientific.

most unanswerable yet underused weapon in the progressive arsenal. "Little Bessie Would Assist Providence" (1908) listens in as a precocious three-year-old innocently asks her devout mother questions about the nature of God. But unlike most of us, Bessie follows inadequate answers with more and more questions, until her poor mother is forced to simply order her into silence.*

My essay "Of Curious Women and Dead Cats" looks at the way the fear of curiosity—especially the fear of curious women—has been baked into the religious narrative since time immemorial, and makes the case for putting this fear to rest at long last.

Katherine Miller brings the mind of a scientist, parent, and wonder-enthusiast to the teaching of evolution in "Repurposing Noah's Ark: How to Inspire Your Kids with the Science of Evolution."

After Yip Harburg weighs in on the musings of a gorilla, I argue against counterfeit wonder, and the chapter concludes with author James Herrick's exploration of one of the great avenues for the expression of human meaning and purpose—the arts—focusing especially on the place of literature in understanding the human condition.

■ ■ ■ ■ ■ ■ ■ ■ ■ ■ ■ ■ ■

---

*This excerpt is only a single chapter of Twain's hilarious satire. Though unpublished during Twain's lifetime, *Little Bessie* is available in an early biography of Twain by Albert Bigelow Paine, as well as the compilation *Fables of Man*, edited by John S. Tuckey (University of California Press, 1972).

LITTLE BESSIE WOULD ASSIST PROVIDENCE

MARK TWAIN

Little Bessie was nearly three years old. She was a good child, and not shallow, not frivolous, but meditative and thoughtful, and much given to thinking out the reasons of things and trying to make them harmonize with results. One day she said:

"Mamma, why is there so much pain and sorrow and suffering? What is it all for?"

It was an easy question, and mamma had no difficulty in answering it: "It is for our good, my child. In His wisdom and mercy the Lord sends us these afflictions to discipline us and make us better."

"Is it *He* that sends them?"

"Yes."

"Does He send *all* of them, mamma?"

"Yes, dear, all of them. None of them comes by accident; He alone sends them, and always out of love for us, and to make us better."

"Isn't it strange!"

"Strange? Why, no, I have never thought of it in that way. I have not heard anyone call it strange before. It has always seemed natural and right to me, and wise and most kindly and merciful."

"Who first thought of it like that, mamma? Was it you?"

"Oh, no, child, I was taught it."

"Who taught you so, mamma?"

"Why, really, I don't know—I can't remember. My mother, I suppose; or the preacher. But it's a thing that everybody knows."

"Well, anyway, it does seem strange. Did He give Billy Norris the typhus?"

"Yes."

"What for?"

"Why, to discipline him and make him good."

"But he died, mamma, and so it *couldn't* make him good."

"Well, then, I suppose it was for some other reason. We know it was a *good* reason, whatever it was."

"What do you think it was, mamma?"

"Oh, you ask so many questions! I think it was to discipline his parents."

"Well, then, it wasn't fair, mamma. Why should *his* life be taken away for their sake, when he wasn't doing anything?"

"Oh, I don't know! I only know it was for a good and wise and merciful reason."

"What reason, mamma?"

"I think—I think—well, it was a judgment; it was to punish them for some sin they had committed."

"But *he* was the one that was punished, mamma. Was that right?"

"Certainly, certainly. He does nothing that isn't right and wise and merciful. You can't understand these things now, dear, but when you are grown up you will understand them, and then you will see that they are just and wise."

After a pause:

"Did He make the roof fall in on the stranger that was trying to save the crippled old woman from the fire, mamma?"

"Yes, my child. *Wait!* Don't ask me why, because I don't know. I only know it was to discipline someone, or be a judgment upon somebody, or to show His power."

"That drunken man that stuck a pitchfork into Mrs. Welch's baby when . . ."

"Never mind about it, you needn't go into particulars; it was to discipline the child—*that* much is certain, anyway."

"Mamma, Mr. Burgess said in his sermon that billions of little creatures are sent into us to give us cholera, and typhoid, and lockjaw, and more than a thousand other sicknesses and—mamma, does He send them?"

"Oh, certainly, child, certainly. Of course."

"What for?"

"Oh, to *dis*cipline us! Haven't I told you so, over and over again?"

"It's awful cruel, mamma! And silly! And if I . . ."

"Hush, oh *hush*! do you want to bring the lightning?"

"You know the lightning *did* come last week, mamma, and struck the new church, and burnt it down. Was it to discipline the church?"

(Wearily). "Oh, I suppose so."

"But it killed a hog that wasn't doing anything. Was it to discipline the hog, mamma?"

"Dear child, don't you want to run out and play a while? If you would like to . . ."

A NOSE IS A NOSE IS A NOSE

YIP HARBURG

Mother, Mother,
Tell me please,
Did God who gave us flowers and trees,
Also provide the allergies?

"Mamma, only think! Mr. Hollister says there isn't a bird or fish or reptile or any other animal that hasn't got an enemy that Providence has sent to bite it and chase it and pester it, and kill it, and suck its blood and discipline it and make it good and religious. Is that true, mother—because if it is true, why did Mr. Hollister laugh at it?"

"That Hollister is a scandalous person, and I don't want you to listen to anything he says."

"Why, mamma, he is very interesting, and I think he tries to be good. He says the wasps catch spiders and cram them down into their nests in the ground—*alive*, mamma!—and there they live and suffer days and days and days, and the hungry little wasps chewing their legs and gnawing into their bellies all the time, to make them good and religious and praise God for His infinite mercies. I think Mr. Hollister is just lovely, and ever so kind; for when I asked him if he would treat a spider like that, he said he hoped to be damned if he would; and then he . . ."

"My child! oh, do for goodness' sake . . ."

"And mamma, he says the spider is appointed to catch the fly, and drive her fangs into his bowels, and suck and suck and suck his blood, to discipline him and make him a Christian; and whenever the fly buzzes his wings with the pain and misery of it, you can see by the spider's grateful eye that she is thanking the Giver of All Good for—well, she's saying grace, as he says; and also, he . . ."

"Oh, aren't you ever going to get tired chattering! If you want to go out and play . . ."

"Mamma, he says himself that all troubles and pains and miseries and rotten diseases and horrors and villainies are sent to us in mercy and kindness to discipline us; and he says it is the duty of every father and mother to *help* Providence, every way they can; and says they can't do it by just scolding and whipping, for that won't answer, it is weak and no good—Providence's way is best, and it is every parent's duty and every *person's* duty to help discipline everybody, and cripple them and kill them, and starve them, and freeze them, and rot them with diseases, and lead them into murder and theft and dishonor and disgrace; and he says Providence's invention for disciplining us and the animals is the very brightest idea that ever was, and not even an idiot could get up anything shinier. Mamma, brother Eddie needs disciplining, right away: and I know where you can get the smallpox for him, and the itch, and the diphtheria, and bone-rot, and heart disease, and consumption, and—Dear mamma, have you fainted! I will run and bring help! Now *this* comes of staying in town this hot weather."

▪▪

OF CURIOUS WOMEN
AND DEAD CATS

DALE McGOWAN

A strange and disturbing character pops up in religion and folklore around the world and throughout history: the curious and disobedient woman. A god/wizard gives a woman total freedom, with one exception—the one thing she must not do/eat/see. She battles briefly with her curiosity and loses, opening/eating the door/jar/box/apple and thereby spoiling everything for everybody.

Curiosity didn't just kill the cat, you see. It unleashed disease, misery, war, and death on the world and got us evicted from a Paradise of blank incuriosity and unthinking obedience.

Bummer.

Traditional religion isn't the source of human hatreds, fears, and prejudices so much as a repository for them, the place we put them for safekeeping against the sniffing nose of inquiry. They sit protected by a veil of sacredness to which nothing is so threatening as curiosity. And since the story of the curious, disobedient woman includes three things powerfully reviled by most religious traditions (curiosity, disobedience, and women), it's not surprising to find them conveniently bundled into a single high-speed cable running straight to our cultural hearts.

I could do pages on Eve alone and her act of disobedient curiosity with the fruit of the tree of knowledge of good and evil: Was she really punished for wanting to know the difference between right and wrong, or just for disobedience? How could she know it was wrong to disobey if she didn't yet have knowledge of good and evil? Then there's Lot's wife, poor nameless soul, a woman (check) who was curious (check) and therefore disobeyed (check!) instructions to not look back at her brimstoned friends and loved ones.

It's not just a Judeo-Christian thing. Islam even coined a word for a disobedient woman—*nashiz*—and decreed an assortment of punishments for her in sharia law.

But neither Eve nor Mrs. Lot was the first *nashiz* woman to cross my path. That honor went to lovely, nosy Pandora.

Pandora was designed for revenge on humanity by the gods, who were angry at the theft of fire by Prometheus. According to the Greek poet Hesiod, each of the Olympians gave her a gift (Pandora = "all-gifted"). She was created by Hephaestus in the very image of Aphrodite. Hermes gave her "a shameful mind and deceitful nature" and filled her mouth with "lies and crafty words." Poseidon gave her a pearl necklace (which, unlike the deceitful nature, for example, was at least on her registry).

But the real drivers of the story were the last two gifts: Hermes gave her an exquisitely beautiful jar (or box) with instructions not to open it, while Hera, queen of the gods, blessed her with insatiable curiosity.

Nice.

Long story short, once on Earth, Pandora's god-given curiosity consumed her, and she opened the jar/box, releasing war, disease, famine, and talk radio into the world. Realizing what she had done, she clamped the lid on at last, with Hope alone left inside.

This tendency in our mythic history to revile women and blame them for evil makes me angry. But if we want to improve on what we've inherited, we have to move past anger to comprehension. As a parent, I want to encourage the same impulse in my kids—not just railing against our more unfortunate tendencies but saying, "Why are we that way?" By knowing why an idea came into being in the past, we can look at the present and decide whether it makes any earthly sense to keep those ancient ideas alive. That's freethought in a nutshell.

By disallowing curious questions, sacredness does the opposite—it allows bad ideas to be retained as readily as good ones.

Though I grew up in a churchgoing family, I was lucky that my parents never pushed any metaphysical answers on me. Instead, they instilled a strong curiosity about the world that made me burn to find real answers. This is a key point. I sometimes feel a sense of urgency from nonreligious parents to pack as much truth as possible into their kids' heads so there won't be any room for nonsense. When a free-thinker's child floats a wrong hypothesis, this little tic begins at the corner of the parent's mouth. "Kill the Wrongness," says a little voice, "before it takes root." Sure, that might get the Rightness installed in that moment—but what about all the future moments, including 10,000 times when you won't be in the room?

I blew this moment many times when my firstborn was young. That's what firstborns are for. But by the time his younger sister came to me in kindergarten and said she had figured out how the earth turns, and I asked how, and she said, "I think it's the wind blowing against the mountains," I didn't lean in and say, "Actually . . ."

Here's the thing. Erin was never going to be 45 years old and still thinking that this (frankly captivating) idea is true. She would eventually learn what turns the world. Less certain in that moment was whether she would become a curious and disobedient woman, pursuing her questions wherever they led.

So instead of correcting her, I said, "Cool, I never thought of that!"—because it was and I hadn't. Then instead of walking away with a stroke of red pen across her mind, she glowed, happy in the act of figuring the world out and all the more likely to do it again.

So no, we don't have to fill our kids' heads with the right answers. Instead, give them a curiosity that won't rest until they find answers on their own, then revisit and revise them for the rest of their lives.

As a bonus, their self-acquired answers will have more staying power than authoritative answers from Mom and Dad. If I just give my kids a lot of answers that I discovered, tied up with a ribbon, they are robbed of the ownership that comes from the process of acquiring it. They end up standing on a foundation full of holes, knowing answers without knowing why they are true.

That's one reason I'm raising freethinkers instead of atheists. If kids have autonomy over their own process, fueled by a ravenous curiosity about the world, they will know each brick in their worldview because they placed it themselves. That's the road less traveled that my own parents put me on—and that has made all the difference.

■ ■

REPURPOSING NOAH'S ARK: HOW TO INSPIRE YOUR KIDS WITH THE SCIENCE OF EVOLUTION

BY KATHERINE MILLER, Ph.D.

When our kids turn their irresistible little faces to us and ask about snack time, soccer practice, or the location of the remote, we parents can more or less handle the question. But when they focus their penetrating laser eyes on us and ask, "Where did humans come from?" we may wish for an easier question, or possibly a stiff drink. When did they get to be so inquisitive?

Introducing kids to biological evolution can be daunting. If you feel that way, you've come to the right place. If you don't feel that way, you've also come to the right place. Grab a beverage, put up your feet, and read on for some strategies on how to bring evolution into your kids' lives.

Don't Be Intimidated

This is the first and most important strategy. Many people believe that understanding biological evolution involves conquering several barbed-wire intellectual fortresses. While such fortresses do exist—genetics, paleontology, geology—they tend to frighten children and grown-ups. Steer clear.

If you can read this book, you can understand enough about evolution to present it to children. If your grasp feels shaky, then the best course is to teach yourself alongside your kids. Do some Googling together, or read some of the recommended books. Not only will you learn about it yourself, but you will also model the process of fearless investigation. We don't know how evolution works? Great, let's go find out, kids! Nothing here to be intimidated by, and definitely no shame in saying, "I don't know."

Keep It Simple

At its heart, the evolution of life through natural selection is simple. In a nutshell:

Animals change slowly over time because the ones that have traits that help them survive are the ones that go on to have the kids. Because those kids have the same traits as their parents, they can also survive well. Some of the kids might also be a little different from their parents, in ways that make them even better able to survive than their brothers and sisters. Meanwhile, the animals that can't survive die off before they can have any kids. Carry that on over many, many, many generations and voila, animals have shapes and organs that suit them to their environments.

The handy acronym VIST sums up four central concepts of evolution: variation, inheritance, selection, and time. The above description contains all these concepts, but in plain language. As long as these concepts show up in your conversations with your kids, jargon is unnecessary.

Over the years I have collected many explanations of evolution by natural selection. I give points for brevity, clarity, and friendliness. Charles Darwin's *On the Origin of Species*, even though it kicked off this whole party, loses points for its length, density, and solemnity. One brilliant winner is a double-page illustration involving frogs in *Life on Earth* by Steve Jenkins, written for ages seven to ten.

I also give points to this exquisitely brief explanation, understandable by people aged 1 to 100: When you make copies of something, then there are more of them.

Keeping evolution simple for children is just like presenting any other complex subject. We teach six-year-olds about government not by reading them the Constitution but by explaining one-person-one-vote. We teach them about the solar system not with Newtonian physics but with a plastic model of the sun and planets. These descriptions of a complex underlying reality are oversimplified but not grossly incorrect, and we wouldn't berate ourselves for omitting the gritty details. We also wouldn't say that these subjects are just too complicated and not appropriate for kids to even contemplate. Most importantly, kids grasp these simpler explanations. Let's do the same for evolution.

Make It Routine

Kids learn best about any topic when it is woven into daily life, discussed repeatedly, and treated as normal. Once my two sons basically grasped evolution, we were amazed at how frequently it came up day to day. Here are some examples:

Looking at some sparrows clustered at our bird feeder, the kids noticed that some birds pushed in toward the food more aggressively than others. There it is: The more aggressive ones get the food, which makes them more likely to survive and eventually produce pushy, aggressive little baby birds.

The *Star Trek* episode "Amok Time" involves Mr. Spock traveling back to Vulcan to mate, but his wife excitedly orders him into a fight to the death with Captain Kirk instead. The whole thing ends up being a textbook example of evolutionary pressure through sexual selection. Watch the episode, you'll see.

Why, my kids whined, do they have to get flu vaccines every single year instead of just once like other vaccines? Well, kids, it's because viruses evolve so quickly that our bodies are facing new strains all the time. By next year, the flu viruses that survive this year will have evolved into something else.

So give it a try. Once your ears are pricked to listen for it, you'll find evolution everywhere.

Play Up the Awe and Wonder

Truly, the evolution of life is mind-blowing. It is a sweeping creation story, complete with thrilling battles, unexpected reversals, and epic upheavals, played out over hundreds of millions of years with an immense cast of fascinating characters. If ever there was purely secular awe, this story will inspire it.

Each kid is connected to the history of all life on earth. And not just connected: We literally embody the history of life. Inside our genes are a bunch of Neanderthal genes, trilobite genes, hell, even jellyfish genes! How strange and cool is that?

Take a look around at our lavish living world, kids. There are lemurs, bacteria, baobab trees, hammerhead sharks, luna moths, ostriches—and on an on. All this extravagant life took hundreds of millions of years to develop. What stunning luck that we should be alive now to see it all, and how wonderful that this rug of life will keep unfurling long after us.

Play Down the Nasty Bits

That said, evolution is also a cold, purposeless process in which countless cute animals that would have made excellent plushy toys have met with grisly extinction. How to break this to the kids?

I have three suggestions. First, call on your larger strategy for dealing with death. Personally, my strategy as a secular parent is pretty prosaic: Death is part of life, kids. When you die, nothing happens, just like before you were born. Looked at this way, the brief time we have to live on this planet gains richness, importance, and purpose. All those cute fuzzy animals did die, yes, but they also had their rich, important time on this earth, just like us.

Second, remind the kids that evolution also generates the beauty of the living world. Every time your child gasps at a peacock's display, laughs at an axolotl, or snuggles with the family cat, she is reveling in the wonderful products of evolution, inseparable from the vicious parts. In other words, the bad is inseparable from the good.

Third, although the evolutionary process is generally indifferent to the survival of offspring, we parents are not. As *Homo sapiens*, we have evolved a ferocious, protective love of our progeny, so our kids need not fear that they face grisly deaths. Also, they can look forward, if they have their own kids one day, to feeling that ancient ferocious love as well. It's pretty great.

Think Through Competing Views

Like it or not, the social context of evolution in the United States is fraught. Perhaps Grandma believes that God made all the animals in their current form, or the kids at school ask why there are still monkeys if we supposedly evolved from them. Evolutionary biology attracts this homespun skepticism more than other sciences, even though other fields propose much freakier ideas, like infinite multiple universes or time flowing backward. But no matter.

Since we have to live with this social context, at least we can put it to use as a critical thinking exercise for the kids. In a scientific worldview, competing ideas are always welcome, and they are always treated to the same essential scrutiny: How well does this idea correspond with what we can observe about the world? The idea of Helios driving the sun chariot across the sky each day was a pretty good match for the daily observations of the ancient Greeks, but our observations are so much richer now, and Helios's chariot no longer cuts it.

Likewise, our vast observations of animals, fossils, rocks, and genes need some splainin'. This is your chance to think it through with the kids: Which explanation best fits what we see in the world? Challenge them to go get the scoop from Grandma, hear out the kids at school, talk to anyone about it. Have the kids gather information about competing theories and try to convince you, or more importantly try to convince themselves. What makes the most sense?

For help on specific arguments arising from creationism or intelligent design, see the Wikipedia page on Objections to Evolution or TalkOrigins' archive of creationist claims and refutations.

Avoid Common Myths

We don't need to be biologists to present evolution to our kids, and we don't need to get every point scientifically correct down to a gnat's knees. Yet certain misconceptions about evolution just seem to persist in this country. Let's do the future a favor and get rid of these myths as we raise the next generation.

Myth: Evolution Is Purposeful

Cognitive science tells us that very young children have a teleological view of the world, meaning they naturally assign intentions to inanimate things and processes. To a child, wind in the trees may seem, for example, like a purposeful force trying to push the trees down. This thought pattern is probably itself an evolved trait, deeply baked into our brains and difficult to counteract in kids as well as adults.

Evolution is a process that takes in random events like genetic mutations or environmental changes and spits out creatures of astounding order. How can that be? We naturally assume that evolution works according to some purposeful agenda, yet in truth it is just a series of inevitable consequences with no purpose at all. A great analogy for children is a sieve, which perfectly and efficiently sorts out larger pebbles from the sand at the beach, yet is no more purposeful than, well, a sieve.

Myth: Humans Are the Pinnacle of Evolution

This myth goes hand in hand with thinking evolution is purposeful. If evolution has some kind of intention behind it, then of course humans would have to be the ultimate aim of that intention, being as brilliant, charming, and good-looking as we are, right? Actually, we're just one of the zillions of species that have come and gone, no more or less important than any other.

Myth: Humans Evolved from Monkeys

This one exasperates me. Humans are apes, yes, and monkeys are cousins of apes. We all evolved from an unknown common ancestor that is now extinct. Any illustration of the tree of life will show this clearly enough for any child of reading age. And there are still monkeys in the same way that kids still have cousins.

Myth: Individuals Evolve

A puppy will become a dog, a caterpillar will morph into a butterfly, and a delightful baby will turn into an insufferable teenager. These transformations, so easy for kids to witness and grasp, are also easy to mistake for evolutionary change. Individual creatures may change form during their life cycle, but evolution happens only on the group level, across generations.

When we say, "Fish evolved to have legs," kids often take it to mean that one individual fish one day sprouted some legs. Instead we mean that over many, many generations the fish who had more leg-like fins were more likely to survive and breed than others. So a million years later, all the fish being born were the ones with legish fins. Species evolve, not individuals.

If your kids play the trading card game Pokemon, you may be in trouble on this one. In that game, a variety of cute imaginary critters have three body forms that they grow through in their life cycle, akin to the human cycle of infant-child-adult. The game uses the word *evolution* for this process, as one individual critter can "evolve" from one form to the next. Beware this poorly named game mechanism. Next time your kids are playing, try poking at them with something like, "Your Pikachu just evolved? But that's not evolution," and see what happens.

Hitch a Conceptual Ride on the Dinosaurs

The dinosaur obsession swept over my kids right on schedule, lasting from about ages four to nine. It was a wonderful time, abundant with dino books, figurines, movies, music, and museums. When this happens to your kids—and I hope it does—take the opportunity to slide in some evolutionary ideas while they aren't looking.

The variation in dinosaurs is fantastic: the huge guys with the long necks, the fierce guys with the tiny arms and gigantic teeth, the armored guys with bony frills and spikes. Many kids love to sort their dinosaur toys by size and shape, like tiny taxonomists, noticing what makes them different from each other. Kids can perhaps see the survival advantage of these various traits: that ankylosaurus's tail looks pretty nasty in a fight, and that apatosaurus's neck probably let her reach tall trees for food. Then of course there is the vastness of time. The dinosaurs lived mainly over three geologic periods, the Triassic, Jurassic, and Cretaceous. Your kids don't have to know or pronounce those words, but they can notice that certain families of dinos lived in the first part (Triassic), other kinds in the middle part (Jurassic), and still others in the last bit (Cretaceous). Look how those body shapes morphed into each other over time! And best of all, despite the best efforts of that meteorite 65 million years ago, descendants of dinosaurs still live among us as birds. If your kids have trouble seeing the bird-dinosaur connection, just Google archaeopteryx. Once they get it, they will never look at a sparrow the same way.

Repurpose Your Noah's Ark

In the biblical story of Noah, a man collects a bunch of animals into a boat and changes the world forever. Hmm, sounds like the story of Charles Darwin, too.

If your kids have a Noah's ark play set, you can hijack that narrative. Put a piece of masking tape on the ark and relabel it the HMS *Beagle*, the ship that transported Darwin to the Galapagos Islands and elsewhere. Rename the Noah figure as Charles and have him board the ship not because of divine commandment but out of curiosity and love of the natural world. Instead of saving the animals from disaster, Darwin studied their lives in their home environments, taking samples on board when he could. (No need to emphasize that Darwin's samples were—ahem—mostly dead, and that the *Beagle*'s crew killed and ate Galapagos tortoises with abandon.) Darwin disembarked with his animals not onto Mount Ararat but into his home laboratory, where he went on to basically blow up the worlds of science and religion with his magnificent ideas. Kids, when you grow up, you could do the same!

See the book recommendations for more on Darwin's voyage, mainly the excellent and engrossing *Inside the* Beagle *with Charles Darwin*, by Fiona Macdonald and Mark Bergin.

Make a Butcher Paper Timeline

For this you'll need a roll of butcher paper, available at any craft store; some books on evolution (see recommendations later in this chapter); some Magic Markers or crayons; some kids; and a rainy afternoon. Find the longest hallway you can and unfurl the paper as much as possible. Then mark one end as "Today" and the other end as, say, "400 million years ago." Make lines along your timeline at intervals of 50 million years or so, keeping in mind that fun is way more important than precision.

Then have the kids open any book and choose the weirdest, biggest, ugliest, or silliest creature they can. Bust out the Magic Markers, and they can draw the creature on the timeline, placing it at about the time that it lived. Many grown-ups like joining in on this one. And if you leave the timeline out for several days (or weeks, as it lasted in our house), the kids can keep adding creatures, perhaps as a bedtime ritual. Eventually you will have a one-of-a-kind work of art, and your kids will have a visceral understanding of the kinds of life that existed over the geologic ages.

Get Some Fun Stuff

If you go on Amazon.com and search under "Toys and Games" for "evolution," you'll find bike helmets, *Star Wars* merchandise, and Pokemon. Fail. But if you search a little deeper, you'll find some great things to buy to support the kids' evolution habit. Plenty of books are available now, for all ages and dispositions. Also, basically any dinosaur merchandise can be repurposed for evolution education. Here are some other treats:

◆ "Evolution" board game from Northstar games, with several expansions (ages 10+)

◆ "Tree of Life Puzzle" from EuroGraphics (1,000 pieces)

◆ "Evolution of Man" play set from Safari Ltd. (figures of *Australopithecus afarensis, Homo habilis, Homo erectus,* Neanderthal, and Cro-Magnon)

◆ "Prehistoric Man Evolution Science Kit" from Clementoni (Italian company, may be hard to find in the United States)

Do Some Fun Stuff

Any natural history museum is basically a temple to evolution. Do not miss—please do not miss under any circumstances—a chance for your kids to visit any of the big three: the American Museum of Natural History in New York, the Field Museum in Chicago, or the Smithsonian National Museum of Natural History in Washington, D.C. Their little minds will be blown. Many smaller cities also have natural history museums and are definitely worth a day trip.

Zoos and aquariums are also monuments to evolution. At your next visit, try playing some simple games with the kids. When they see an animal, for example, the kids have to find a trait that might help that animal survive in the wild. What about that giraffe's long neck? What about the shark's big teeth or the cheetah's fast legs? You can also try picking out the closest cousins in the family tree. That macaroni penguin looks a lot like that chinstrap penguin, so they are probably close cousins on the tree. The elephant doesn't look much like either of them, so elephants must be more-distant relatives. Who is close and who is far away?

Do Some Serious Learning

If you are homeschooling or if your kids show a deeper interest in learning about evolution, you will need some more in-depth educational resources:

The "Understanding Evolution" website from the University of California Museum of Paleontology is a marvel (evolution.berkeley.edu). It offers full curricula and lessons for kindergarten through high school, plus a vast array of tools for teachers and parents to better understand evolution themselves. Go here first.

The PBS program *NOVA* has an excellent online "evolution lab" with games, videos, quizzes, and other tasty educational morsels for kids and adults alike (pbs.org/wgbh/nova/labs/lab/evolution/).

The academic journal *Evolution: Education and Outreach* is on the cutting edge of evolution teaching practices, with the aim to "promote accurate understanding and comprehensive teaching of evolutionary theory for a wide audience." Highly readable and freely downloadable, its articles often include instructions for novel games or lessons teaching various evolutionary concepts at all levels, from kindergarten to 12th grade. Go poke around; you'll be intrigued (link.springer.com/journal/12052).

Book Recommendations

A fair number of children's books on evolution are available, in a broad enough selection to require curating. Some of my highest recommendations:

- *Cartoon History of the Earth* series, by Jacqui Bailey and Matthew Lilly (A & C Black Publishers)

- *The Story of Life: A First Book About Evolution,* by Catherine Barr, Steve Williams, and Amy Husband (Frances Lincoln Children's Books, 2015)

- *When Bugs Were Big, Plants Were Strange, and Tetrapods Stalked the Earth*, by Hannah Bonner (National Geographic Children's Books, 2004)

- *When Fish Got Feet, When Bugs Were Big, and When Dinos Dawned*, by Hannah Bonner (National Geographic Children's Books, 2015)

- *Prehistoric World,* by Fiona Chandler, Jane Bingham, and Sam Taplin (Usborne, 2000)

- *Evolution (Eyewitness),* by Linda Gamlin (Dorling Kindersley, DK, 2009)

- *Evolution: The Story of Life on Earth,* by Jay Hosler, Kevin Cannon, and Zander Cannon (Hill & Wang, 2011)

- *The Sandwalk Adventures: An Adventure in Evolution Told in Five Chapters,* by Jay Hosler (CreateSpace, 2013)

- *Life on Earth: The Story of Evolution,* by Steve Jenkins (HMH Books for Young Readers, 2002)

- *Evolution: How We and All Living Things Came to Be,* by Daniel Loxton (Kids Can Press, 2010)

- *Inside the* Beagle *with Charles Darwin,* by Fiona Macdonald and Mark Bergin (Enchanted Lion Books, 2005)

- *The Beast in You! Activities & Questions to Explore Evolution,* by Marc McCutcheon and Cindy Blobaum (Kaleidoscope Kids Books, 1999)

- *Totally Human: Why We Look and Act the Way We Do,* by Cynthia Pratt Nicolson and Dianne Eastman (Kids Can Press, 2011)

- *Our Family Tree: An Evolution Story,* by Lisa Westberg Peters and Lauren Stringer (HMH Books for Young Readers, 2003)

- *Evolution: Why Did Fish Grow Feet? and Other Stories of Life on Earth,* by Anne Rooney (TickTock Books, 2014)

- *Bones, Brains and DNA: The Human Genome and Human Evolution,* by Ian Tattersall, Rob DeSalle, and Patricia Wynne (Bunker Hill Publishing, 2007)

- *The Kingfisher Book of Evolution,* by Stephen Webster (Kingfisher, 2000)

KATHERINE MILLER is a scientist and mother whose fieldwork included researching women's reproductive health, largely in sub-Saharan Africa. She holds a Ph.D. in demography from the University of Pennsylvania and a master's in public health from Columbia University. In 2008 she founded Charlie's Playhouse, a company creating educational toys and games that help children learn about evolution.

■ ■

WE'VE COME A LONG WAY, BUDDY

YIP HARBURG

An ape, who from the zoo broke free,
Was cornered in the library
With Darwin tucked beneath one arm,
The Bible 'neath the other.
"I can't make up my mind," said he,
"Just who on earth I seem to be—
Am I my brother's keeper
Or am I my keeper's brother?"

TEACHING KIDS TO YAWN AT COUNTERFEIT WONDER

DALE McGOWAN

A lot of people believe that you can't experience wonder without religious faith. The life of a person without supernatural beliefs is thought by some to be cold, sterile, and devoid of any sense of wonder.

If that were the case, this book would have to sound the alarm. Childhood is our first and best chance to revel in wonder. If parenting without religion meant parenting without wonder, I might just say to heck with reality.

Funny, though, how often I've experienced something that seemed an awful lot like wonder, and it never had even a pinch of religion in it. I always found the biblical version of wonder rather flat and hollow, even as a kid. It never moved me even as metaphor, rendered pale by its own vague hyperbole.

Instead, try these on for size:

> - If you condense the history of the universe to a single year, humans would appear on December 31 at 10:30 p.m.; 99.98 percent of the history of the universe happened before humans existed.
> - Look at a gold ring. As the core collapsed in a dying star, a gravity wave collapsed inward with it. As it did so, it slammed into the thundering sound wave heading out of the collapse. In that moment, as a star died, the gold in that ring was formed.
> - We are star material that knows it exists.
> - Our planet is spinning at 900 miles an hour beneath our feet while coursing through space at 68,400 miles per hour.
> - The continents are moving under our feet at three to six inches a year. But a snail's pace for a million millennia has been enough to remake the face of the world several times over, build the Himalayas, and create the oceans.
> - Through the wonder of DNA, you are literally half your mom and half your dad.
> - A complete blueprint to build you exists in each and every cell of your body.

> ‣ The faster you go, the slower time moves.
> ‣ Your memories, your knowledge, even your identity and sense of self exist entirely in the form of a constantly recomposed electrochemical symphony playing in your head.
> ‣ All life on Earth is directly related by descent. You are a cousin not just of apes but of the sequoia and the amoeba, of mosses and butterflies and blue whales.

That, my friends, is wonder.

I was a teenager when I was first introduced to genuine, jaw-dropping, mind-buzzing wonder by Carl Sagan. He was a master of making conceivable the otherwise inconceivable realities of the universe, usually by brilliant analogy, taking me step by step into a true appreciation of honest to goodness wonder. I was aware, for example, that humans were relative newcomers on the planet, but it wasn't until I came across Sagan's astonishing calendar analogy at age thirteen—the one above that puts our arrival at 10:30 p.m. on New Year's Eve—that I actually got it, and reeled with wonder.

A little precision can make all the difference in the experience of wonder. Merely knowing that the universe is really, really, really, really big is one thing, but that only rated a two on the wow-meter for me as a child, as it does for my son and daughters. A few more specifics, though, can snap it into focus, and up goes the meter.

Find a large open space. Put a soccer ball in the middle to represent the sun. Walk 10 paces from the ball and stick a pin in the ground. That's Mercury. Take nine more full steps and drop a peppercorn for Venus. Seven more steps, drop another peppercorn for Earth. An inch away from Earth, stick another pin in the ground for the moon, remembering that this inch is the farthest humans have been so far. Another fourteen steps, drop a very small peppercorn for Mars, then continue another 95 steps and drop Jupiter, a Ping-Pong ball. After 112 more paces, place a large marble for Saturn. Uranus and Neptune are still farther apart, and recently demoted Pluto would be a pinhead about a half mile from the soccer ball.

> 66 [We inhabit] a universe made of a curved fabric woven of space and time in which hydrogen, given the proper conditions, eventually evolves into Yo-Yo Ma. 99

So how far would you have to walk before you can put down another soccer ball for Proxima Centauri, the nearest star to our sun? Bring your good shoes—it's over 4,000 miles away at this scale, New York to Berlin.* That's the nearest star. And there are about a trillion such stars in the Milky Way galaxy alone, and roughly 100 billion such galaxies, arrayed through 12 billion light-years in every direction, a universe made of a curved fabric woven of space and time in which hydrogen, given the proper conditions, eventually evolves into Yo-Yo Ma.

> " Two hundred years ago it was possible, even reasonable, to believe that we were the central concern of the Creator of it all—and therefore reasonable to teach our children the same. "

Two hundred years ago it was possible, even reasonable, to believe that we were the central concern of the Creator of it all—and therefore reasonable to teach our children the same. But anyone who was engaged for the whole process above will still be blank-eyed and buzzing at all we have learned about ourselves and our context in the past two centuries. Just as infants mature into adults by gradually recognizing that they are not the center of the universe, so science has given humanity the means to its own maturity, challenging us not only to endure our newly realized smallness but to find the incredible wonder in that reality.

> " As each complex and awe-inspiring explanation of reality takes the place of "God did it," the flush of real awe quickly overwhelms the memory of whatever it was we considered so wondrous in religious mythology. "

Religious wonder—the wonder we're said to be missing out on—is counterfeit wonder. As each complex and awe-inspiring explanation of reality takes the place of "God did it," the flush of real awe quickly overwhelms the memory of whatever it was we considered so wondrous in religious mythology. Most of the truly wonder-inducing aspects of our existence—the true size and age of the universe, the relatedness of all life, microscopic worlds, and more—are not, to paraphrase Hamlet, even dreamt of in our religions. Our new maturity brings with it some real challenges, of course, but it also brings astonishing wonder beyond the imaginings of our infancy.

---

*This marvelous exercise is adapted from John Cassidy, *Earthsearch* (Klutz, 1994).

There is no surer way to strip religion of its ability to entice our children into fantasy than to show them the way, step by step, into the far more intoxicating wonders of the real world. And the key to those wonders is precisely the skill that is so often miscast as the death of wonder: skepticism.

> *After sleeping through a hundred million centuries, we have finally opened our eyes on a sumptuous planet, sparkling with colour, bountiful with life. Within decades we must close our eyes again. Isn't it a noble, an enlightened way of spending our brief time in the sun, to work at understanding the universe and how we have come to wake up in it? This is how I answer when I am asked—as I am surprisingly often—why I bother to get up in the mornings.*
>
> —Richard Dawkins, *Unweaving the Rainbow*

Nothing wrinkles noses faster than a skeptical attitude—"Why do you have to be so negative, why do you have to tear everything down?"—yet there is nothing as essential to experiencing true wonder in its greatest depth. Skepticism is the filter that screens out the fool's gold, leaving nothing behind but precious nuggets of the real thing. Tell me something amazing and I'll doubt it until it's proven. Why? Because fantasies, while charming, are a dime a dozen. I can tell you my dreams of purple unicorns all day, spinning wilder and wilder variations for your amusement. You'll enjoy it, perhaps even be moved by it, but you won't believe—until I show you one, take you for a ride on its back, prove it's more than just a product of my imagination. Your skepticism up to that point will have served you well; it fended off counterfeit wonder so you could feel the depth of the real thing.

We must teach our kids to doubt and doubt and doubt, not to "tear everything down" but to pull cheap façades away so they can see and delight in those things that are legitimately wonderful. How will they recognize them? It's easy: They're the ones left standing after the hail of critical thinking has flattened everything else. Magnificent, those standing stones.

> *Fling your arms wide in an expansive gesture to span all evolution from its origin at your left fingertip to today at your right fingertip. All the way across your midline to well past your right shoulder, life consists of nothing but bacteria. . . .*

The dinosaurs originate in the middle of your right palm and go extinct around your last finger joint. The whole story of Homo sapiens *and our predecessor* Homo erectus *is contained in the thickness of one nail clipping. As for recorded history— as for the Sumerians, the Babylonians, the dynasties of the Pharoahs, the legions of Rome, the Christian Fathers, Troy and the Greeks . . . Napoleon and Hitler, the Beatles and Bill Clinton—they and everyone that knew them are blown away in the dust from one light stroke of a nail-file.*
—Richard Dawkins, *Unweaving the Rainbow*

Supporters of the scientific worldview are sometimes accused of having "faith" in ideas such as evolution and therefore practicing a sort of religion. The less you know, the more reasonable that assertion is. Evolution by natural selection was positively barraged with skepticism throughout the end of the 19th century and well into the 20th. Darwin and Huxley spent the remainder of their lives answering doubts about the theory. And when the dust cleared, the theory remained, intact, beautiful in its inevitability, awe inspiring not because it drew no fire but because it drew the fire and survived spectacularly. That is what is known as the truth, or our best approximation of that elusive concept. It is so precious to get a glimpse of real knowledge, so breathtaking, that no lesser standard than trial by skepticism will do. It leaves behind only those things wonderful enough to make us weep at the pure beauty of their reality and at the equally awesome idea that we could find our way to them at all.

A theologian friend of mine once suggested to me that the metaphors of religion are beautiful "responses to mystery." If the metaphor stepped aside each time a mystery is dispelled by real understanding, ceding the ground of wonder to its successor, there would be no problem with such metaphors. The problem—as illustrated by the creation/evolution "controversy"—is that we fall so deeply in love with our metaphors that we are often unable and unwilling to let go when the time comes and mystery is replaced with knowledge. "If you are awash in lost continents and channeling and UFOs and all the long litany of claims," Carl Sagan said, "you may not have intellectual room for the findings of science. You're sated with wonder." It's this all-too-human tendency that presents a challenge for parents wishing to raise independent thinkers: the magnetic power of the lovely metaphor, standing in the doorway, impeding progress toward

> ❝ We fall so deeply in love with our metaphors that we are often unable and unwilling to let go when the time comes and mystery is replaced with knowledge. ❞

real answers.

The most compelling cases of preferring fact to fiction are the most practical. All the prayer, animal sacrifice, and chanting in the world couldn't cure polio— the Salk vaccine did. And how did we find it? Through rigorous, skeptical, critical thinking and testing and doubting of every proposed solution to the problem of polio until only one solution was left standing. Let others find uncritical acceptance of pretty notions a wonderful thing. I'm more awestruck by the idea of ending polio because someone cared enough to find more wonder in testable reality than in wishful fantasy.

Some would protest, rightly, that science stops at the measurable, that those things that cannot be quantified and calculated are beyond its scope. That's entirely true. But the foundation of reality that science gives us becomes a springboard to the contemplation of those unmeasurables, a starting point from which we dive into the mystery behind that reality. Our reality has astonishing implications and yields incredible mystery, questions upon questions, many of them forever unanswerable. But is it not infinitely better to bathe in what we might call the genuine mystery behind our actual reality, instead of contemplating the "mystery" behind a mythic filial sacrifice, or transubstantiation, or angels dancing on the head of a pin?

It's easy to get a child addicted to real wonders if you start early enough. Simply point them out—they are all around us—and include a few references to what was once thought to be true. Take thunder. Explain that a bolt of lightning rips through the air, zapping trillions of air molecules with energy hotter than the sun. Those superheated molecules explode out of the way with a *crack!* Then the bolt is gone, and all those molecules smash into each other again as they fill in the emptiness it leaves behind. That's the long rumble—waves of air swirling and colliding like surf at the beach.

I find that completely wonder-full.

Then explain that people once thought it was a sound made by an angry god in the sky, and enjoy your child's face as she registers how much less interesting that is.

Repeat steps one and two until college.

■ ■

PARENTING AND THE ARTS

JAMES HERRICK

NOTICE

Persons attempting to find a motive in this narrative will be prosecuted; persons attempting to find a moral in it will be banished; persons attempting to find a plot in it will be shot.

By Order of the Author
Per
G. G., Chief of Ordnance

(On the forepage of Mark Twain's *Huckleberry Finn*)

If you are looking for comfort, if you are looking for consolation, if you want the meaning of life handed to you on a plate—don't go to the arts. Whether it is for parents or children, or their interaction, the arts can disturb and should not avoid the difficult areas of life. But art is not to be feared, for it can also stretch the imagination—art is wonderfully elastic, and it can stir creativity. Art is a wonderful stirrer, and a stirrer of wonder.

I intend to consider art and its effect and value, looking particularly at literature, the art with which I am most engaged. I will refer to four children's/adult texts that seem relevant—*Huckleberry Finn* by Mark Twain, *A Gathering Light* by Jennifer Donnelly, *Northern Lights* by Philip Pullman, and folk tales—a phrase I prefer to *fairy tales*, which sounds effete when in fact the tales are often knotty and tough. I shall consider the range of arts and the range of their practice particularly to children. And I shall conclude by returning to the value in art which we can all take—parents, children, citizens.

For a nonreligious parent or child, art can become an integral part of understanding the world and other people and of creating a meaning in life. Art is not a substitute for religion—no such thing is necessary. But it brings to us all the excitement and danger of being alive, the intensity and delight of love and human relationships, the lasting enhancement of beauty, and the perception of extraordinary wonder.

> 66 Art is not a substitute for religion—no such thing is necessary. But it brings to us all the excitement and danger of being alive, the intensity and delight of love and human relationships, the lasting enhancement of beauty, and the perception of extraordinary wonder. 99

Art is not just challenging—it can be dangerous. Do not enter if you feel queasy. Kafka wrote in his diary of 1916, "If I am condemned, then I am not only condemned to die, but also condemned to struggle till I die." The artist is then condemned to struggle, and to some extent the reader or observer may need to struggle, too. Potted biographies of artists are not much use, but an understanding of the Herculean struggle through which some artists go to hammer out their art is worth having. Humanism is a questing, questioning attitude to life, which may not always be easy.

Humanism in the arts involves looking at communality, diversity, human sympathy, otherness, freedom, and truth.

We are essentially social animals; it is our place in the community that establishes us as living, feeling, thinking people. Some art is social in nature—joining with others to watch a play or a film, which gives a very different experience from watching television or a PlayStation on one's own. Laughter together is a liberating force, and no harm if the laughter is subversive. Singing in a choir or playing in an orchestra or a band or group (both experiences I have had at some stage in my life) are social experiences that require intellectual discipline and deep feeling at the same time.

George Eliot, perhaps the greatest of all British 19th-century novelists, created a complete community in *Middlemarch*. There is a reality to that place and those people that compares with the complete reality of a Dutch painting. Within that town are people struggling: to change the medical establishment, to come to terms with their own dishonesty, to allow great idealism to clash with dry pedantry. Eliot was an agnostic, but one who believed deeply in human values, the power of good. In contrast, Mikhail Bulgakov, a Russian novelist of the first half of the 20th century who fought against repression and censorship, portrayed in *The White Guard* a city in disarray, with civil disorder in the face of the Bolsheviks. But Bulgakov has the long perspective of the artist: "Everything passes away—suffering, pain, blood, hunger and pestilence."

These literary masters create worlds in which human values, ambitions, loyalties, and longings compete—worlds that may then be compared quite meaningfully to our own place and time. In this way, literature can serve much the same purpose for secular audiences as scriptural tales do for the religious, providing narratives upon which we reflect and against which we view our own lives and choices.

Equally important to art are the more individual qualities of universal sympathy and human diversity. If we cannot enlarge our understanding by the scrutiny of others—depicted on screen or canvas, on printed page or raised platform—there is a failure of communication. It is the "otherness" of the world around that is so important. We are easily immersed in ourselves, and this leads to a diminishment of our identity. To be aware of the other—the other people, the other places, the other events—is a creative act. It enhances a sense of awe at the world and, indeed, the universe.

Human diversity is seen abundantly in the texts we will shortly consider. Huck's friendship with the black Jim in *Huckleberry Finn*, and the two gay angels in the trilogy *His Dark Materials* by Pullman illustrate the need for children and adults to accept the variety of the human race. Attempts to stifle this are found in Arthur Miller's play *The Crucible*, where the persecution of supposed witches represents the unacceptability of those who are different and the hysteria in response to threats. Miller wrote of that play, "The tranquility of the bad man lies at the heart not only of moral philosophy but dramaturgy as well."[1] Art does not propose moral answers but does offer moral issues for our consideration.

Art cannot be cheery—it must face the depths. Consider, for instance, the brilliant *If This Is a Man*, in which Italian author Primo Levi gives an account of his experiences in a World War II concentration camp. He has to tell the truth of his awful experience. If parents can face this, so can their children at some stage in their development.

This seems a long way from Twain's *Huckleberry Finn*, but growth and development are characteristics of the three central characters in the three texts I shall look at. Huck, who is certainly not of a good background (his father's a drunk), through his travels along the river, through the types that he meets, through his friendship with the "nigger" Jim, develops an awareness of people and the process of living that he had not had at the beginning. The fact that Jim is described as a "nigger"—now a taboo word, but used regularly at the period of the novel—does not signal a derogatory attitude, for Jim is of pure gold, and when Huck thinks Jim has disappeared "he set down and cried." Weaver, the black youth in *A Gathering Light,* living 50 years later, is outraged by being called a "nigger." Thus, we see the development of language and understanding. And language is important to all the texts, Twain being particularly good at expressing the vernacular and Mattie in *A Gathering Light* being a person to whom words are life.

Although Twain wants no moral to his story, he is excellent at portraying the ethical ambivalence Huck inhabits, especially when he decides to help Jim escape from slavery. It is worth remembering that *Huckleberry Finn* was regarded as a subversive book in its day. Pullman's trilogy has likewise caused controversy, particularly in the opposition to religion. The river that is Huck's highway has a largeness and a power that we hold in awe. And Huck and Jim, when they lie looking at the stars, discuss whether they are made or "just happened."

A Gathering Light by Jennifer Donnelly is a remarkable recent novel set at the beginning of the 20th century in a subsistence farming community in New York State. The central character is Mattie, who plays with words and wants to be a writer. A teacher encourages her and tells her that books are dangerous. We need to focus on the fact that art is dangerous. The teacher is herself a poet who has fallen foul of the Comstock Act (which was aimed at suppressing "obscene literature") and faced censorship. (I am reminded of a recent report of the banning of the Cassell *Dictionary of Slang* in a North Carolina school, under pressure from conservative Christian groups.) Parents, let your children explore—and especially explore words.

Like Huck, Mattie has an important interracial friendship. Hers is with Weaver, who, like Mattie, wants a college education. She asks him, "Why aren't people plain and uncomplicated? Why don't they do what you expect them to do, like characters in a novel?" The best novels are not like that. Mattie is unexpected in many ways: her falling in love with a simple would-be farmer, her toughness in seeing her family through illness, her choice of a new word every day from a dictionary, her loyalty to the poor in the community. Rightly, because novels should leave questions, not answer them, we do not know for sure what success she will have.

Northern Lights, the first of Pullman's trilogy, is an "other world" novel where all the characters have demons attached to them for support and where the enemy is the church; at the end of this volume there is the hope of the end of centuries of darkness. Lyra, the central character, is resourceful, imaginative, and determined.* One of the novel's strengths is the great diversity of characters. In a later volume, there is a couple of gay angels of great charm. Just as Huck is aware of the power of the river, so Lyra, when looking at the Aurora, the northern lights, feels "it was so beautiful it was almost holy."

Folk tales are often told to young children, but they have resonance for parents as well. Tales such as *The Arabian Nights* have a richness and wonder, delineating the magic and unexpected in life and reminding us of the richness of Islamic culture. Grimm's tales are much darker, including children who might be shoved into an oven and eaten, the threat of being boiled to death by a witch, the loss of sight when jumping from a tower into thorns. Freud and his disciples had a field day with these tales. Some say they are too grim for children—but children do have dark fantasies and dreams, and it helps them to accept them, or make sense of them, to have them read to them in a controlled way. And the darkness is often followed by an ingenious rescue. Angela Carter, the novelist and storyteller, has praised Perrault, the French fairy story writer, for his "consummate craftsmanship and his good-natured cynicism. . . . From the work of this humane, tolerant and kind-hearted Frenchman, children can learn enlightened self-interest . . . and gain much pleasure besides."[2]

Other arts are equally important. Music, theater, film, and other visual arts are all valuable for young and old alike. There have been increasing attempts at outreach by professional artists into schools and community groups. As an example, a group of difficult adolescent youths were taken for some weeks dancing—creating a dance drama. They went back to class completely transformed and ready to learn. Journalist Will Hutton has pointed out that "today's society does not equip boys with the emotional intelligence to come to terms with their feelings."[3] Schools and families can be harsh and lacking in understanding. They need more democracy and participation and listening—and more artistic activity. Music, for example, teaches

> " Schools and families can be harsh and lacking in understanding. They need more democracy and participation and listening—and more artistic activity. "

---

*See Shannon and Matthew Cherry, "Doule Vision: Teaching Our Twins Pride and Respect," in chapter 4 for another appearance of Lyra.

self-discipline, working together with others, perseverance, cooperation—and gives great rewards. Why, then, has musical education declined? The state should encourage arts in schools and homes, partly
because it pays off in producing balanced, imaginative citizens, and
partly because it leads to fulfilled individuals.

W. H. Auden points the right way in the poem "Leap Before You
Look":

> *The sense of danger must not disappear:*
> *The way is certainly both short and steep,*
> *However gradual it looks from here;*
> *Look if you like, but you will have to leap.*[4]

Danger is important to life and to art, as we have seen. There is the
need to leap into the arts as well as into life.

I finish with Thoreau on the value of knowledge and the arts and
sciences—and then ultimately the value of not knowing.

KNOWLEDGE
> *Men say they know many things;*
> *But lo! They have taken wings—*
> *The arts and sciences,*
> *And a thousand appliances;*
> *The wind that blows*
> *Is all that anybody knows.*[5]

*JIM HERRICK worked for 30 years in the humanist movement in the
United Kingdom. He is former editor of* New Humanist *and* Interna-
tional Humanist. *His writings include* Vision and Realism: A Hundred
Years of The Freethinker; Against the Faith: Some Deists, Skeptics and
Atheists; *and* Humanism: An Introduction. *He is a cofounder of the
Gay and Lesbian Humanist Association and has written theater reviews
regularly for various journals. Now retired, Jim writes, gardens, and
plays the oboe.*

■ ■

ADDITIONAL RESOURCES FOR "WONDERING AND QUESTIONING"

Dawkins, Richard. *The Magic of Reality: How We Know What's Really True*. Free Press, 2011. A brilliant and accessible introduction to what we know about the universe around us and how we came to know it. Built around the real, hard-won answers to 12 big questions. Hardcover edition (2011) includes illustrations; 2012 paperback is text only. Ages twelve and up.

Harris, Annaka. *I Wonder*. Four Elephants Press, 2013. A tribute to curiosity by the cofounder (with husband Sam Harris) of Project Reason, this lovely book reinforces the simple virtue of wondering. Preschool and up.

Stock, Gregory. *The Kids' Book of Questions*. Workman, 2015. A kids' version of the classic *Book of Questions* for adults, this is a collection of more than 200 open-ended questions to get kids to articulate their own values and preferences: "If you could change one thing about your parents, what would it be?" "If you knew you wouldn't get caught, would you cheat by copying answers on a test?" Several are great conversation-starters for religious questioning: "Of all the things you've heard about God and religion, what do you think is true and what do you think is just a story?" "Do you believe in God? If not, why do you think so many people do?" Ages eight–eighteen.

Law, Stephen. *The Complete Philosophy Files*. Orion, 2011. An excellent introduction to philosophical questions in engaging dialogic form.

Clayton, John C. *Alexander Fox and the Amazing Mind Reader*. Prometheus, 1998. A con man calling himself Mr. Mystikos has come to town, telling fortunes, reading minds, knowing things he couldn't possibly know about the people of the town—and parting the gullible townsfolk from their cash. Young Alexander Fox is plenty impressed at first—until he starts thinking carefully. A terrific illustration of the power of skepticism. For years after reading it, you're kids will turn to you every time they see a faith healer or other huckster on TV and say, "It's Mr. Mystikos!" Ages six–ten.

Law, Stephen. *The War for Children's Minds*. Routledge, 2006. In this powerful book that has been called "a defense of the philosophically liberal life," Stephen Law calls for a rejection both of right-wing demands for a return to authoritarian religious morality and postmodern relativism. He advocates instead that children be educated in ethics based in the philosophy of the Enlightenment. For adults.

Cool and Wonder-Inducing YouTube Channels (Search by Name)

- **Smarter Every Day**—An engineer puts himself through every imaginable kind of experiment. Search for a special favorite of mine: The Backwards Brain Bicycle.

- **ASAP Science**—Obsessively watchable white board videos about basic (and not so basic) questions in science.

- **Minute Physics**—More brilliant whiteboard videos, this time on more serious questions, like whether you can outrun a fart, what happens when you die—that kind of thing.

- **Vsauce**—There's just no describing it. Fun, fascinating, awesomely edited videos on such questions as, "Will we ever run out of new music?"; "Is your red the same as my red?"; and "What if everyone jumped at once?"

- **Kurzgesagt/In a Nutshell**—Complex ideas explained amazingly well with great animations and voice-over.

- **Captain Disillusion**—A quick, smart, fun debunking of all kinds of visual trickery, from faked videos and photos to magic tricks and other phenomena.

. . . and One on Its Own Site

- **The Kid Should See This** (http://thekidshouldseethis.com/)—Rion Nakaya is not a content creator but a brilliant search-and-collector of the best videos on the web "for curious minds of all ages." Her mantra, "We don't underestimate kids around here," captures it perfectly: Instead of the usual dumbed-down, condescending content intended for children, most of the 2,400-plus videos curated on the site were "not made for kids, but perfect for them." Trust me, this one is a gem.

CHAPTER

7

Community and Identity

INTRODUCTION

Two are better than one, because they have a good reward for their toil. For if they fall, one will lift up the other; but woe to one who is alone when he falls and does not have another to help.

—Eccl 4:9–10

There's plenty of bad advice in the Bible, but when the authors of Ecclesiastes said two are better than one, they were on to something. After three chapters bemoaning God's fixed plan for humanity—"it is an unhappy business that God has given to human beings to be busy with—all is vanity and a chasing after wind"—they offer this glimpse of nothing less than humanist community. Toil all you want under God's blind eye, they say—but if you expect support when you fall, you have only each other to turn to.

We need each other. Prolonged isolation is, for most of us, one of the most difficult ordeals to endure. Not for nothing is solitary confinement sometimes considered cruel and unusual. Occasional solitude can be a precious gift—but if it goes on too long, it can begin to erode our sense of ourselves, since much of that ongoing definition takes place relative to our fellow human beings.

One of the great advantages of membership in a religious community is in that second word, *community*: the ability to surround oneself with an extended family, others who care for, support, nurture, and encourage one's own way through the world, who lift each other up when they fall. This chapter focuses on the many ways such community can be achieved without compromising what we hold to be true.

Among the more interesting developments in this area is nontheistic religion. You read that right: religious organizations without gods. Theology is only one part of the religious impulse, as you've known now for 300 pages or so. There's the predefined set of values, the common lexicon and symbology, rites of passage, a means of engendering wonder, comforting answers to the big questions, and consoling explanations to ease experiences of hardship and loss—and an established community in which to experience these benefits. Most Christians attend church not to worship but to enjoy these benefits. "God" is simply the frame in which these concepts are hung. Remove the frame, and the beautiful picture—which is the point of it all, of course—remains.

We've mentioned Unitarian Universalism in passing more than once, a denomination that grew out of two separate heresies: Unitarianism (the idea that God is one thing, not three) and Universalism (the notion that everyone is loved equally by God and that all receive salvation). They merged in the 1960s as one of the most liberal Christian denominations, opening their doors to all people regardless of belief, but by the 1990s had become majority nontheistic. The specific character varies tremendously from one UU fellowship to another, but having visited more than a dozen, I can make the following observations: UUs tend to be wonderfully warm, welcoming, and relaxed people; though creedless, they are powerful social activists, opposing violence and supporting civil rights for all; and most fellowships give no special place to Christian teaching or symbols—some even avoiding them entirely. Religious literacy is an important part of the UU fellowship—not indoctrination, but study and appreciation, the kind of approach that makes religion downright interesting rather than threatening. Again, by recognizing the validity of many expressions of humanness, you deny any one of them the high ground.

Another example of nontheistic religion is Secular Humanistic Judaism, a fully secular expression of Jewish culture founded 50 years ago by Rabbi Sherwin Wine. Most readers will be familiar with the idea of cultural Jewishness. Humanistic Judaism provides a unifying community for this expression—again, the beautiful picture without the obsolete frame.

There has been a strong revival of interest in a third (essentially) nontheistic religion: Liberal Quakers. And the reason is wonderful. Millions of people have taken the Belief-O-Matic quiz (at www.beliefnet.com), only to discover that their beliefs identify them not with the Methodist, Baptist, Episcopal, Catholic, or Lutheran churches to which their families and offerings go, but with the Liberal Quakers. Quaker organizations have reported as much as an eightfold increase in inquiries since the Belief-O-Matic went online. And that's good news, since Liberal Quakers believe that one's beliefs cannot be dictated by another person—one's relationship with whatever reality there is is one's own and cannot be mediated. In other words, no indoctrination, no evangelism, no dogmatic nonsense—just another community devoted to nonviolence, positive social action, building community, and alleviating suffering. While Southern Baptists were forming their denomination around the biblical support of slavery, Quakers were among the most prominent abolitionists. While Catholics in the United States represented the single largest organized opposition to women's voting rights, Quakers were in the streets getting arrested in defense of those rights. Quakers have been in the forefront of every antiwar movement. Funny what the absence of dogma will do.

Many Quaker schools have been established around the United States, and freethinkers should feel entirely comfortable if they choose to enroll their children there. They will be exposed to models of positive moral action, not indoctrination.

Finally there is the Ethical Culture movement, "a humanistic religious and educational movement inspired by the ideal that the supreme aim of human life is working to create a more humane society."[1] Like UUs, Ethical Culture societies focus on service to the community, encouraging the knowledge, practice, and love of ethical behavior and deepening the collective sense of the spiritual—again, without supernatural overtones.

If every church in America began its service this week with the announcement that the congregation would continue meeting every Sunday, continue singing songs and sharing hopes and offering solace and acceptance and the occasional chance to do good works and to be a part of something larger than oneself, but that these tokens of love and joy and togetherness would henceforth be directed to each other rather than to the idea of a god—after the initial shock and rending of garments, I honestly doubt it would take long to adjust.

Most people attend church first and foremost for humanistic reasons, not to worship an abstraction. And if that's the part of religion we really need, a nontheistic religion might not be such an oxymoron after all. "A passionate and committed atheism can be more religious than a weary or inadequate theism," says religious historian Karen Armstrong, who further quotes Albert Camus's deeply humanistic assertion that "people should reject God defiantly in order to pour out all their loving solicitude upon mankind."* It is to that passionate, committed vision of loving human community that this chapter is devoted.

Then there's identity. . . .

In 2011, I posted this question on the Parenting Beyond Belief Facebook page: "How do you help your kids achieve a sense of belonging?" I'd been thinking about this as my son, Connor, entered high school. He seemed a little disconnected from others in an unhelpful way.

The comment thread quickly devolved into two camps. Some expressed outrage at the question. It brings to mind tribalism, division, us versus them. One said, "This doesn't sound like something an atheist parent should even ask! It sounds like a question from a religious parent!" Another said it was "very disappointing. I'm a member of the human race, that's all I need."

Yeah, I always loved that idea. I'm a member of the human race, a citizen of the world. Leave all that toxic parochialism behind. "The world is my country, all mankind are my brethren, and to do good is my religion." Thomas Paine. Imagine there're no countries . . . and no religion, too. This is the dream, right?

But the other half of the thread said, "Yes, please. This is a big issue for us. We really struggle with this. I'd love to see this discussed." And for all the good things we did for our kids, I think we didn't consider early enough how we could help them establish the part of their identity that tangibly connects them to other people.

I'm not a social person myself, not a belonger. I'm an introvert and perfectly happy that way. I'd rather spend three hours in a book than one hour at a party. So when I rejected religion intellectually, I was also able to walk away from the social and emotional benefits, the multilayered sense of belonging that religious people enjoy, just because of who I am.

---

*Both quotes are from Karen Armstrong's *A History of God*.

There's been some great sociology done about the benefits of congregational life. You know the old finding that churchgoers are happier than nonchurchgoers? A 2010 study put an asterisk on that.

The people with the highest life satisfaction were churchgoers with close friends in the congregation. Next were nonchurchgoers. The lowest level of life satisfaction in the study: churchgoers without close friends in the congregation.

One of the researchers said, "[The life satisfaction boost] is almost entirely about the social aspect of religion, rather than theology. People are more satisfied with their lives when they go to church IF they build a social network within their congregation and gather on a regular basis for activities that are meaningful to the group. The sense of belonging seems to be the key to the relationship between church attendance and life satisfaction."[2]

Though most of the time I'm satisfied with being a "citizen of the world," there are other times when I've felt vulnerable and alone—and I just couldn't wrap my mind around the whole world. I needed a subset of humanity to turn to, a community within that whole that I could identify with. And that is what we need to help our kids find as well.

Music ensembles can do this for kids. So can sports. Clubs built around shared interests. Volunteering. All of these are examples of gathering on a regular basis to participate in meaningful activities that connect us to others. And they can all serve to supplement our humanist philosophy with a positive tribe of passion and purpose.

Belonging isn't just a religious thing—it's a human thing that religion has addressed. And just like charity, and the search for meaning, and meditation, and comfort in times of loss, and all sorts of other valuable things, we need to help kids in nonreligious families find other ways to satisfy that need to connect with others.

Writer and journalist Katherine Ozment begins our final chapter by addressing the question of identity in a nonreligious context: what it is, why it matters, and how we can help our kids find it when they need it. Sociologist Phil Zuckerman, whose books *Society Without God* and *Living the Secular Life* have provided invaluable insights into secular community, addresses that aspect of the search for context and belonging without religion.

Amanda Metskas and August Brunsman return with an update on Camp Quest, the summer camp for kids of nonreligious families.

Finally, the inspiring force of nature that is Sanderson Jones, cofounder of the Sunday Assembly movement, introduces that extraordinary development in secular community and invites us all to participate.

Religious community builds on millennia of tradition, rooted in the age when humanity believed a supernatural intelligence was running the show. By comparison, the effort to create secular community—to come together as a loving, compassionate human family in the light of our new understanding of reality—is in its infancy. More than anything, this chapter can serve as an invitation for you to join courageous people like Sanderson, Amanda, August, Katherine, Unitarian Universalists, Humanistic Judaism, Nontheist Friends, and all the rest who are working not to displace religion but to provide secular alternatives for the growing numbers who have set religion aside.

■ ■ ■ ■ ■ ■ ■ ■ ■ ■ ■ ■ ■

"WHAT ARE WE?"

KATHERINE OZMENT

When I was growing up, most of the kids in my neighborhood were from Italian-Catholic families. They had long, musical last names and skin that tanned easily in the summer. Little crucifixes hung on the walls in their houses. And every Sunday morning their families piled into their station wagons and drove off to attend Mass. On Sunday mornings, my two older brothers and I stayed home. We'd drag our comforters from our bedrooms into the living room and camp out in our pajamas all morning, watching *Scooby Doo* and playing cards. Later I'd go outside with my mother to help her weed the garden or tend the tomato plants. We were Christian—a mix of Presbyterian and Methodist, to be exact—but not the churchgoing kind.

Though I couldn't have articulated it then, I envied my Catholic friends their strong ties to religion and ethnic heritage. Their families had something mine didn't: a place to go on Sundays, a set of beliefs and practices, and a tether to their roots that seemed stronger and more lasting than my own. They were something, and that something gave structure and meaning to their Sundays, perhaps their entire lives.

I had no idea where my own family had come from any farther back than my grandparents' small town in Arkansas. My father once pronounced, apropos of nothing, that we were of Turkish origin, *Oz* being a common Turkish prefix. I was thrilled for the few months before he recanted, saying his research indicated that we sprang from Germany instead, which was a little less exciting. Meanwhile, my mother's side of the family clung to the belief that we were descended from a dark-eyed Cherokee princess, an idea I brought out at cocktail parties in my twenties to easy "oohs" and "aahs." (That was until I met an actual Cherokee leader for a research paper I was writing in graduate school, and he told me that such false claims were so common among whites that they were widely ridiculed among Native Americans.)

I was left to embrace the bland and clunky *Protestant*, a word my father used to describe us when I asked why we didn't go to Mass and after-school religion classes like so many of the other kids in our neighborhood. When my parents divorced, my mother and I joined a

Presbyterian church. I didn't believe the church teachings, and warbling through the hymns was an exercise in awkwardness for an already awkward teen. But I dutifully memorized the Nicene Creed and studied the Bible and was confirmed in a white dress on a bright spring day. I loved having a label and telling people what I was. It meant that I was something after all.

But as the years went on, that something thinned. For some reason, organized religion never really took with me. By the time I entered my thirties, married a secular Jew, and had children, I'd stopped calling myself Christian, Protestant, or Presbyterian—really anything at all. For a long time I forgot how much I longed for a label to describe who I was, what I valued, and where I fit. Then one night, when my son was nine, we were watching a religious procession across the street, and I explained that the people holding candles and singing songs were Greek Orthodox, and that this was their tradition. When he asked, "What are we?" I racked my brain for an answer before blurting out, "Nothing."

I felt terrible about it, like I had let him down. He was longing for an answer—for a name—and I couldn't give him one. Didn't my son need a clear label for himself, as I had once wanted a name for myself? Without religion, I wasn't sure where to find the same strong sense of identity.

Perhaps it's not too embarrassing in this day and age to say that I first turned to the Internet for answers. I found a website called Belief.net and took the Belief-O-Matic quiz, which promised to tell me what I was. Within minutes of answering the series of questions about my beliefs and values, I received an email with my answer. I was a Secular Humanist, 100 percent. It was a strange feeling. I'd heard the words before but didn't really know what they meant. And yet I was 100 percent of this thing I didn't understand. How could that be? Had it been lurking beneath my skin all these years, just waiting for me to discover it? Why hadn't I found it before?

For the next three years I wrote a book exploring secular humanism, a philosophy that values human life here and now, science, reason, and protecting the earth. I visited secular humanist communities, partook in secular rituals, and learned its rich history. I also studied other nonreligious or quasi-religious groups: Ethical Culture, Humanistic Judaism, Unitarian Universalism, and a range of more individualized pursuits among the atheist, agnostic, and spiritual-but-not-religious set that makes up a growing proportion of the country. As I set off to visit the community meetings of these various groups, I felt the way I always imagined my Italian-Catholic friends felt when they piled into their station wagons and headed to Mass: like I had somewhere to be, a people to join hands with, a way to express who I was and what I valued outside the confines of my own family and home.

I soon realized that I wasn't alone. Millions of Americans were wrestling with the loss of religious identity and a desire to form new language and labels to encompass the complexity of who they are. I realized, too, that my striving to find the right label for myself was really a wish to belong to some larger, lasting whole. But I'd been going about it all wrong. My attempts to adopt an identity—Turkish, Presbyterian, Cherokee princess descendant, or the many others I tried and discarded through the years—were a backward approach. What I needed to consider first was what I believed and valued—not try to glom onto the values and beliefs of others. The reason the Belief-O-Matic quiz worked was that it started with my own answers to the questions, not someone else's answers.

> " My attempts to adopt an identity—Turkish, Presbyterian, Cherokee princess descendant . . . was a backward approach. What I needed to consider first was what I believed and valued—not try to glom onto the values and beliefs of others. "

What I found in the humanist communities I visited was a kind of radical acceptance I hadn't experienced before. Those people, I realized, were my people because I could be myself. I learned through exploring the rich landscape of secular humanism that we don't have to satisfy ourselves with identities that don't fit, and there is no one group that can answer every question you have or pang that you feel. Maybe, as more and more people leave religion, and the walls that have long separated us start to fall, we'll find that a more fluid sense of identity is not necessarily a bad thing.

> " What I found in the humanist communities I visited was a kind of radical acceptance I hadn't experienced before. "

A year and a half ago, my family and I moved from Boston to Chicago. My husband and I worried that our kids, ages four, nine, and twelve, would struggle to fit in in our new city. And, in the beginning, there were middle-of-the-night wakings, dramatic door-slammings, and tears (so many tears!). But then something wonderful began to happen. Each of our children, in his or her own way, started to find that sense of belonging. And my husband and I also started to find the pieces and the people that make up a home.

We are lucky. We live in a neighborhood that fits us. Our part of the city is dominated by a university but also by a distinctive culture that values what we value: diversity, education, reason, charity. And so we found belonging in that: a neighborhood that valued our secular humanism. And our kids feel that sense of belonging even as they continue to unfold into their own people, with identities all their own.

At first, our younger daughter approached her preschool classroom tentatively, with arms wrapped tightly around my legs and tears pooling in the corners of her eyes. But then there was a classroom tortoise and a kind teacher and girls who loved Disney princesses as much as she did. Soon she was shoving me out the door when I dropped her off at school, and friends were taping pictures of hearts and rainbows on her cubby door.

Our older daughter finds a sense of belonging in midair. In the first week after we arrived, I took her to a gymnastics tryout at the place we hoped would be her new gym. I watched her walk tentatively across the expanse of blue carpet toward a coach she'd never met. She touched his elbow from behind, and when he turned she raised her hand in a shy half wave and mumbled her name. A year and a half later, she cheers the loudest at team meets, laughs with the girls around their lockers after practice, and says she would sleep at the gym if she could. Recently she told me that she has three religions: Christianity, Judaism, and Gymnastics.

> 66 Our older daughter finds a sense of belonging in midair. 99

Our son, who wondered what we were, shows us every day. Recently I was sitting in the bleachers watching his seventh-grade basketball team play its last game of the season, and I was struck by how comfortable he looked on the court, a feeling hard won through years of practices and games. When he dribbles, he does this dramatic shoulder roll that makes him look like he's trying to drive the ball through the floorboards of the court. He loves to fake to the left then drive right. And his defense is tenacious.

The team won by a single point at the buzzer that night, and the boys leaped into the air and embraced midcourt, crushing each other to the floor as they whooped and yelled. Without thinking, I jumped up and raised my arms in the air, shouting myself nearly hoarse. And why wouldn't I? My son had built something inside himself that he could take to any court, anywhere and feel like he belonged. If he ever felt homesick, this was one way to quell it. If he needed community, he could start with this.

They say you have to lose the self to feel ecstatic transcendence. But you have to find yourself first. Saint Paul converted to Christianity when he fell off his donkey on the road to Damascus. It seemed to me that a cold, hard, metal gym bench was at least as humble a starting point. Years ago, when my son had asked me what we were, I shouldn't have searched outside our window for an answer or even gone on the Internet to find out. I should have turned to him and said, "You tell me."

KATHERINE OZMENT's *work has appeared in the* New York Times, Salon, *and* Fitness. *She is the author of* Grace Without God: The Search for Meaning, Purpose, and Belonging in a Secular Age *(HarperWave, 2016).*

■ ■

BEING SECULAR, FINDING COMMUNITY

PHIL ZUCKERMAN, Ph.D.

In 1897, David Emile Durkheim published the first great work of empirical sociology, *Suicide*. Rife with theoretical insights and oozing with data, the underlying argument was that those societies characterized by a high degree of individualism have significantly higher rates of suicide, while those societies characterized by a high degree of social integration have significantly lower rates of suicide. In other words, when people are not well connected to others and don't have lots of social interactions, there is a higher chance of self-destruction. And conversely, when people have lots of social connections and ongoing interactions with others, the likelihood of suicide goes down. Individualism, it seems, can be hazardous to your health.

Today, we know that a major buffer against potentially dangerous anomie and alienation is a high degree of social capital—positive social networks, social connections, and friendly/neighborly relations—all of which correlate with various indicators of healthy human flourishing.

The fact that humans thrive amid other humans and suffer when away from other humans makes bioevolutionary sense. After all, we have always been pack animals. We evolved in groups, and it has been in groups—and as groups—that we have always existed and developed. Individual isolation has often meant not merely loneliness and boredom but much worse—when we are all alone, we typically go insane. So being with other people has always been pretty damn crucial to our species' health and well-being.

For centuries, religion has met humanity's need for community head-on. Religion has been a major source of establishing a sense of group belonging, reinforcing that sense of belonging with rituals and traditions, maintaining that sense of belonging via the organic development of heritage and intergenerational ties, and ultimately making people feel like they are part of a loving, purposeful, meaningful communal endeavor that existed before them and will continue to exist after they are gone.

Consider, for example, a local church in my neighborhood where several of my friends are members. OK, first off, you've got the big building, with its impressive architecture. Then there is the community garden out back, dubbed "Peace and Carrots." The church also has a large gym with a basketball court where games are played on a regular basis. Sometimes they hold a dance or banquet in there as well. The church also hosts a monthly dinner for local college students. There are also women's groups that gather regularly. And men's groups. And youth groups. And fireside chat groups. And an elder/retirees group. There is also an LGBT group. And a "going green" environmental action group. And a social justice group. There is also a preschool. There are also frequent cultural events, such as musical concerts, guest lectures by professors, readings by poets and authors, and hands-on workshops led by local or visiting artists. There's a book club that meets once a week, and a cinema club that also meets once a week. As for charity—there are a host of ongoing charitable events throughout every year, which allow people to donate time and/or money to various causes of goodwill. Indeed, an underlying ethical imperative of compassion undergirds this entire congregation; people feel like their ongoing involvement with this congregation has a deep moral meaning and significant purpose beyond their own individual needs and desires. There is also a sense of history and heritage that pervades the place; many of the people there are third- and fourth-generation members whose grandparents or great-grandparents founded the church. Oh, and there are also worship services with a lot of stuff about God and Jesus. Prayer is big at this church. As is baptism. And the Bible. And sin. And salvation. Amen.

Clearly, the need for meaningful communal engagement is one of the main reasons people are religious. In fact, I suspect that many people are actively religious not because of God, Jesus, fear of hell, or philosophical questions but simply because they like being part of a religious community and the security, comfort, and camaraderie that it sustains. And they are right to enjoy it; numerous studies have shown that people who are regularly involved in religious communities experience higher levels of subjective well-being and lower levels of depression than the unaffiliated. Being congregationally affiliated seems to be good for you.

So what if you want to experience all the goodness and well-being that comes along with religious involvement—but you simply can't stomach all the nonsense about God, Jesus, prayer, heaven, hell, etc.? What can people do who want to experience community, but without the supernatural nonsense?

To be frank, there's no readily available, easy solution here. There are no obvious, well-established secular equivalents to the kind of "Peace and Carrots" church some of my friends attend. That said, if I had to give advice to secular folks seeking community but without the supernatural nonsense, here are my best suggestions:

1. **Join a religious congregation where God and other supernatural elements are minimal, marginal, or nonexistent.** The top contender here would be a Unitarian Universalist congregation. The vibe of UU congregations certainly varies from town to town; some are more "spiritual" than others. But the few UU congregations that I have visited were notable for their lack of reference to God or anything supernatural, their lack of concern about an afterlife, and a focus on ethical conduct and charitable works, positive children's programs and youth groups, great hymns (often about morning dew), great live music (covers of "Imagine" and the like), and a sense of belonging to a larger network of over 1,000 UU congregations nationwide, many of which have existed for a long time; indeed, there is a real sense of heritage and history. You'll also find a large proportion of atheists, agnostics, and humanists in the aisles. A second possibility would be to join a Humanistic Judaism congregation. Humanistic Judaism congregations celebrate Jewish culture and heritage, but without any supernatural elements. No God. No prayer. Just holiday fun, humanistic rituals, charitable opportunities, family time, talks and lectures, singing, eating, and schmoozing. Being Jewish is not necessary to join, but rather an openness to being part of the community.

2. **Join Sunday Assembly.** Founded by British humanists Pippa Evans and Sanderson Jones in 2013, Sunday Assembly now has approximately 500 congregations in over 30 cities worldwide. They usually meet one Sunday a month, and these gatherings are all about creating a religion-like communal experience but without anything supernatural. You get songs, sermons (in the form of educational talks about some humanistic theme), charitable opportunities, and an upbeat atmosphere, but without the God stuff. And there's cake and coffee after each meeting, of course.

3. **Join the Ethical Movement, also known as the Ethical Culture Society.** Founded back in the 1800s by Felix Adler, Ethical Societies are focused on supporting one another to be better people, making

the world a better place, and meeting regularly for educational and communal fellowship. Most congregations are in the New York area, but others can be found in Chicago, Baltimore, and Austin, etc.

4. **Join or create a humanist meetup group.** According to my latest perusal of humanism.meetup.com, there are over 330,000 individuals signed up online and more than 1,000 different groups to choose from. Humanist Hikers of Southern California has more than 2,500 members, Houston Atheists has 2,800, Phoenix Atheists has more than 2,500, Seattle Atheists/Agnostics has more than 2,300—and there are many more out there, of varying types. And there are humanist meetup groups that specifically cater to people of color, people of different sexual orientations, and so on.

5. **Get involved with a secular humanist organization.** There are plenty to pick from, including Center for Inquiry, American Humanists Association, Council for Secular Humanism, Americans United for the Separation of Church and State, Secular Coalition of America, Freedom From Religion Foundation, Skeptic Society, American Atheists, and African Americans for Humanism. If you've got kids, then getting involved in your local Camp Quest—a summer camp for the children of atheists, agnostics, humanists, and freethinkers—is highly encouraged.

6. **Pursue a hobby with a decidedly social element.** Consider your local community theater. Join a sports team or get involved with your child's sports team. Join a biking, hiking, or dancing group. Join a book club. A quilting group. An orchestra or band. Something that involves more than doing some activity by yourself.

7. **Social justice.** Get involved in an organization that is focused on ending inequality; or protecting the environment; or fighting racism, sexism, or homophobia; or advocating for workers' rights or the rights of children; or improving our nation's prisons.

It is essential to recognize, however, that none of the possibilities above is perfect. For example, the UU congregation in your neighborhood may talk about the soul or the spirit more than you like. The Ethical Culture group may be too intellectual for your tastes. American Atheists may not have a youth group. The secular meetup group in your area may just be a bunch of white guys in their 50s griping about religion—not that there's anything wrong with that, but if it's not what you're looking for, well, you know.

Personally, I have found a very enriching community through playing soccer every Sunday morning. There's a pickup game in my neighborhood for men and women in their 40s—or thereabout—that has been going on for over a decade. I've been playing every week for these past three years and loving it. I've made new friends, many from different ethnicities, races, and class backgrounds. I've gotten in better shape. And I really enjoy the way it punctuates my weekend with fresh air, sweat, and competitive camaraderie. But it certainly isn't the perfect substitute for a religious congregation—it isn't something my spouse or kids share in; there is no sense of history, heritage, or ritual; and there's no altruism or charity taking place.

Finding and creating communities that are equivalent to religious communities—but without the supernaturalism—may, in fact, be one of the greatest challenges facing the growing population of secular people today. The very real possibility of iPads, iPods, smartphones, and computers sucking away every last waking hour of our lives— and the concomitant diminishing of social capital that breeds—looms large. And without the purposeful, structured gathering of people, across generations, for the sake of ritualizing life's transitions, sustaining traditions, deepening ethical commitments, and providing cake and coffee in the courtyard, secular life will be ever so emptier and less humane.

PHIL ZUCKERMAN, Ph.D., is a professor of sociology and secular studies at Pitzer College. He is the author of several books, including Living the Secular Life *(Penguin, 2014) and* Society Without God *(New York University Press, 2008).*

■ ■

SUMMER CAMP BEYOND BELIEF

AMANDA K. METSKAS
AND AUGUST E. BRUNSMAN IV

Summer camp. Ahh, the thought brings back memories: swimming in the lake, toasting marshmallows, riding horses, meeting new friends, singing songs around the campfire. Many of us recall fondly our summer camp experiences as kids. For most of us, those camps probably had some religious component, as minor as prayers before meals and "Kumbaya" around the campfire, or as involved as daily chapel and Bible study. If only parents could give their kids all of the positive benefits of summer camp—and there are many—without the accompanying religious messages. While in some parts of the country, particularly the Northeast and West Coast, parents may find comprehensive summer camps that fit this bill, in many other parts of the country, options like this may be practically nonexistent. It was with this in mind that Camp Quest, the first residential summer camp in the United States for children from nonreligious families, was founded in 1996.[1]

Sending kids off to summer camp is an American tradition stretching back over 140 years.[2] According to a study commissioned by the American Camping Association and conducted by Philliber Research Associates, the camp experience makes kids more comfortable trying new things, increases their ability to make new friends, allows them to develop independence and maturity, and increases their self-esteem.[3] "For many children, sleep-away camp is the first time they have been away from home for any appreciable amount of time. The weeks at camp become a chance to grow up—at least a little," reports Dr. Marie Hartwell-Walker.[4]

Despite these benefits, the nature of summer camp in America is changing, with an increasing number of specialty camps devoted to helping kids develop skills in an activity they are already interested in, such as soccer or horseback riding. As one *Washington Post* columnist complained, "Whatever happened to camp camp?"[5] Summer camps are also dealing with increased pressure from parents to be in touch with their kids while they are at camp, including parents who hide cell phones in their camper's suitcases, hoping counselors won't find the banned electronic devices.[6] Both of these developments potentially threaten the benefits that a traditional comprehensive summer camp provides kids—independence, self-esteem, and a chance to try new things.

At Camp Quest, children experience all sorts of activities common to traditional summer camps—horseback riding, swimming, arts and crafts, canoeing, ropes courses, singing songs by the campfire—all in an environment free from the pervasive religious messages in the rest of American society. But Camp Quest isn't just a traditional summer camp minus God. In addition to typical activities, campers there learn about famous freethinkers from around the world. These include people they may have heard of, like Thomas Jefferson and James Madison, the deist authors of the U.S. Constitution, and people they may be less familiar with, like A. Philip Randolph, an African American civil rights leader who organized the March on Washington at which Martin Luther King Jr. gave his famous "I Have a Dream" speech. Kids learn that there are many people like their families, people who are skeptical of religious belief and have done great things. It gives them people to look up to and lets them know that they and their families are not alone.

Camp Quest also focuses on critical thinking, scientific reasoning, and ethics. Campers are given challenges where they work together as a cabin to design and perform a skit that answers a question given to them on the opening night. Past questions include, "Did some being design our planet and us? Wouldn't it take an intelligence of some sort or other to put together something as complicated as living things? Many say there are no other possible good explanations for how we got here. Is that true? What do you think, and why?" and "Let's say that you could start everything all over again. Imagine that you suddenly have no rules or laws of any kind. Imagine that you have no countries and no religions—but that you do have many different races and many different languages. Please make up 10 rules that everyone on the planet Earth would have to obey at all times. These must be rules everyone will agree with, and they must be rules that will make life better for everyone all the time." While the questions may be serious and lead to serious discussion in the cabins, the skits that result are often hilarious and entertain the entire camp at the closing campfire.

Other Camp Quest programs involve discussions with campers about what they tell their friends about their beliefs and how they handle situations like saying the Pledge of Allegiance at school. Counselors leading these discussions serve only as moderators, giving the kids a chance to talk about things they have experienced and strategies they have used. Following on the motto used at Camp Quest Classic in Ohio one year, "Reason and Compassion in Action," campers worked on ways they could get involved in improving their communities.

Camp Quest is careful not to indoctrinate campers, letting them come to their own conclusions in a supportive environment. In answer to a question on her camp evaluation form about what she learned at Camp Quest, one camper wrote, "I learned that it is okay not to believe in god." Note that she didn't say she learned there is no god; she learned that it is okay not to believe. That is probably the most important thing Camp Quest offers: an environment where kids can be kids and have fun without compromising their beliefs and without controversy. They build lasting friendships with fellow campers from all over the country. When they go back home, they are a little more comfortable with who they are, a little more confident in their abilities, and a little more willing to branch out.

> " In answer to a question on her camp evaluation form about what she learned at Camp Quest, one camper wrote, 'I learned that it is okay not to believe in god.' Note that she didn't say she learned there is no god; she learned that it is okay not to believe. "

Camp Quest has expanded substantially in the number of campers it serves and in the variety of sessions offered. It has grown from one Ohio location in 1996 to 17 locations in 2016—in the states of Arizona, Virginia, Colorado, Kansas, Michigan, Minnesota, Washington, Ohio, Oklahoma, Tennessee, South Carolina, Texas, and California, as well as two camps in the United Kingdom, one at Lake Lucerne in Switzerland, and one in Norway. Each of the camps is independently operated, but all follow the same mission. All offer some of the same activities, but each also has its own feel and flavor.

Camp Quest is run entirely by volunteers who devote a week to being on camp staff and other time throughout the year developing programs and performing administrative and support roles. The organization also strives to be affordable for every child by raising money to provide full or partial camperships so that no camper is turned down for financial reasons. Camp Quest is open to any child from the age of eight to seventeen. For more information, please go to www.camp-quest.org. Links to all of the Camp Quests are available there.

AMANDA K. METSKAS received her MA in political science from Ohio State University in 2005. She graduated magna cum laude from Brown University in 2002 with honors in international relations. Amanda co-authored Raising Freethinkers *(2009) and is the executive director of Camp Quest.*

AUGUST E. BRUNSMAN IV has been executive director of the Secular Student Alliance since 2001. In 1997, he founded Students for Freethought at Ohio State University. He graduated Phi Beta Kappa from there in 2001 with a major in psychology and minors in mathematics and cognitive science. August has volunteered in a number of roles for Camp Quest Classic since 1999.

August and Amanda married in 2005 and live together in Columbus, Ohio.

■ ■

LIVE BETTER, HELP OFTEN, AND WONDER MORE

SANDERSON JONES

The entire global Sunday Assembly movement started with two people having a conversation in a car.

Pippa Evans and I were on the way to our comedy gig in Bath, England, when we discovered we both wanted to do something that was like church but totally secular and inclusive of all—no matter what they believed.

We started with 180 people in London in January 2013. By the end of the year, we were up to 350 people meeting twice a month. Our motto then and now—"Live Better, Help Often, and Wonder More"—has stayed right at the heart of things.

Soon after our first go in London, people all over the world were asking to start their own Sunday Assembly chapters. Now there are over 70 chapters in eight countries where people sing songs, hear inspiring talks, and create community together.

Everything we have ever done in Sunday Assembly is down to one thing: We are incredibly grateful to be alive humans. Life is short, it is brilliant, it is sometimes tough, so we build communities that help everyone live life as fully as possible.

We are obsessed with trying to help you—yes, YOU!—live your life as fully as possible.

But not just you. Not even just everyone who is in the room at a Sunday Assembly gathering. We want to build that joyful world where everyone—young and old, families and singles, poor and rich, north and south, up and down—lives life as fully as possible. In addition to celebrating life at our meetings, we're volunteering in our communities and supporting each other in times of need. We're even designing life courses modeled on the evidence-based work of positive psychology.

Why are we doing this? Because the problems we are facing are very bloody real.

This is where I get serious.

One in ten people in the United Kingdom have no friends or family, meaning we have ten percent of the population with zero social support. The numbers are not much different throughout the developed world. Helping these people would be transformative—not only personally for them, but in our increasingly atomized, individualistic, isolated culture, it would be transformative at a societal level. That's why:

- We want to work with ex-offenders and in schools.
- We want to let the socially isolated know there is a space for them.
- We want to visit those who are too ill to leave their houses.
- We want to tell an alternative story about the world that might make extremist radicalization just that bit harder.
- We want to be the best in the world at creating joyful, meaningful lives.
- We want to provide hundreds of activities and small groups.
- We want our community to vibrate with excitement.
- We want to give everyone their right to community.

Why are we confident that we can make a difference? Not just because we've done so well so far. It's also because we are basing our work on an excellent model. The congregational community—pioneered by mosques, synagogues, churches, temples, and so many more—is one of the most effective ways of building communities that change people, transform towns, and spawn movement.

Learning from religions has been effective in the past: In 1976, a guy called Jon Kabat-Zinn thought that using *vipassana* meditation could help patients who were suffering from pain in his hospital. He was a doctor and an excellent Buddhist practitioner. He knew he couldn't make them become Buddhists, so he found another way to teach them. He:

- Made it secular—so it is not tied to a religion
- Made it inclusive—so anyone of any belief could do it
- Measured its social impact—creating an evidence base for it

Thus, he created mindfulness, which you can now find in the National Health Service, boardrooms, your smartphones, and a ton of other places.

We are now looking at congregations and want to do the same thing:

- Make it secular—so it is not tied to a religion.
- Make it inclusive—so anyone of any belief could do it.

- Measure its social impact—creating an evidence base for it.
- Add pop songs (because singing "Livin' on a Prayer" is good for the soul).

Do you and your friends and family want to be part of this adventure? Do you want to live in this vision? Does this sound like the joyful, secular community celebration of life you've wanted your kids to be part of?

We hope the answer is yes, because we need you.

The congregational community model is built around creating connections that unleash the human being's inner desire to help. Taking people out of the fight-or-flight mode helps to promote kindness, altruism, and compassion. All of these systems are built around human commitment to that ideal.

And going for it has been the most glorious experiment that we could possibly have done.

SANDERSON JONES is a British stand-up comedian and cofounder of Sunday Assembly. Learn more about Sunday Assembly and find a meeting near you at https://www.sundayassembly.com/.

■ ■

ADDITIONAL RESOURCES FOR "COMMUNITY AND IDENTITY"

Zuckerman, Phil. *Living the Secular Life: New Answers to Old Questions.* Penguin, 2015. In the past decade, Dr. Phil Zuckerman has done more than anyone to illuminate the secular life as it is lived today. The insights from his fieldwork and research are captured with brilliant clarity in *Living the Secular Life.* Highly recommended for teens and adults.

Ozment, Katherine. *Grace Without God.* HarperWave, 2016. There's nothing like putting yourself in the hands of a writer who rewards that decision on every page. Katherine Ozment is such a writer, and *Grace Without God* is just that good. An engagingly personal exploration of parenting without religion that's clear and honest, thoughtful and deeply felt, and a brilliant addition to the growing chorus of voices in nonreligious parenting.

Grayling, A. C. *The Good Book: A Humanist Bible.* Walker Books, 2011. British atheist philosopher A. C. Grayling had an arresting thought: How would world history have been different if the writers of the Bible used Greek and Roman philosophy instead of local religions as their sources? But they didn't, so Grayling did. The result is *The Good Book: A Humanist Bible.* Grayling didn't mean for his humanist bible to shove the Bible bible aside. He wanted to create a secular contribution to the age-old conversation humanity has with itself about the good. So he did what the creators of the Bible did: selected texts from a number of different sources, then edited them, wove them together, and added a bit of his own thoughts to make it flow.

But here's the twist: It's not just a collection of excerpts, an approach that's been done a thousand times before. Instead, Grayling put everything into a kind of biblical structure, with chapters and verses, allowing the reader to really imagine that the original may have turned out very differently with different sources. If you know Plato and Aristotle, you'll see their ideas pop up in this or that verse, but without citation. It's a completely different way of experiencing their work, and you get the same kind of narrative flow you get from scriptures. Adults and advanced teens.

Introductions to Nontheistic Religious Communities

Seid, Judith. *God-Optional Judaism: Alternatives for Cultural Jews Who Love Their History, Heritage, and Community.* Citadel, 2001. An excellent introduction to secular Judaism for those who wish to remain connected to traditions and history of Judaism but do not believe in God.

Dant, Jennifer. *Unitarian Universalism Is a Really Long Name.* Skinner House, 2006. Introduction to the UU denomination for ages five through nine, including answers to questions like, "Do We Pray?" and "What Do We Believe?"

Boulton, David, ed. *Godless for God's Sake: Nontheism in Contemporary Quakerism.* Dale's Historical Monographs, 2006. An anthology of writings by twenty-seven nontheistic Quakers in four countries.

Sunday Assembly. The world's greatest experiment in joyful human community without religion. https://www.sundayassembly.com/.

Blogs and Books Especially for Nonreligious Parents

- **Greater Good** www.greatergood.berkeley.edu/family_couples. An inexhaustibly brilliant multicontributor blog of the Greater Good Science Center at UC Berkeley. Focus is on moral and intellectual development, meaning, and purpose, all in the context of science.

- **Grounded Parents** www.groundedparents.com/. Not just a great blog—a whole busy and smart network of 30 great bloggers writing about nonreligious parenting and everything remotely related to it.

- **Godless Mom** www.godlessmom.com/. An intelligent, fun take on nonreligious parenting from a mom who's been there and knows how to tell the story.

- **Natural Wonderers** www.patheos.com/blogs/naturalwonderers/. A smart and irreverent blog by Wendy Thomas Russell, one of the great rising voices in nonreligious parenting.

- *Relax, It's Just God* by Wendy Thomas Russell (Los Angeles: Brown Paper Press, 2015). The smart, irreverent companion book to Wendy's blog.

- *Growing Up Godless: A Parent's Guide to Raising Kids Without Religion* by Deborah Mitchell (New York: Sterling Ethos, 2014). One of the best of the newer voices in nonreligious parenting.

- *Raising Freethinkers: A Practical Guide for Parenting Beyond Belief* by Dale McGowan, Molleen Matsumura, Amanda Metskas, and Jan Devor (AMACOM, 2009). The practical companion to the book you're holding, built around 100 questions and answers, along with resources and activities.

GLOSSARY

These are terms mentioned in this book that are either especially important or so unimportant that few people will know their meaning.

AGNOSTIC: One who withholds judgment on the existence or nonexistence of supernatural entities on the grounds that it cannot be known with any certainty. Coined by 19th-century biologist Thomas Huxley.

ATHEIST: One who does not believe in the existence of a god or gods.

BAHA'I: A religion born in the mid-19th century as an offshoot of Babism (which was an offshoot of Shia Islam, which was an early division of original Islam). Has many admirable humanistic tenets, including equality of sexes, abolishing racial and religious prejudice, and universal education.

BRIGHTS: A recent attempt at a positive term for those whose worldview is naturalistic, without supernatural or mystical elements. Philosopher Daniel Dennett has suggested SUPERS as the corresponding name for those who believe in the supernatural.

CHRISTADELPHIANS: Also known as Brethren of Christ, this sect was founded by a British physician in 1848 around the need for a return to primitive Christianity. Doctrines include equal importance of Old and New Testaments, conscientious opposition to war, and eternal life only for believers. Nonbelievers cease to exist.

EVANGELICAL: Any Christian denomination that stresses the personal, born-again conversion experience; holds the Bible in high authority; and considers it important to convert others to their beliefs.

EXISTENTIAL: Relating to questions of individual human existence. Questions about individual existence, mortality, life, death, freedom, and choice are all existential questions.

FREETHINKER: One who does not passively accept views or teachings, especially on religion, preferring to form opinions as a result of independent inquiry.

FUNDAMENTALISM: In current usage, refers to conservative Protestant Christian practice and beliefs, including the infallibility and literal interpretation of the Bible, salvation through faith alone, and damnation for nonbelievers.

HUMANISM: A concern with the well-being and interests of humanity as opposed to supernatural beings and ideas. Humanism most often includes the rejection of all supernatural beliefs, including belief in God. Sometimes "secular" precedes it to make clear that this more precise meaning is intended.

JAINISM: A religion originating in India around the same time as Buddhism, and, like Buddhism, essentially atheistic. Embraces nonviolence, education, and moral conduct.

METAPHYSICAL: Concerning the nature of ultimate reality and existence, including consideration of abstract concepts and intangible things.

MUGGLETONIANS: A small Protestant sect formed when an English tailor had a vision and "commissioning from God" in 1652. Focused on the imminent second coming of Christ. The last practicing Muggletonian died in 1979.

NONTHEIST: Generally synonymous with "atheist," though some people prefer "nontheist" to indicate disbelief without implying active rejection. Others prefer it because "atheist" has been used as a hostile term by believers for so long. Many atheists find the label pusillanimous.

PENTECOSTALISM: A loosely affiliated fundamentalist Christian denomination emphasizing the imminent second coming of Christ and the personal, ecstatic experience of the Holy Spirit, often marked by speaking in tongues and uncontrollable bodily movements. Faith healing is also a common feature.

PROSELYTIZE: To actively attempt to convert another person to one's own religious beliefs.

SEVENTH-DAY ADVENTISTS: A large Protestant denomination (10 million members worldwide) with principles that include the Bible as sole authority, the imminent return of Christ, living a healthy lifestyle, avoiding dancing and theaters, and worshipping on Saturdays (attending church on Sunday is called "the mark of the Beast").

SKEPTIC: One who requires sufficient evidence before accepting a conclusion.

SUNDAY ASSEMBLY: A global movement of congregational meetings without religion, intended to encourage everyone to "live better, help often, and wonder more."

SUPERS: Those who have a worldview including supernatural beliefs. Coined by Daniel Dennett. Opposed to BRIGHTS (see p. 285).

TRANSUBSTANTIATION: The Catholic doctrine that Communion bread and wine become, when consecrated, the actual body and blood of Jesus Christ.

UNITARIAN UNIVERSALISM: A religious denomination that attempts to capture many of the best features of religious communities without demanding a single belief or creed of its members. UU churches are creedless and nondogmatic. Most members and attenders are nontheistic.

NOTES

PREFACE

1. American Religious Identification Survey 2008, http://commons. trincoll.edu/aris/files/2011/08/ARIS_Report_2008.pdf; Pew Center Religious Landscape Survey 2015, www.pewresearch.org/fact-tank/2015/11/03/5-key-findings-about-religiosity-in-the-u-s-and-how-its-changing/.

Chapter 1: Personal Reflections

INTRODUCTION

1. Richard Dawkins, "Religion's Misguided Missiles," *Guardian,* September 15, 2001.

Excerpt from the Autobiography of Bertrand Russell

1. Russell, Bertrand. *The Autobiography of Bertrand Russell.* Abington (UK): Routledge Edition (2009).

Raised Without Religion

1. All quotes from personal correspondence of the author.

Authentic Secular Parenting: Letting Children Choose

1. Summary at "America's Changing Religious Landscape," Pew Research Center, May 12, 2015, www.pewforum.org/2015/05/12/americas-changing-religious-landscape/.

Chapter 2: Living with Religion

INTRODUCING KIDS TO THINGS WE DON'T BELIEVE

1. Hirsch, E.D. The New Dictionary of Cultural Literacy: What Every American Needs to Know. Boston: Houghton Mifflin Harcourt (2002).

2. "Religion in the Public School Curriculum: Questions and Answers." In Journal of Law and Religion, Vol. 8, No. 1/2 (1990), pp. 309–312.
3. Esther Boyd, "Religious Literacy: Knowledge vs. Understanding," State of Formation, June 4, 2014, www.stateofformation. org/2014/06/religious-literacy-knowledge-vs-understanding/.

Parenting Across the Belief Gap

1. Quoted in Fishblatt, E.N. (1880), "Maladies Involving the Genital Functions," in *New York Medical and Surgical Journal* (later Northwestern Medical Journal), v. 6, 525.
2. American Academy of Pediatrics Task Force on Circumcision, "Circumcision Policy Statement," *Pediatrics* 103, no. 3 (March 1999): 686–693, pediatrics.aappublications.org/content/103/3/686. full; American Academy of Family Physicians, "Neonatal Circumcision," www.aafp.org/patient-care/clinical-recommendations/all/circumcision.html; Douglas Gairdner, "The Fate of the Foreskin: A Study of Circumcision," *British Medical Journal* 2 (1949): 1433–1437, http://www.cirp.org/library/general/gairdner/.
3. *Book of Common Prayer*, 298.
4. *Book of Occasional Services* (2003), 159.
5. Website of the Episcopal Diocese of New York, "Concerning Baptism," http://www.dioceseny.org/administration/for-clergy/liturgical-and-sacramental/concerning-baptism/.
6. Rabbi Joshua M. Davidson, letter to the editor, *New York Times*, Nov. 6, 2013, A28.
7. Summary available online at http://www.pewforum.org/files/2008/06/report2religious-landscape-study-key-findings.pdf.
8. Sutrakritinga; Wisdom of the Living Religions #69, 1:2:33.
9. Udanavarga 5,18.
10. Plato, *Crito* (49c).
11. Mahabharata 5,1517.
12. Confucius, *Analects* 15, 23.
13. Matthew 7:12.
14. Talmud, Shabbat 3id.
15. Azizullah, Hadith 150.
16. T'ai Shang Kan Ying P'ien.
17. Baha'u'llah, Gleanings, 66:8.
18. The Wiccan Rede.
19. Quoted in Beth Pearson, "The Art of Creating Ethics Man," *Herald* (Scotland), January 23, 2006.

Choosing Your Battles

1. Staver, Matthew. "Bringing Good News to Public Schools," *National Liberty Journal Online.* Sept 2005. Cited at http://www.jewsonfirst. org/06d/goodnewsclubs01.html.

Secular Schooling

1. Madison, James. *Memorial and Remonstrance Against Religious Assessments,* June 1785. Available online at http://founders.archives. gov/documents/Madison/01-08-02-0163.

Chapter 3: Holidays and Celebrations

Put the Claus Away

1. Bettelheim, B. "Dialogue with mothers." *Ladies Home Journal.* 1971; 88:14.
2. Quoted in Turner, Francis, *Encyclopedia of Canadian Social Work.* Waterloo ON: Wilfrid Laurier Univ. Press (2009) 66.
3. Richardson, J.G., and Simpson, C.H. "Children, Gender, and Social Structure: An Analysis of the Contents of Letters to Santa Claus." Child Development Vol. 53, 429–436 (1982).

Chapter 4: On Being and Doing Good

INTRODUCTION

1. Quoted in Cohen, Richard, "The Purported Power of Prayer," Washington Post, June 3, 1999. Available online at https://www .washingtonpost.com/archive/opinions/1999/06/03/the-purported-power-of-prayer/d46d4888-f91e 4911-b2bf-9f0a875d8487/.
2. Pearson, "Art of Creating Ethics Man."
3. Grusec, JE and Goodnow, Jacqueline J. "Impact of parental discipline methods on the child's internalization of values: A reconceptualization of current points of view." *Developmental Psychology,* Vol 30(1), Jan 1994, 4–19.
4. Oliner, Samuel and Pearl. *The Altruistic Personality.* New York: Touchstone Books (1992).
5. Pearson, "Art of Creating Ethics Man."
6. Fehr, Ernst, et al. "Egalitarianism in young children." *Nature* 454, 1079–1083 (28 August 2008).

Spare the Rod—and Spare Me the Rest

1. James Dobson, *The New Dare to Discipline* (Carol Stream IL, Tyndale Momentum, 2014), 21, 35, 36, 64, 65, 66, 70.
2. Gershoff, ET. "Corporal Punishment by Parents and Associated Child Behaviors and Experiences: A Meta-Analytic and Theoretical Review." Psychological Bulletin (2002), Vol. 128, No. 4, 539–579.
3. Gershoff, Elizabeth T., and Grogan-Kaylor, Andrew. "Spanking and child outcomes: Old controversies and new meta-analyses." *Journal of Family Psychology,* Vol 30(4), Jun 2016, 453–469.

Behaving Yourself: Moral Development in the Secular Family

1. Austin Dacey, "Believing in Doubt," *New York Times*, Feb. 3, 2006, A23.
2. L. Kohlberg, C. Levine, and A. Hewer, *Moral Stages: A Current Formulation and a Response to Critics* (Basel, Switzerland: Karger, 1983).
3. R. Dobert and G. Nunner-Winkler, "Interplay of Formal and Material Role-Taking in the Understanding of Suicide Among Adolescents and Young Adults. 1. Formal and Material Role-Taking," *Human Development* 28, no. 5 (1985): 225–239.
4. S. Baron-Cohen, "From Attention-Goal Psychology to Belief-Desire Psychology: The Development of a Theory of Mind, and Its Dysfunction," in S. Baron-Cohen, H. Tager-Flusberg, and D. Cohen, eds., *Understanding Other Minds* (New York: Oxford University Press, 1993), 59–82.
5. Ibid.
6. M. Lewis, *Shame: The Exposed Self* (New York: Free Press, 1992).
7. J. Grusec and J. Goodnow, "Impact of Parent Discipline Methods on the Child's Internalization of Values: A Reconceptualization of Current Points of View," *Developmental Psychology* 30 (1994): 4–19; G. Kochanska, "Beyond Cognition: Expanding the Search for the Early Roots of Internalization and Conscience," *Developmental Psychology* 30 (1994): 20–22.
8. K. Aunola and J.-E. Nurmi, "The Role of Parenting Styles in Children's Problem Behavior," *Child Development* 76, no. 6 (2005): 1144–1159.
9. G. Ezzo and R. Bucknam, *On Becoming Babywise* (Sisters, OR: Multnomah Books, 1995).

Take Two Tablets and Call Me in the Morning

1. Harburg, Yipsel. *Rhymes for the Irreverent*. Madison WI: Freedom From Religion Foundation (2006).

Chapter 5: Death and Consolation

INTRODUCTION

1. From the collected letters and diary of Thomas Henry Huxley, entry for 23 Sept 1860. Available online at http://aleph0.clarku.edu/huxley/letters/60.html.

Helping Your Child Live with Grief Without Religion

1. Donna M. Burns, *When Kids Are Grieving: Addressing Grief and Loss in School* (Thousand Oaks, CA: Corwin, 2010).
2. J. W. Worden, Ph.D., "Talking to Your Child About the Loss of a Loved One, Part 1," PsychCentral.com, accessed February 25, 2016, psychcentral.com/library/child_death.htm.
3. Barbara Coloroso, *Parenting Through Crisis: Helping Kids in Times of Loss, Grief, and Change* (New York: HarperCollins, 2000).
4. Alan Wolfelt, *Healing the Bereaved Child: Grief Gardening, Growth Through Grief, and Other Touchstones for Caregivers* (Ft. Collins, CO: Companion Press, 1996).
5. George A. Bonanno, *The Other Side of Sadness: What the New Science of Bereavement Tells Us About Life After Loss* (New York: Basic Books, 2009).

Chapter 6: Wondering and Questioning

INTRODUCTION

1. William O'Grady, *How Children Learn Language* (London: Cambridge University Press, 2005).
2. Dawkins, Richard. *Unweaving the Rainbow: Science, Delusion, and the Appetite for Wonder* (Boston: Houghton Mifflin Harcourt, 2000), 142–3.

Parenting and the Arts

1. Miller, Arthur. *Collected Plays* (Viking Press, 1957), Introduction.
2. Carter, Angela. *The Bloody Chamber* (New York: Penguin, 1990), Introduction.
3. Hutton, Will. "Boys Today? We're Doing Their Heads In." *The Guardian,* 3 June 2006.
4. Auden, W.H. "Leap Before You Look." In *Collected Poems: Auden* (New York: Vintage, 1991).
5. Thoreau, Henry David. Excerpt from *Walden,* in *Walden and Civil Disobedience* (New York: Penguin Classics, 1983), 85.

Chapter 7: Community and Identity

INTRODUCTION

1. Available online at http://www.noves.org/article/17/about-noves/ what-we-are/statement-of-purpose.
2. Lim, Chaeyoon, quoted in Pappas, Stephanie, "Why Religion Makes People Happier (Hint: Not God)." LiveScience, Dec 6, 2010. Available online at http://www.livescience.com/9090-religion-people-happier-hint-god.html.

Summer Camp Beyond Belief

1. Camp Quest, www.camp-quest.org.
2. Douglas Belkin, "Cutting Ties That Digitally Bind," *Boston Globe,* August 18, 2006.
3. American Camp Association, "Directions: Youth Development Outcomes of the Camp Experience," 2005, www.acacamps.org/resource-library/research/ directions-youth-development-outcomes-camp-experience
4. Marie Hartwell-Walker, Ed.D., "What's So Great About Summer Camp?", PsychCentral.com, www.psychcentral.com/library/id211. html.
5. Ruth Marcus, "Camping Alone; Ready for S'More Networking Billy?" *Washington Post,* July 19, 2006.
6. Douglas Belkin, "Cutting Ties That Digitally Bind," *Boston Globe,* August 18, 2006.

INDEX

abortion, 68
Abrahamic mythologies, 42
abstinence, teacher focus on, 94
Adam and Eve, 53
Adler, Felix, 272
afterlife, 16, 175, 185
    child's perception of, 191–192
    religion's focus on, 217
agnostic, 285
alienation, buffer against, 270
Allen, Norm R., *African-American Humanism*, 182
American Academy of Family Physicians, 71
American Academy of Pediatrics, 71
American Camping Association, 275
Angier, Natalie, 185
answers, search for, 232
apologizing, 167
April Fool's Day, 119–120
The Arabian Nights, 255
Arent, Ruth P., *Helping Children Grieve*, 220
Armstrong, Karen, 262
    A Short History of Myth, 107
arrogance, 172
arts, 196
    as dangerous, 252, 254
    literature, 252–253
    music, 255–256, 263
    parenting and, 251–256
atheism, 18–19, 37–39
    history of, 85
atheists, 3, 23, 285
    charity by, 177–178
    in Christian family, 56
Auden, W.H., "Leap Before You Look," 256
authoritative parenting, 158
authority, 9, 11, 26, 92–93
Autumnal Equinox, 122
Aveni, Anthony, *The Book of the Year*, 132
ayatollahs, in Muslim religion, 11

Babbitt, Natalie, *Tuck Everlasting*, 215, 221–222
Baha'i religion, 87, 285
baptism, 56–57, 72–75
bar/bat mitzvah ceremony, 85, 115
Barker, Dan, 2, 31–36
    Godless, 40
    Maybe Right, Maybe Wrong, 182
    "My Father's House," 31
Barr, Bob, 135

battles, choosing wisely, 96–97
Baumrind, Diana, 88
Beliefnet, 108, 266
Belief-O-Matic, 261, 266, 267
beliefs, 5–6, 48
    diversity of, 103
    freedom to form, 62
    good and bad reasons for, 8–15
    honesty in sharing, 54
    loss of, 20
    parenting across gap, 68
belonging, 262, 263, 268
Bennett, Helen, *Humanism--What's That?*, 107
Bergin, Mark, *Inside the Beagle with Charles Darwin*, 240
Berkowitz, Marvin, 136, 137, 139–145
Bettelheim, Bruno, 126–131
Bible Gateway, 108
biblical literalists, 69
Big Bang theory, 200
birth control, 68–69
    education, 94
The Blank Slate (Pinker), 35
Bonanno, George, 197
Borba, Michele, *Building Moral Intelligence*, 182
Boston Medical Center, Good Grief Program, 222
Boxing Day, 124
Boyd, Esther, 47
Brethren of Christ, 285
Brights, 285
Brooklyn Society for Ethical Culture, 23
Brooks, Arthur, 178
Brunsman, August, 263–264, 275–278
Buckner, Ed, 99–106
Buddha, 49
Buddhism, 29, 87
Bulgakov, Mikhail, *The White Guard*, 252
bullying, 55
burial, 7
Butler, Samuel, 146

camouflage egg hunt, 120–121
Camp Quest, xiv, 263–264, 273, 275–278
Carter, Angela, 255
Carter, Neil, 43, 55–61
Catholics, 68, 261, 265
    childhood, 3
    school, 91

celebration, 109–133
    of life, 279
cemetery, 7
censorship, 254
ceremony, 111
    bar/bat mitzvah, 85, 115
    coming of age, 114–115
    for death in family, 210–211
    humanist, 111–117
    naming, 74, 113–114
    wedding, 113, 115
character, 140
Cherry, Matt, 138, 166–171
Cherry, Shannon, 138, 166–171
Child Evangelism Fellowship (CEF), 90
children
    choices, 54
    discussion on God's existence, 199–201
    freedom for decisions, 64
    impact on religious/nonreligious
        relationship, 75
    as observers, 168–170
    traditional information and, 14
Chinese New Year party, 124
Chisholm, George Brock, 126
choice, 30
Christadelphians, 285
Christianity, 87
    branches, 10
    early church virtues, 171
    mythologies, 44
    reaction to atheist teaching, 81
    role in ceremonial events, 111–117
    see also Catholics; Protestants
Christmas, 49, 118, 124
church
    bond between child and, 74
    children's attendance, 82–84
    curiosity about, 28
    reasons for worship, 262
church and state, separation of, 102–106
classroom proselytizing, 93–95
Clay, Michelle, 23
Clayton, John C., *Alexander Fox and the
    Amazing Mind Reader*, 257
clergy as parent, 32
coexistence, with religion, 42
collaboration, 168
Coloroso, Barbara, 26
Columbine High School shootings, 135
comfort, for grieving child, 194
coming of age, 85–86
    ceremonies, 111, 114–115
communication, with other adults about
    grieving child, 195
Communion, First, 86
community, 259–263
    advice for seeking, 272–273
    secular, 264
    Sunday Assembly, 279–281
compromise, 95
conception, nonexistence before, 187
condemnation, 61
confirmation, 86
conflict, between family generations, 66

Confucianism, 87
confusion, in children, 80
connecting to others, 263
Conrad, Heather, *Lights of Winter*, 133
conservative social philosophy, 176
continents, movement, 245
continuity of life, affirming, 214
conviction, 54
corporal punishment, 66, 146–149
courage, 174–175
creationism, 18
critical thinking, 29, 171
    Camp Quest focus on, 276
    teaching skills for, 60
cultures, holidays from other, 124
curiosity, 230–233

danger, 256
Darwin, Charles, 239–240
    On the Origin of Species, 234
Darwin Day, 118, 133
Dawkins, Richard, 1, 8–15, 38, 77, 224
    The God Delusion, xiii, 34
    The Magic of Reality, 257
    Unweaving the Rainbow, 185, 248–249
Day of the Dead, 124
death, 4, 16–17, 175, 180
    affirmations needed, 211–214
    child's view of, 201–202
    in difficult situations, 214–215
    discussion with child, 190
    fear of, 218
    inclusion of children, 116
    of Jesus, 79
    naturalistic view of, 201–203
    of pets, 204–205
    responding to religious doctrines and
        cultural images, 218–219
    in secular family, 208–219
deceiving children, about Santa Claus, 126–127
deconversion stories, 177
dedication, 73
demandingness, 141–142
Dennett, Daniel, 60, 285
dinosaurs, 239
discipline plan, 149
disease, death from, 215
dissonance, 62–67
distress, 160
diversity, 42, 170, 253
    embracing, 176–177
DNA, 245
Dobson, James, *The New Dare to Discipline*,
    147–148
Donnelly, Jennifer, *A Gathering Light*, 251, 254
doubt, 248
Dougy Center, *35 Ways to Help a Grieving
    Child*, 221
Dougy Center for Grieving Children & Families,
    222
Durkheim, David Emile, *Suicide*, 270

Earth Day, 121
Earth Day Network, 133
Easter, 118, 119, 120–121

Easter Bunny, 33
Ecclesiastes, 259
education, secular schooling, 99–106
Eliot, George, *Middlemarch*, 252
emotional development, 158–160
emotions, validating child's, 193–194
empathy, 45, 163, 173–174
  for believers, 174
empowerment, 142–143
Emswiler, James and Mary Ann, *Guiding Your Child Through Grief*, 220
environment, child's study of, 16
Epicurus, 187
Espeland, Pamela, *Knowing and Doing What's Right*, 182
ethical behavior, 87
ethical children, 139–145
Ethical Culture movement, 261, 272–273
  coming-of-age programs, 86
Ethical Movement, 272–273
Ethical Society, 22–23
evangelical Christianity, 56, 285
evangelist, 91
Evans, Pippa, 272
Eve, disobedient curiosity of, 231
evidence, 8, 12, 13
evil, 137–138, 150–154
evolution, 38–39, 63, 216
  awe and wonder of, 235–236
  book recommendations, 242–243
  camouflage egg hunt, 120–121
  Christianity and, 69
  dinosaurs, 239
  natural history museum, 241
  by natural selection, 249
  as part of routine, 235
  science of, 233–242
  simplicity in explanation, 234–235
  toys and games for studying, 240–241
Evolution: Education and Outreach, 242
existential, 285
expectations
  of conformity, 63
  parents creating, 141
experience, death as end, 187
exploration, 78

facial expressions, 159
fairness, development of, 137
fairy tales, 251
faith, 37, 52
  child's choices, and parental love, 29
  as choice, 27
  dialogue about, 28
  profession of, 56
faith literacy, 48
fallibility, embracing, 176–177
family, faith of, 53
fear
  from death discussion, 191
  from religion, 42
feelings, 12–13
Festivus, 123–124
First Communion, 86
Flynn, Tom, 126–129

folk tales, 255
force, vs. reason, 148
Foundation Beyond Belief, xiv, 178
Franklin, Benjamin, 90
freedom, 89
Freedom From Religion Foundation, 33, 95
freethinking, 32–34, 96, 286
  B. Russell and, 20
  by child, 25–30, 232–233
Freethought Today, 33
fundamentalism, 286
funeral ceremonies, 113, 116
  inclusion of children, 116

gay marriage, 68
gay rights, 68
Gaylor, Annie Laurie, 33, 95
  Women Without Superstition, 182
generosity, 177–178
Gershoff, Elizabeth Thompson, 148–149
GI Bill educational benefits, 100
Gibbon, Edward, 24
Gibbons, Kendyl, 188, 208–219
Girl Scout Promise, 52
God, 53, 58
  anxiety over, 52
  discussion of existence, 199–201
  and moral development, 102, 152–154
  and Santa, 131
The God Delusion (Dawkins), xiii, 34
The God Who Wasn't There (DVD), 40
godparents, 113
gods, as stories, 66
gold, 245
good, being and doing, 135–183
grandparents, relationship with, 65–67
gratitude, 178–179, 279
Grayling, A.C.
  The Good Book, 282
  Meditations for the Humanist, 182
Greece, myths, 41–42
grief, 209
  helping child with, 190–198
  learning, 204–205
  of parents, 192
  processing, 193
Grief Beyond Belief (group), xiv, 188, 190, 222
grief counseling, 196
Grimm's tales, 255
Grusec, Joan, 88, 136
Grych, John, 141
guilt, 162

Hamilton, Virginia, *In the Beginning: Creation Stories from Around the World*, 107
Harburg, Edgar Yipsel "Yip," 138
  "Before and After," 189
  "A Nose Is a Nose Is a Nose," 229
  "Small Comforts," 207
  "Take Two Tablets and Call Me in the Morning," 165
  "We've Come a Long Way, Buddy," 244
Harris, Annaka, *I Wonder*, 257
Hartwell-Walker, Marie, 275
Haught, James A., *2000 Years of Disbelief*, 183

Haven, Kendell, *New Year's to Kwanzaa*, 133
heaven, 5, 53, 57, 58, 69
    belief in, 84
    discussion of, 218–219
    family discussion, 65
    as lie, 191
hell, 57, 76–77, 84–85
    discussion of, 65, 218–219
Henry, Patrick, 104
Hensler, Rebecca, 188, 190–198
Hera, 231
Hermes, 231
Hesiod, 231
Hinduism, 87
Hirsch, E.D., *Dictionary of Cultural Literacy*, 45
hobby, with social element, 273
holidays, 109–133
holy, 153
homeschooling, vs. school, 66
homosexuality, 68
honesty, 175–176, 186
    in dealing with grief, 190
hubris, 162
human goodness, 139
human judgment, limitations of, 103
human nature, pessimistic view by Christianity, 35
humanism, 166, 286
    in arts, 252
humanist epiphany, 177
humanist groups, coming-of-age rituals, 86
humanist meetup group, 273
Humanist Society, 74
Humanistic Judaism, 272
HumanLight, 123
humans, evolution and, 238
humility, 172–173
Humphrey, Sandra McLeod, *If You Had to Choose*, 181–182
Hutton, Will, 255
Huxley, Thomas, death of son, 186–187
hypothesis, 9

identity, 266–267
idolatry, 51–52
Ig Nobel Awards, 17
Ignatius Loyola (saint), 37
ignorance, from religion, 42
imagination, 33–34
imagination memory, 192
immorality, silence on, 42
independence, 168
    summer camp and, 276
independent thinking, xv–xvi
    see also freethinking
individualism, and suicide, 270
individuality in children, 25–30
    celebrating, 213–214
indoctrination, 88
induction, 143–144
infancy, emotional aspects of morality, 158–190
influence, 4–5
Ingersoll, Robert G., 112
intellectual freedom, 21
intolerance, 55

Islam, 87
    on disobedient woman, 231
    isolation, 259, 270

Jainism, 87, 286
JAMA (Journal of the American Medical Association), 17
Jenkins, Steve, *Life on Earth*, 234
Jesus, 79
Jesus Christ Superstar (DVD), 108
Jewish culture
    bar/bat mitzvah, 85, 115
    mythologies, 44
    secular expression of, 260, 282–283
Jillette, Penn, 1, 37–39
joint attention, 159
Jones, Sanderson, 264, 272, 279–281
Judaism, 87

Kabat-Zinn, Jon, 280
Kellogg, John Harvey, 71
Kids are Worth It! (Coloroso), 26
Knight, Margaret, "Morals Without Religion," 180
Kohlberg, Lawrence, 157–158
Kohn, Alfie, *Unconditional Parenting*, 181
Konner, Melvin, *The Tangled Wing*, 203
Kurtz, Paul, 175

language, 254   z
    tradition and, 13–14
Law, Stephen
    The Complete Philosophy Files, 257
    The War for Children's Minds, 257
laws, 157
laying on of hands, 17
Levi, Primo, *If This Is a Man*, 253
Libby Anne, 43, 62–67
liberal philosophy, 176–177
life messages, for children, 26, 28
life satisfaction, 263
listening, to grieving child, 193
literature, 252–253
Lot's wife, 231
love, 149
    evidence of, 13
lying, 126–127

Macdonald, Fiona, *Inside the Beagle with Charles Darwin*, 240
Madison, James, *Memorial and Remonstrance Against Religious Assessments*, 104–105
Mary (mother of Jesus), Roman Catholic beliefs, 10–11
masturbation, 71
Mather, Anne, *Character Building Day by Day*, 182
Matthews, Gareth, 138, 150–154
McKerracher, Be-Asia, 2, 25–30
Secular Parenting in a Religious World, 107
Medhus, Elisa
    Everyday Heroes, 181
    Raising Children Who Think for Themselves, 181
memories, 4–5, 213

Mercer, Jean, 138, 155–165
metaphysical, 286
Methodist church, 76–77
Metskas, Amanda, 263–264, 275–278
Mill, John Stuart, *Autobiography*, 200
Miller, Arthur, *The Crucible*, 253
Miller, Katherine, 233–242
Miller, Matt, *Facing Cancer Without God*, 220
mindfulness, 280
minister as parent, 32
mixed marriage, 43, 68, 70, 75–76
    and christening, 72–75
    and circumcision, 70–72
    survey of, 79
    surviving, 95–96
modeling, 144–145
    parents behavior, 167
monkeys, evolution and, 238
moral, 140
moral development, 153, 158–160
    education, 101–102
    national conversation on, 135–137
    research, 88
    secular approach, 163–164
    in secular family, 155–165
moral reasoning, 155, 163
    development of, 156–158
morality
    and evil, 150–154
    learning about, 22
mortality
    confronting, 216–218
    see also death
mother's faith, honoring, 53
Muggletonians, 286
music, 255–256, 263
Muslim religion, ayatollahs in, 11
myth, 41–42, 44
    avoiding common, 237–238

naming ceremonies, 74, 113–114
natural history museum, 241
natural selection, evolution by, 234, 249
Nature (journal), 137
Nazi era, 136
neutral views, 21
new ideas, sharing with children, 59–60
Newman, Emily, 24
nice actions, 6–7
Noah's Ark, 239–240
nonconformity, courage for, 175
nonexistence, 175, 187
nonreligious population, xiii–xiv
nontheistic religious communities, 286
    introductions, 282–283
Norway, 114
    Humanist Confirmation program in, 86
Nova (PBS), 242
Nucci, Larry, 88, 135
nurturance, 143

obedience to rules, teaching questioning, 136
observation, 8–9
Oliner, Pearl, 136
Oliner, Samuel, 136

organized religion, loss of interest in, 266
otherness
    feelings of, 46
    of the world, 253
Ozment, Katherine, 263, 265–269
    Grace Without God, 282

pagans, 64
    rituals, 118
Pandora, 231
Parenting Beyond Belief, 262
parenting for character, 141
    empowerment, 142–143
    induction, 143–144
    modeling, 144–145
    nurturance, 143
parents
    blogs and books for nonreligious, 283
    of ethical children, 139–145
    and moral development, 162
    motivation for philosophy, 146
    as role models, 144–145, 161
    role of, 31
    shared experience of, 80
Patheos, 108
Pearce, Jonathan, 21
peer interactions, and moral development, 88
Pentecostalism, 286
pets, death of, 204–205
Pew Forum, 82–83
Pew Research Center, Religious Landscape
    Survey (2014), 27, 68
Pfeffer, Wendy, *The Shortest Day*, 132–133
Philliber Research Associates, 275
philosophy, consolations of, 187
Pinker, Steven, *The Blank Slate*, 35
Plato
    Euthyphro, 153
    philosophy, 87
Pledge of Allegiance, 6, 18, 52, 93, 276
pope, as authority, 11
prayer, 65
prediction, 9
preschool, 76–77
pretending, 33–34
pride, 162
    teaching, 166–171
    as virtue, 168
private schools, 100–101
Prometheus, 231
proselytize, 286
Protestants, 68–69, 265
Proverbs, 146
public schools, 38
    role in moral education, 101–102
    separation of church and state, 102–106
    support of, 99–101
Pullman, Philip
    His Dark Materials, 253
    Northern Lights, 251, 254–255
punishment, 158, 161–162, 163
    and right vs. wrong, 157
purity obsession, 61

Quakers, 261, 283

questions, 92, 223, 232
    freedom to ask, 65
    on Santa Claus, 130

Ramadan, 49
Randi, James, 17
Randolph, A. Philip, 276
reason, 187
    vs. force, 148
reasoning, 90–91, 136
    Camp Quest focus on, 276
religion, 51–55
    children learning about, xv–xvi
    children raised without, 21–24
    as dangerous, 1
    exposure to many, 51
    and hatred, fear, and prejudice, 230
    as human response, 41
    humanizing, 49
    and need for community, 270–271
    options for challenging intrusions, 98
    and response to human condition, 174
    secular parents sharing about, 45
    social aspects, 263
    traditions and, 14–15
Religion in the Public School Curriculum, 45
religious community, 259–260
religious discussions
    age for, 48
    engaging children in, 47–50
religious holidays, 49
religious identity, child's, 77–82
religious liberty, 103–104, 260
    protecting, 102, 105
religious literacy, 45–50, 82–84
religious people, diversity in, 42
religious relatives, dissonance with, 62–67
religious wonder, 247
religious zealots, 90
religiously unaffiliated, xiii–xiv
    marriage to religious partner, 43
    religious partner of, 68
religious/nonreligious couple
    see mixed marriage
resilience in grief, 197
respect, 47, 55
    for boundaries, 62
    from children, 97
    teaching, 166–171
responsibility, 177
Réveillé-Parise, Joseph-Henri, 71
revelation, 9
    belief and, 12–13
right vs. wrong
    reward and, 157
    variations in, 161
rites of passage, 111, 114–115
ritual, 112
    for death in family, 210–211
    see also ceremony
rod, 147
Roman Catholics, beliefs on Mary, mother of
    Jesus, 10–11
Rome, myths, 41–42
Rosa, Emily, 2, 16–19

Rosh Hashanah, 49
Rothman, Juliet Cassuto, A Birthday Present for
    Daniel, 221
rules, 157
    complying with, 156
Russell, Bertrand, 126–127, 223
    Autobiography, 20
    Why I Am Not a Christian, 200
Russell, Wendy Thomas, 45–50, 51–55
    Relax, It's Just God, 43

sacred, 24
sadness from death, validating child's, 212
Sagan, Carl, 246, 249
Santa Claus, 16, 33, 126
school
    administrators, 105–106
    classroom proselytizing, 93–95
support of public, 99–101
science, 9, 38, 51–52, 187
    of evolution, 233–242
    and humility, 172
Scientific American Frontiers, 17
scientific worldview, 249
Sears, William, 147
"secular," 102
secular community, 264, 270–274
secular family, death in, 208–219
secular humanism, 266, 267
secular Judaism, 260, 282–283
secular parenting, xiv, xv, 16–19
    approaches, 1–2
    authentic, 25–30
secular schooling, 99–106
Secular Seasons, website, 119, 133
secular virtues, 171–179
    courage, 174–175
    empathy, 173–174
    generosity, 177–178
    gratitude, 178–179
    honesty, 175–176
    humility, 172–173
Seidel, Andrew, 24
self-confidence, 168
self-discipline, 149
self-esteem, 168
    summer camp and, 276
self-image, negative, 35
selfishness, 128
self-respect, 166
separation of church and state, 102–106
Seventh-Day Adventists, 286–287
shame, 162
Shragg, Karen, A Solstice Tree for Jenny, 132
silence, on immorality, 42
simplicity, in evolution explanation, 234–235
skepticism, 248, 287
social approval, 157
social capital, 270
social contract, level of moral reasoning, 157
social emotions, positive or negative, 162
social experiences, in arts, 252
social justice, 273
social support, 279–280
socializing children, 5

solar system, 246
solitude, 259
Southern Baptists, 261
    on separation of church and state,
        103
space, child's need for, 195
spanking, 146–149
spiritual fitness, 23
St. Patrick's Day, 118
Stock, Gregory, *The Kid's Book of Questions*,
    257
stories, sharing, 53
suicide, and individualism, 270
summer camp, 275–278
Summer Solstice, 121–122
Sunday Assembly, xiv, 264, 272, 279–281,
    283, 287
Sunday school, 76–77
Supers, 287
superstition, 20
Sweeney, Julia, 1, 3–8
    Letting Go of God, 40
sympathy, 253

Tanquist, Stu, 90
Taoism, 87
teachers
    personal meeting with, 96–97
    religion restrictions, 105
Ten Commandments, for talking about religion,
    51–55
Thanksgiving, 122
theism, 59
theology, 260
    consolations of, 187
theory of mind, 159–160
Therapeutic Touch (TT), 17–18
Thomas, Pat, *I Miss You; A First Look at Death*,
    220–221
Thomas Aquinas, 171
Thoreau, Henry, on knowledge, 256
thunder, 250
time, choices for using, 217
timeline, on butcher paper, 240
tolerance, 45, 47, 90, 176
toys and games, for evolution study,
    240–241
traditions, 9–10
    holidays from other, 124
    importance of, 13
    of others, 170
    in Roman Catholicism, 11
transubstantiation, 287
traumatic death, 214–215
Trooien, Chrystine, *Christian Mythology for
    Kids*, 44, 107
Trozzi, Maria, *Talking with Children About
    Loss*, 221
trust, 37, 224
    in children, 15, 19
    evidence and, 13
    in Jesus, 57
truth, 37, 175–176
Twain, Mark, 224–225
    Huckleberry Finn, 251, 253–254

"Little Bessie Would Assist Providence,"
    227–230

unconditional love, 149
Unitarian Universalist (UU) movement, 33, 65,
    86, 283
    characteristics, 188, 272
    definition, 287
    focus on good, 64
    formation, 260
United Nations, agreements on freedom of
    conscience, 170
Universal Declaration of Human Rights, 78
universal ethical principles, 157
universe, 246–247
    history of, 245
unknown, acknowledging, 212–213

values, 156
    importance of, 63
    teaching of, 86–88
values assessments, 93–95
vernal equinox, 119
violence, death by, 214–215
virtue, 140
vocabulary, development of, 223
volunteer work, 263
    in grieving process, 196–197
vouchers, 100–101

Walters, Sheila, 23
websites, 108
    on secular celebrations and holidays, 133
    "Understanding Evolution," 241
    YouTube channels, 258
wedding ceremonies, 113, 115
welcoming ceremonies, for baby or young
    child's arrival, 113–114
Weldon, Louise, *Character Building Day by
    Day*, 182
White, E.B., *Charlotte's Web*, 221
Wicca, 87
Willson, Jane Wynne, 109, 111–117
    Funerals Without God, 132
    New Arrivals, 132
    Parenting Without God, 40
    Sharing the Future, 132
Wine, Sherwin, 260
Wing, Natasha, *The Night Before Easter*, 132
Winter Solstice, 123
Wolfelt, Alan, *Healing the Bereaved Child*, 196
women
    blame for evil, 231
    reproductive rights, 68
wonder, 223–225, 245–250
World Religions Conference (2005), 35
worship, reasons for, 262
Wykoff, Jerry, *20 Teachable Virtues*, 182

youth group, 18

Zuckerman, Phil, 270–274
    Living the Secular Life, 263, 282
    Society Without God, 263

ABOUT DALE McGOWAN

Dale McGowan is the author and editor of books including *Raising Freethinkers* (2009), *Atheism For Dummies* (2013), and *In Faith and in Doubt: How Religious Believers and Nonbelievers Can Create Strong Marriages and Loving Families* (2014).

He founded Foundation Beyond Belief, the world's largest humanist charitable and service organization. He was Harvard Humanist of the Year in 2008 and FBB's Humanist Visionary in 2015.

Dale and his wife Becca live near Atlanta with their three children. For more about Dale's work, visit www.dalemcgowan.com.